Waste Manage.

WASTE MANAGEMENT IN EUROPEAN LAW

THE EXAMPLE OF NAPLES AND CAMPANIA

IOANNIS K. PANOUSSIS AND HARRY H.G. POST (EDS.)

eleven
international publishing

Published, sold and distributed by Eleven International Publishing
P.O. Box 85576
2508 CG The Hague
The Netherlands
Tel.: +31 70 33 070 33
Fax: +31 70 33 070 30
e-mail: sales@budh.nl
www.elevenpub.com

Sold and distributed in USA and Canada
International Specialized Book Services
920 NE 58th Avenue, Suite 300
Portland, OR 97213-3786, USA
Tel.: 1-800-944-6190 (toll-free)
Fax: +1-503-280-8832
orders@isbs.com
www.isbs.com

Eleven International Publishing is an imprint of Boom uitgevers Den Haag.

ISBN 978-94-6236-115-7
ISBN 978-94-6094-967-8 (E-book)

© 2014 The authors | Eleven International Publishing

This publication is protected by international copyright law.
All rights reserved. No part of this publication may be reproduced, stored in a retrieval system, or transmitted in any form or by any means, electronic, mechanical, photocopying, recording or otherwise, without the prior permission of the publisher.

Printed in The Netherlands

With the support of the Fondation Cardinal Paul Poupard.

Table of Contents

Preface	ix
List of Contributors	xiii
Abbreviations	xv
Introductory Remarks *Ioannis K. Panoussis & Harry H.G. Post*	xvii

Part I Introduction

1	Waste Management in EU Legislation: An Introduction *Harry H.G. Post*	3
2	Waste Management in the ECHR: An Introduction *Ioannis Panoussis*	17

Part II Jurisprudence

3	The 'Waste Crisis' in Campania before the European Court of Human Rights: Some Remarks on the Case *Di Sarno and Others v. Italy* *Mario Odoni*	33
4	EU Case-Law and Waste Management in Campania *Leonardo Massai*	45

Part III Assessment and Evaluation

5	Implementation of EU Waste Law: Just as Difficult as Enforcement of EU Law in Other Domains? *Marc Clément*	63
6	The Legal Paradox of EU Waste Management *Aurélien Raccah*	73

7   Opportunities and Pitfalls for Sustainable Materials Management
    in EU Waste Law   97
Geert van Calster

Annexes
Directive 2008/98/EC of the European Parliament and of the Council   109
Affaire Di Sarno et Autres c. Italie   153

Preface

The world's population will continue to grow in the coming decades as will the consumption from emerging middle classes worldwide. This will have a direct consequence for the global extraction of resources which is expected to increase by 75% in the next 25 years. Today already, the European Union imports six times more materials and resources than it exports.

To keep our economy operating today, we use 16 tonnes of materials per person per year. Of that amount, 6 tonnes per person becomes waste and almost half of those 6 tonnes is going to landfill.

But what is encouraging is that when we ask people to name things that they can do for the environment, amongst the top answers is 'recycling'. This reflects public interest and engagement. But it also shows that we have to move from today's linear economy, where we mine, manufacture, use and throw away, towards a circular economy, where one industry's waste becomes another's raw material. It is about building a sustainable industry that can prosper for many years to come and where waste is ultimately eliminated.

The circular economy has a role to play in getting us out of the economic crisis: through a resource efficient, green economy the markets and societies in this resource-constrained and crowded world in the long-term will become more resilient and competitive.

The EU waste legislation sets very clear requirements, notably the waste hierarchy gives priority to prevention, re-use and recycling, and it also establishes key binding targets concerning recycling and landfill diversion.

The Roadmap to a Resource Efficient Europe[1] outlines how we can transform Europe's economy into a sustainable one by 2050. It proposes ways to increase resource productivity and to decouple economic growth from resource use and its environmental impact. It illustrates how policies interrelate and build on each other. The Roadmap includes clear orientations promoting the use of waste as a resource.

Building on the strategy set out by the Resource Efficiency Roadmap, the 7th Environment Action Programme[2] for the period up to 2020 confirms this approach and lists several waste-related objectives:

- Existing waste legislation based on a strict application of the waste hierarchy is fully implemented in all Member States;
- Absolute and per capita waste generation is in decline and a comprehensive strategy to combat unnecessary food waste is developed by the Commission;

---

1 European Commission, *Roadmap to a Resource Efficient Europe*, Brussels, 20 September 2011, COM(2011) 571 final.
2 Decision No .../2013/EU of the European Parliament and of the Council of 20 November 2013 on a General Union Environment Action Programme to 2020 'Living well, within the limits of our planet'.

PREFACE

- High quality recycling is ensured and recycled waste is used as a major, reliable source of raw material for the Union;
- Energy recovery is limited to non-recyclable materials;
- Landfilling of recyclable and recoverable waste is phased out.

For sure, these objectives may appear very ambitious. Nevertheless, there are also opportunities to seize: better waste management means job creation and economic growth. Just implementing existing waste legislation properly could create 400,000 jobs in the EU according to a recent study.[3]

The revision of the EU Waste Directive, the corner stone of EU Waste policy, has led to a different way of thinking about waste: From an unwanted burden it may become a valuable resource. That change of perspective is still far from being realised. When we have a look at the statistics from EUROSTAT, the picture which emerges is rather contrasted. Landfilling is the worst option under the waste hierarchy. Yet, 37% – more than a third – of all municipal waste in the EU goes to landfills. Seven Member States are burying more than 80% of their waste; three of them bury more than 90%. The better news is that we are moving in the right direction. Just 10 years ago more than half of municipal waste – 56% – was landfilled. The landfilling rate has therefore experienced a 19% reduction. Our recycling and composting rates have increased – from 17% to 25% and from 10% to 15%, respectively. More importantly, already today 6 Member States are landfilling less than 5% of the waste they generate and four Member States are recycling over 60% of their municipal waste. More and more success stories and best practices are known in terms of prevention, recycling and especially the use of economic incentives, like pay-as-you-throw-away schemes, or landfill and incineration taxes, as well as extended producer responsibility.

The long-standing waste problems in the area of Naples provide a good illustration of the impact that inadequate and bad waste management can have. The current book provides a thorough analysis of the waste crisis in Naples, using it as example to understand the legal and policy issues related to the management of waste in practice and its potential effect on the quality of life and the environment in modern society. The book also shows the complexity of waste management and the constant need to critically evaluate the policy and legislative efforts undertaken in respect to it. I congratulate Professors Panoussis and Post together with the other authors, for providing such a timely and welcome contribution to our understanding of this complicated and ever evolving subject.

Julio García Burgués
Brussels, November 2013

---

3   BIO Intelligence Service, *Implementing EU Waste Legislation for Green Growth*, Final Report prepared for European Commission DG ENV, 29 November 2011.

Preface

The Poupard Foundation was established in order to promote studies and actions in the field of culture and understanding of the main challenges aiming to promote a more just world, based on a sustainable economy. It is in this perspective that was created the Chair in 'Social Issues and Prospects' in the Catholic University of Lille, which aims to deliver specialized lectures, seminars and research on the above topics.

The Protection of the Environment is a crucial question nowadays. It implies mobilization locally, nationally and internationally. Many actors are now stakeholders in environmental debates: private companies, civil society, states, intergovernmental organizations . . . Since the mobilization of the sixties and seventies, and particularly the publication of the famous report of the Club of Rome (*The Limits to Growth*), the environmental challenges have become more complex, their approach has also become more scientific and technical.

That is why the Poupard Foundation and the Chair in 'Social Issues and Prospective' warmly welcomed the proposal of Professor Ioannis Panoussis and Professor Harry Post to analyze the problem of waste management in Europe. Under their direction, an international workshop was organized in Lille, where eminent European lawyers had the opportunity to exchange their points of view. This book reflects the final conclusions of the participants. The Foundation is very grateful to Professors Panoussis and Post and is pleased to be associated with the publication of this work.

Giuseppe Musumeci
President of the Poupard Foundation
November 2013

List of Contributors

Marc Clément	Judge at the Administrative Court of Appeal of Lyon, France
Julio García Burgués	Head of the Waste Unit, European Commission, Directorate-General for Environment, Brussels, Belgium
Leonardo Massai	Visiting Professor, Faculté Libre de Droit, Université Catholique de Lille, France
Mario Odoni	Assistant Professor, Dipartimento di Giurisprudenza, Università degli Studi di Sassari, Sassari, Italy
Ioannis K. Panoussis	Senior Lecturer, Faculté Libre de Droit, Université Catholique de Lille, UNHCR Expert/Judge at the National Court for Asylum (France) representing the UNHCR
Harry H.G. Post	Professor of International Law, ret., University of Exeter, UK; Visiting Professor, Faculté Libre de Droit, Université Catholique de Lille, France; Guest Professor at the Faculteit Rechtsgeleerdheid, KU Leuven, Belgium
Aurélien Raccah	Lecturer and Researcher in EU Law, Faculté libre de droit, Université Catholique de Lille, France
Geert van Calster	Professor, and Head of the Department of European and International Law, KU Leuven; Member of the Brussels Bar (practising)

ABBREVIATIONS

ADEME	Agence de l'Environnement et de la Maîtrise de l'Energie *(French Agency for Environment and Energy Management)*
BGBl	Bundes Gesetz Blatt
CEDH	Convention Européenne des Droits de l'Homme
EAP	Environment Action Program
EAR	Elektro-Altgeräte Register
EC	European Community
EEC	European Economic Community
EEE	Electrical and Electronic Equipment
ECJ	European Court of Justice
ECR	European Community Reports
ELV	End-of-live-vehicles
EU	European Union
ECtHR	European Court of Human Rights
ECHR	European Convention of Human Rights
ILC	International Law Commission
MARPOL	1973 (London) Maritime Convention for the Prevention of Pollution by Ships
NEA	Nuclear Energy Agency
NGO	Non-governmental organisation
OJ	Official Journal of the European Union
PIC	Prior Informed Consent
RDF	Refuse-derived fuel
REACH	(Regulation on) Registration, Evaluation, Authorisation and Restriction of Chemicals
RoHS	Restrictions of the Use of certain Hazardous Substances (RoHS Directive)
SEPA	Scottish Environment Protection Agency

Abbreviations

TEU	Treaty on the European Union
TFEU	Treaty on the Functioning of the European Union
WEEE	Waste Electrical and Electronic Equipment Directive (WEEE Directive)
WFD	Waste Framework Directive

Introductory Remarks

That the organisation of waste is not a simple matter became abundantly clear during the 2007 waste disposal crisis which struck in Naples and the Campania and could be followed on a daily basis on Italian television. Although by 2010 a newly elected mayor of Naples could report progress towards bringing its most obvious manifestations under control, that year there still existed a Neapolitan waste crisis. In fact the waste problems in the region date already from the 1990s.

Apparently, such matters are not easy to resolve (at least not for the Italian region of Campania). Is this due to a lack of clarity or, perhaps, over-complexity of European regulations and principles, or is it all the fault of remarkable Italian politics?

The European Court of Justice (ECJ) repeated and emphasised the legal limits set to, in particular, waste disposal in its 2010 judgement in Case C-297/08 *Commission v. Italy*. The Court found, *inter alia,* that the Italian Government had not adopted all the measures necessary for the disposal of waste in Campania. This judgement, and so have done others, to some extent further clarifies the discretion left to the Member States in light of the existing Community legislation on waste. It also demonstrates how complicated and often, indeed, unclear and out-dated, legal regulation can be for this extremely dynamic and changing subject matter. In recent years the European Commission has undertaken several steps to initiate new legislation and policy. It launched a 'Thematic Strategy on the Prevention and Re-cycling of Waste',[4] and on that basis attempted to integrate and clarify existing waste legislation. This culminated in a new 'Framework' Directive 2008/98, adopted in 2008. The Member States had until 10 December 2010 to implement this Directive which was certainly a challenge, not in the least for Italy and its Regions.[5]

One of the established purposes of EU policy regarding waste disposal is 'self sufficiency', more in particular that the Member States become self-sufficient individually. In order to achieve such self-sufficiency the Member States shall draw up waste management

---

[4] European Commission, *Taking Sustainable Use of Resources Forward: A Thematic Strategy on the Prevention and Recycling of Waste*, Brussels, 21 December 2005, COM(2005) 666 final.

[5] Directive 2008/98/EC of the European Parliament and of the Council of 19 November 2008 on Waste and Repealing Certain Directives, OJ 2008 L 312/3.

plans and, of course, more in general abide by the relevant European law. Article I of the new 2008 Framework Directive on waste,

> [...] lays down measures to protect the environment and human health by preventing and reducing the adverse impacts of the generation and management of waste and by reducing overall impacts of resource use and improving the efficiency of such use.

Waste should as much as possible be prevented (Art. 9), the principles of self-sufficiency and proximity will govern the responsibility of the member States for their waste management (Arts. 16 and 15) and movements of waste should be reduced. There will be extended producer responsibility (Art. 8). Within such parameters, however, Member States still have discretion in how they organise their national management of waste (notably the disposal of waste on their territory). In Italy, the primary objectives mentioned above together with some other purposes and duties embodied already in EU waste instruments preceding the 2008 Framework Directive have been implemented into legislation which delegates a considerable part of the management competence to the Italian Regions (Legislative Decree No. 152 of 3 April 2006).

In this book the legal limits of the discretion of the Member States to manage waste will be a central topic of consideration. However, in respect to the management of waste the law of the European Union is not the only European law limiting that discretion. The European Court of Human Rights in Strasbourg has determined that waste management policies may also lead to violations of human rights of citizens for which the States parties to the European Convention of Human Rights can be held responsible. The Court has made this clear in the 2012 judgment in *Di Sarno and others v. Italy*.

Part I of the book introduces both the European Union Law applicable to waste management and the relevance of the European Convention of Human Rights for the subject. In Chapter I, Harry Post shows the considerable width but also the intricacies of the EU instruments in respect to waste management. Notwithstanding a very considerable effort on the part of the European Commission to simplify and in particular to make the applicable EU law to waste management more comprehensive, the problems are still abound. On the one hand this is due to the nature of the subject matter. The technological developments in the area of waste are fast and complex and the law notoriously lags behind. However, on the other hand, from the very beginning of the Community's involvement with waste management important issues like the definitions of even fundamental aspects of the subject matter (like the definition of waste itself) have proved controversial. That was not only due to inherent shortcomings but also to a lack of co-operation on the part of Member States: there has been tension between a proper regulation of waste management at the

European level and the hesitancy of Member States to give up their powers in the field. Nevertheless, gradually the objective and desirability of Community and Union regulation have come to prevail. In the process the protection of health and the environment have become the primary purpose of European waste management now prevailing over its trading aspects ('waste as a good and a product'). Still the tension between the two has never disappeared and shows itself often in the way waste management has been regulated and also in the numerous questions still remaining to be answered. Quite a number of these research questions are inherited from the past, Post argues, like issues of definition or the meaning and scope of the principles of proximity and self-sufficiency. But other issues result from new technological development, like the conditions to be set for the process of using waste as fuel for energy production. In some areas of waste management the precise scope of national discretion is still to be determined, like in respect to radio-active waste. This is a kind of waste which special legal treatment by way of Euratom demands specific attention: it is largely separate from 'normal' European law regarding waste management, but to what extent precisely?

In Chapter 2 Ioannis Panoussis explains how waste management can be a subject to be addressed within the European Convention of Human Rights, although the Convention does not even mention the environment. He provides a survey of the jurisprudence of the European Court of Human Rights where 'environment' as a factor has been taken into account. In early cases the Court recognised that an environmental issue may arise under Article 8 of the Convention, the protection of private and family life, but could not conclude to a violation. In the 1990s the Court did convict for violations under Article 8 on the ground of industrial pollution. In one such case it also stated a positive public obligation to inform individuals about environmental risk. This particular duty came back in the recent *Di Sarno* case where waste management in the Campania, the Region of Naples was the core matter. Panoussis introduces this *Di Sarno* case and concludes his chapter by a detailed analysis of the nature of the relevant obligations in respect to waste management States have under the European Convention.

In Part II, *Jurisprudence*, Mario Odoni provides background to the *Di Sarno* case and a further legal analysis. This case is at the heart of international involvement and assessment of Italy's dealing with the waste crisis in the Campania region. In Chapter 3 Odoni explains critically and in great detail what the waste crisis in Campania involved and what approach the Italian government choose in order to cope with the problems. He concludes that the main purpose of the applicants in the case could not so much be recovering damages. Their satisfaction would consist of a declaratory judgement that Italy had failed to fulfil its obligations under the Convention and that is what they got. The main issue seemed to have been, as Odoni believes, the rather ineffective 'emergency' approach chosen by the Italian government.

INTRODUCTORY REMARKS

In Chapter 4 in this same Part II, Leonardo Massai, discusses the jurisprudence on waste management of the European Court of Justice in Luxembourg. Also here cases against Italy relating to the same waste crisis in Campania take central stage. Massai illustrates the rather weak implementation in Italy of EU waste law in particular regarding the region of Campania, by way of the legislation on disposal by landfill. This has led the Commission to the application of infringement procedures against Italy and to bring cases before the ECJ. He then proceeds to discuss and analyse the substance of the jurisprudence on waste management, including of the two most important cases against Italy.

In Part III *Assessment and Evaluation*, Marc Clément opens his contribution with a discussion of the crucial role of the European Commission in the implementation of European waste law. In this Chapter 5, Clément analyses the Campania waste crisis within the wider context of enforcement of EU law. He reminds that the infringement procedure managed by the Commission is only an alternative to enforcement of EU law within the legal systems of the Member States. In fact for all practical purposes the latter is the prevalent mode of enforcement. He identifies the various problems that are perceived to be attached to this system of parallel national and European legal enforcement, but concludes to their full compatibility. He then continues to assess in detail the merits and problems of the infringement procedure, in particular since in 2007 the Commission has presented a new infringement strategy. In the light of these developments the problems with the implementation of EU waste law are not exceptional. Enforcement in this field relies strongly on the cooperation of national authorities as well as of citizens and associations in respect to the complex facts at stake. Clément submits that therefore direct submission to the national courts seems the most appropriate and efficient way to enforce EU waste law. However this enforcement path presumes that access to justice is not subjected to all kinds of legal and practical barriers as it still often is.

In Chapter 6 Aurélien Raccah evaluates EU waste management regulation and submits that it has a paradoxical nature: it states objectives that are not achievable in most national systems but nevertheless presumes effective implementation. He illustrates his thesis by way of a detailed discussion of the development of EU waste policy evaluating to what extent in its various manifestations specific objectives have been realised. He concludes that 100% implementation is simply not possible. These (unrealistic) policy objectives legally lead to infringement procedures and considerable case-law. In the second part of his Chapter Raccah provides two explanations for the problems of EU waste law. He identifies the 'multi-level governance' of the EU law as the first, general, explanation: European representatives, mainly from the Commission and the EU Council of Ministers, seem primarily impressed by ambitious political objectives which can simply not be achieved in the time allowed. The second reason is of an economic nature: EU waste law is very costly and at the local level in particular there is insufficient financial capacity to support and realise the European objectives. In order to address these problems the author welcomes a study of the European Commission to be published before the end of 2013 which aim is "to assist Member States in improving waste management based on an assessment of their waste policy performance".

In the final suggestive Chapter 7 of the book, Geert van Calster's essay examines some of the most relevant legal aspects of sustainable materials management in EU waste law. A clear pitfall ('a first elephant in the room' as the author calls them) he identifies, is the ever problematic definition of waste. Industrial practice continues to produce challenges. In particular the development of 'end-of-waste criteria' and criteria for by-products, are subject of discussion. Also in a more general sense, the application of the waste definition continues to cause problems, *e.g.*, in the context of reverse logistics for defective and otherwise not adequate products). Another elephant in the room is the 2011 REACH Regulation on the registration, evaluation and authorisation of chemicals, from which application waste is explicitly exempted. This led to attempts to classify products as waste in order to avoid the application of REACH. Complicated arguments were the result involving in the end both the Commission and the Court. As a third area of complications Van Calster mentions the shipment of waste Regulation in its relation to Treaty articles on the free movement of goods. Ambiguity in some of the provisions of the Regulation has led to complaints by industry about potential partiality of its application in allowing in-and export of waste. The author notices a parallel development at the World Trade Organization. He further points to issues of ownership of waste which have become more salient since waste is increasingly seen as a 'resource'. He concludes his chapter with a detailed section on 'use restrictions and waste management' and divergent national environmental laws. He provides a number of examples illustrating the thesis that sound science should be the basis for use restrictions with an impact on trade. More clarification by the Court would be helpful here.

On Friday 30 March 2012 an International Workshop/Journée d'Etude Internationale on 'Waste management and European Law; Reflections sur l'exemple Italien' took place in Lille (France). It was hosted by the Faculté Libre de Droit, Université Catholique de Lille, supported and funded by the Faculty and by the Fondation Poupard. The Workship in Lille was a successful meeting as a result of the highly interesting contributions of an excellent group of speakers, but also due to the often engaging participation of a large interested audience. It also showed, as was cited by several speakers, how 'curiously engaging' the subject matter is, and why it gets so much attention from the European Court of Justice. The contributions demonstrated once more how extremely important and really difficult waste management is in modern society. This book is to quite some extent the fruit of the reports presented and of the comments they drew at the Lille Workshop.

Introductory Remarks

The editors of this book wish to express their gratitude to each one of the contributors and also to those who so generously supported in the organisation of the Workshop and the publication of the book. Besides the authors whose work is published in this volume, we would like to thank in particular, the Dean of the Faculté Libre de Droit, Université Catholique de Lille, Dr Alexis Massart for the support of the Faculty and the members of the International and European Law Department (IELS) for their precious help. Ing. Cédric Caravetta deserves special thanks for his excellent contribution to its organisation and the publicity for the Workshop. We would further like to express our special gratitude to the Fondation Cardinal Poupard. The Fondation has generously supported both the Workshop and the publication of this book.

We would also like to thank the staff of Eleven International Publishing for their help, competence and patience in the publication of this book and Carol Post for her thorough language revision.

Ioannis K. Panoussis and Harry H.G. Post
Lille-Bologna, October 2013

Part I
Introduction

1 Waste Management in EU Legislation: An Introduction

Harry H.G. Post

In particular in the industrialised developed world, waste management is one of the most important subjects of the environmental policy of States. Staying in a sensible way on top of the growing mountains of waste of all kinds produced by manufacturers, energy producers, consumers or agriculture is perhaps not the most pleasant but certainly a great challenge in modern societies. Managing hazardous, including radioactive forms of waste may be the most difficult problem to deal with, but the complexity of the trade in, and the processing – disposal, recycling, re-using – or transport of other forms of waste is often technically so great that such more 'ordinary' waste causes problems that are just as complicated. The 'ordinary' waste crisis in the region of Naples illustrates as much. National as well as international regulation in respect to almost all forms of waste appears to suffer from forms of inadequacy or is at least lagging behind technical and economic developments. Although also accomplished for other reasons, the adoption of a new Framework Directive on waste in 2008 while the Member States of the Union had hardly transposed the previous 2006 Framework into their national legislation is somewhat telling. To quite some extent the (growing) jurisprudence of national and international courts reflects the problems and dynamics of the field, not in the least the technical complications the judges have to deal with.

In the last decade, the legal and policy developments in respect to waste management in the European Union, as they have successively been laid down in Community instruments have thus been numerous and often very interesting. One reason is that they continuously have been expanding to more kinds of waste, addressing ever more specific and detailed aspects of its management. However, it should not be forgotten that the EU is not at all the only body trying to cope with the ever growing quantities of waste modern societies produce. Organisations ranging from the Organisation for Economic Cooperation and Development (OECD) to UN Specialised Agencies, like, notably, World Trade Organization (WTO), International Maritime Organization (IMO), International Atomic Energy Agency (IAEA) and World Health Organization (WHO), and regional organisations inside and outside Europe have been developing their own approaches and policies to cope with the management of waste. The differences in approaches including in national, for instance US, waste policies converge to some extent in international treaties to which Member States and/or the European Union are a Party. The next step in the EU is then that such international obligations are expressed in proper European (and Member State) legislation. The 1989 Basel Convention on the Control of Trans-boundary Movements of Hazardous Waste and their Disposal (particularly in its 1995 amended and modified form) is an important example of such an international treaty which is implemented by and within the EU.[1]

Even if waste management is addressed only from the European and international legal point of view as is the case in the following pages, it has a wide scope. These introductory pages focus on a few of the most important parts of the legislation on waste management. Often, they still contain elements of (considerable) controversy. Firstly, in Section 1.1, following brief remarks on the development of the Community's involvement in the area (section 1.1.1), some of the rather intricate issues of definition of terms and principles in the basic Framework legislation on waste management are introduced, as well as its main procedures and mechanisms. In section 1.2, EU legislation on hazardous waste management (section 1.2.1), including of radioactive waste (section 1.2.2) is discussed. In section 1.3, transport of waste (section 1.3.1), of hazardous waste (section 1.3.2) and of radioactive waste (section 1.3.3) are addressed. Finally, section 1.4 contains some concluding remarks.

1.1 Basic Principles, Terms and Definitions of Waste Management

1.1.1   Towards the 2008 Framework Directive

In European Union policy and law, waste management all along has been marked by tension between trade interests and objectives, on the one hand ('waste as a product'), and environmental and health concerns, on the other hand. Now the latter can be said largely to prevail. Article 1 of the newest Framework Directive 2008/98 expresses this shift when it says that the directive

> [...] lays down measures to protect the environment and human health by preventing and reducing the adverse impacts of the generation and management of waste and by reducing overall impacts of resource use and improving the efficiency of such use.

---

1   The 2006 dumping of toxic waste in Côte d'Ivoire from the *Probo Koala*, a ship leased by the Trafigura Company, is a case to keep in mind. The undue disposal of the toxic waste upon arrival in Abidjan from Amsterdam, led to the death of fifteen people and thousands affected by various illnesses attributed to the toxic waste. On 23 July 2010 the Trafigura Company was penalised €1 million in a Dutch Court (confirmed on appeal on 23 December 2012). Other court procedures are still pending. Trafigura, reportedly had already concluded two indemnity agreements to the value of €152 million in Côte d'Ivoire and €33 million in the United Kingdom (*see* for the EU instruments in respect to the Basel Convention, below, Sections 1.3.1 and 1.3.2).

Prior to the 1985 Single European Act directives on waste were based on the 'trade' Articles 100 and 235 of the EEC Treaty (re-numbered 94 and 308 EC, respectively, now Article 114 TFEU), but since the Act entered into force, almost all such directives have been based on the 'environment' Article 130s or 175 EC, now Article 192 TFEU, and only a few on Article 100A or 95 EC, now Article 114 TFEU. The Court agreed with this choice for Article 130s.[2] Since the 1997 Treaty of Amsterdam, the 'ordinary legislative procedure' of Article 289 TFEU applies to 192 TFEU.

Within the trade-environment tensions, a basic purpose of EC and EU policy regarding waste disposal has always remained 'self sufficiency', more in particular in the sense that the Member States should individually be self-sufficient in respect to the management of their waste. In order to achieve such self-sufficiency they had to abide by the relevant European Law and draw up waste management plans accordingly, a very important obligation which is also included in the newest Framework Directive (see below, section 1.2).

The various original European Community pieces of regulation policy on waste management found a more comprehensive format in a 1989 strategy document where general priorities for all kinds of waste were established whether intended for disposal or for recycling and re-use. This strategy was seen as necessary for the completion of the internal market and in view of growing concerns regarding the protection of health and the environment. In this document prevention of waste was the first priority, followed by recovery and, finally, by the safe disposal of waste. It thereby introduced the so-called 'waste hierarchy'.[3] Its implementation was to be determined by considering the best solutions for health and environment as well as economic and social costs.[4] The reality of implementation and execution of this policy can best be seen in terms of a balancing act between both kinds of objectives.

The early legislation on waste management and the accompanying jurisprudence show the complexity of what was to be undertaken. Preceding by some fifteen years the 1989 EC policy strategy on waste management, just referred to, the original 1975 Framework Waste Directive laid down, in the first place, the general definitions in respect to waste management. This Directive, as amended several times, and repealed and codified in 2006 as Directive 2006/12/EC, refers thereto to an Annex, where an

---

2 *See, e.g.,* Case C-155/91, *Commission v. Council* [1991] ECR I-939, or Case C-187/93, *Parliament v. Council* [1994] ECR I-2857. A notable, but apparently isolated exception is the Titanium Dioxide judgement (Case 300/89, *Commission v. Council* [1991] ECR I-2867).

3 Art. 4 of the 2008 Framework Directive phrases the waste hierarchy as: The prevention of waste production; preparation for re-use; re-cycling; other means of recovery, such as energy recovery; disposal. Art. 4.2 allows that for certain waste streams a departure of the order if that leads to better environmental outcomes (Directive 2008/98/EC of the European Parliament and of the Council of 19 November 2008 on Waste and Repealing Certain Directives, OJ 2008 L 312/3).

4 SEC(89) 934 and the new Strategy presented by the Commission in 1996, COM(96) 399; *see also* the Council's Resolution of 24 February 1997 on a Community Strategy for Waste Management, OJ 1997 C 76/1.

enumerative definition was chosen, listing the major categories of waste.[5] This attempt clearly did not solve the question of what may and may not be considered waste. Courts in the Community and primarily, the Court of Justice itself, over the years often had to address basic questions regarding the definition and its elaboration (see below, section 1.1.2).[6]

As a first step in the implementation of its most recent 'Thematic Strategy on the Prevention and Recycling of Waste',[7] the European Commission proposed a revision of Directive 2006/12/EC. Subsequently this proposal (COM (2005) 667) has led to the adoption of the new Framework Directive 2008/98/EC providing, since 12 December 2010, the current legislative framework for the management of waste. More comprehensively than before, it lays down its basic concepts, definitions, principles and other characteristics.

1.1.2 The Core Legislation

For the purposes of the 2008 Framework Directive (2008/98/EC) 'waste' means: "[...] any substance or object which the holder discards or intends or is required to discard"; (Art. 3.1).[8] The Framework Directive contains the general rules that apply to all categories of waste. However, Article 2 sums up the exclusions from its scope, and they are not minor ones, like:

- Gaseous effluents emitted into the atmosphere (Art. 2.1.a), which excludes application to carbon emission as well as to CO_2 capture stored underground;
- Radioactive waste (Art. 2.1.d);
- De-commissioned explosives (Art. 2.1.e).

Furthermore, among some others, waste waters, most animal by-products, and waste from prospecting, extraction etc., of mineral resources, are excluded from the rules of the Framework Directive "to the extent that they are covered by other Community legislation" (Art. 2.2). Finally, Article 2.4 stipulates that specific rules "[...] on the management of particular categories of waste may be laid down by means of individual directives" (Art. 2.4). This, of course, does not necessarily mean that the definition of the 2008

---

5 Directive 2006/12/EC of the European Parliament and of the Council of 5 April 2006 on Waste, OJ 2006 L 114/9. The definition of waste has not changed in the 2006 Directive, hence the rather numerous ECJ judgements in which questions of definition were addressed remain relevant.
6 See, e.g., J. Jans & H. Vedder, *European Environmental Law*, 4th edn, European Law Publishing, Groningen, The Netherlands, 2012, pp. 473-485.
7 European Commission, *Taking Sustainable Use of Resources Forward: A Thematic Strategy on the Prevention and Recycling of Waste*, Brussels, 21 December 2005, COM(2005) 666 final.
8 The preceding Framework Directive (2006/12/EC) in Art. 1.1.a had the same definition but with a reference to categories of waste set out in its Ann. I. Annex I ended, in Q 16, with a 'catch all' category: "Any materials, substances or products which are not contained in the abovementioned categories." This effectively declared that all substances not enumerated should also be declared waste.

Framework Directive is not also appropriate for the forms of waste excluded, but its application may not be presumed.

As said above, extensive jurisprudence helps us with the meaning of terms used in the basic definition, or in closely related ones, notably the pivotal 'discard', covering both disposal and recovery.[9] In the *Inter-Environment* case, the Court choose a broad approach deciding "[...] that the concept of waste does not in principle exclude any kind of residue, industrial by-product or other substance arising from production processes".[10] This led again to further finesse about the differences between 'by-product' and waste, making by-products an important exception to waste. In the end, it, *e.g.,* matters very considerably if a substance resulting from the refining of crude oil like petroleum coke, is to be considered a waste substance, a 'residue', or a by-product which technically can be used as a fuel and is therefore excluded from the waste definition. After a number of Court decisions regarding various aspects of this important distinction[11] the 2008 Directive, in Article 5, stipulates considerable and cumulative conditions to be fulfilled for a 'secondary' substance from a production process to be a by-product and not waste.

Furthermore, it is possible and legally acceptable under conditions set in Article 6 that a substance firstly classified as waste may cease to be waste when it is recovered, including being re-cycled thus becoming a real product for the market.[12]

But even the distinction between recovery and disposal can occasionally be complicated to make. An important example is the possibility that waste is combusted to generate energy. Such generation of energy is, according to the Court, in principle a lawful form of recovery.[13] However, such a waste incinerating process has to be properly qualified as 'energy recovering', meeting energy efficiency criteria. When the process does not thus qualify, incineration ends up at an equal footing with landfill or disposal. Hence, as a result of technological development, constant modification and re-classification of substances is needed as the rules covering waste differ very considerably from those regarding marketable products and so do, *e.g.,* the transport regulations that apply. Furthermore, another interpretation of the meaning of waste remains a legitimate choice for individual Member

---

9 Telling is, perhaps, the reported amazement of an experienced judge of the European Court of Justice about the judicial effort put into defining the concept of waste. J. Tieman, *Naar een nuttige toepassing van het begrip afvalstof: over de betekenis en toepassing van kernbegrippen van international, Europees en Nederlands afvalstoffenrecht* [Towards a useful application of the concept of waste: on the meaning and application of core concepts of International, European and Dutch waste law] [in Dutch], Kluwer, Deventer, The Netherlands, 2003, pp. 5 *ff*. Tieman's book by itself provides quite an illustration of Judge Kapteyn's finding. *See also* Jans & Vedder, *op. cit.*, pp. 475-479.
10 Case C-129/96, *Inter-Environnement Wallonie ASBL v. Waals Gewest* [1997] ECR I-7411.
11 *Cf.* Cases C-1114/01, *Avesta Polarit Chrome* [2003] ECR I-8725 and C-235/02, *Saetti* [2004] ECR I-1005.
12 Again *see* Case C-9/00, *Palin Granit and Vehmassalon kansanterveystyön kuntayhtymän hallitus* [2002] ECR I-3533 and Case C-444/00, *Mayer Parry* [2003] ECR I-6163.
13 Case C-228/00, *Commission v. Germany* [2003] ECR I-1439.

States as long as the result is more stringent environmental protection regarding waste treatment. This possibility leads to still other differences in treatment and transport of waste substances.

Article 4 of the Directive contains the waste hierarchy of prevention, preparation for re-use, re-cycling, other means of recovery (such as energy recovery), and, finally, disposal (see below), whereas Articles 8-12 provide the duties of Member States to put it into effect. Article 8 allows Member States to enact producer responsibility schemes or end of life cycle responsibilities, which may also induce more environmentally friendly production. For the whole waste hierarchy cycle, whether re-use, re-cycle, or disposal, Article 13 emphasises that these various ways should not endanger human health or harm the environment. What is precisely meant by Article 13 (and by Art. 4 of the preceding Directive) has been the subject of a score of (mainly Italian) cases about the obligations it gives rise to, the margin of discretion it leaves to the Member States and the possible direct effect of Article 13.[14]

Article 16 re-states the self-sufficiency and proximity principles of older legislation for the integrated and adequate network of disposal installations and recovery installations for household waste. The EU as a whole should be self-sufficient and so should be the individual Member States (Art. 16.2). The waste referred to in the Article should be disposed of or recovered when appropriate, in the nearest installations (Art. 16.3), corresponding to the proximity principle. But the latter principle should not be interpreted too strictly (Art. 16.4), otherwise it might look like an import restriction, which is not allowed as waste is after all a good (within the basic meaning of Art. 34 TFEU). Self-sufficiency and proximity do not apply to waste for recovery.[15] Needless to say, that also Article 16 has given rise to considerable questioning and judicial activity.[16]

Member States are responsible for a sound management of hazardous waste (Art. 17), waste oils (Art. 21) and bio-waste (Art. 22). The Framework Directive replaces the old specific directives on these subjects which are repealed (see, below, section 1.2).

Finally, as in the previous 2006 Framework Directive, this Directive also requires Member States to draw up waste prevention programmes (Art. 29) to be integrated into Waste Management Plans (Art. 28). The latter should be organised and co-ordinated systems and not *ad hoc* projects.[17] The Member States still have (some) discretion how they organise

---

14 See Jans & Vedder, *op. cit.*, p. 481, for an overview and some (carefully phrased) conclusions.
15 As the European Court had already determined in 1998 in the *Dusseldorp* case, C-203/96 [1998] ECR-I-4075, para. 30.
16 See Jans & Vedder, *op. cit.*, p. 482.
17 As the Court had already determined in 2000, in Case C-387/97, *Commission v. Greece* [2000] ECR I-5047, para. 76.

their national management of waste (notably regarding the disposal of waste). But to what extent precisely remains an interesting question to answer.

1.1.3 Processing of Waste

Several directives have been enacted on the incineration and other modes of processing of waste and on the disposal of waste. Proposals for dumping of waste at sea (increasingly considered an illegal or dubious form of processing) have been withdrawn conforming to developments in international law on marine dumping. The 1996 IPPC Directive (on integrated pollution prevention and control) emphasises already that waste production is generally to be avoided, that waste is to be recovered and that, if such cannot be achieved, its disposal must be as environment-friendly as possible.[18] In respect to the landfill of waste, Directive 99/31 has formulated broad environmental objectives and divides landfill according to whether it concerns hazardous, non-hazardous or inert waste.[19]

1.1.4 Various Kinds of Waste and a 'Comprehensive' Approach

Apart from waste management of hazardous waste, the Community originally has been enacting separate legislation on a steadily increasing number of specific kinds of waste: the disposal of waste oils, waste from the titanium dioxide industry, waste from extractive industries, contaminated waste from agriculture (*i.e.* BSE waste), on the use of agricultural sewage sludge, on packaging and packaging waste, on waste of electrical and electronic equipment and on waste from batteries and accumulators.[20] In response to several serious accidents, the EU has also adopted a separate Directive on mining waste. This Directive 2006/21/EC aims at preventing and reducing negative effects of the management of such waste for the environment and for human health. As said, particularly since the adoption in 2006 of the 'Thematic Strategy on the prevention and recycling of waste' the choice has been made in favour of a more comprehensive approach.[21] Several of the separate legislative instruments have now been brought under the regime of the 2008 Framework Directive. This is the case in particular for the existing legislation on waste oils, and bio-waste, but also for hazardous waste to which we will turn in section 1.2.

---

18 Council Directive 96/61/EC of 24 September 1996 concerning Integrated Pollution Prevention and Control, Art. 3(c), OJ 1996 L 257/10.
19 OJ 1999 L 182/1 (later amended).
20 *E.g.*, Directive 75/439/EEC on waste oils, Directive 78/176/EEC on titanium dioxide industrial waste, Directive 86/278/EEC on sewage sludge, Directive 94/62/EC on packaging and packaging waste and Directive 1999/31/EC on the landfill of waste for the period 2001-2003, in COM(2006) 406 final (not yet published).
21 *See op. cit.*, note 7.

1.2 Specific Legislation

1.2.1 Hazardous Waste and Waste Oils

Directive 91/689[22] specifically addressed hazardous waste. The Directive applied to all wastes enumerated in a detailed list of hazardous wastes which was established and regularly modified by Council Decisions.[23] Since 12 December 2010 it is repealed and is replaced by the appropriate provisions of the 2008 Framework Directive.[24] The 2008 Directive basically defines hazardous waste differently. It has codified the findings of the Court in the *Fornasar* case[25] applying to all wastes which are 'explosive', 'carcinogenic' or are characterised by one or more of the other properties listed in Annex III. Legal certainty in respect to the definition of hazardous waste left to be desired under the old Directive 91/689 as not all Member States had adequately transposed its list. However, the new approach clearly also still leaves some room for differences as Article 7.2 of the 2008 Directive gives leeway to Member States to consider waste not listed in Annex III as hazardous.

The Hazardous waste Directive included a special safeguard clause (Art. 7) addressing threats to the population or the environment in cases of emergencies or grave danger. This provision is now replaced by Article 13 of the 2008 Framework Directive entitled 'Protection of human health and the environment'. Article 13 applies to all waste management but for hazardous waste it is strengthened with Article 17 on 'Control of hazardous waste'. Furthermore, Article 18 provides for a ban on the mixing of hazardous waste with other wastes (with some specific exceptions). Article 19 proscribes its packaging and labelling. All establishments for waste treatment are supposed to obtain a permit from Member States. Some exemptions of this general permit requirement are allowed (Art. 24). However in the case of hazardous waste treatment specific conditions are to be fulfilled (Art. 25.2). Finally, for hazardous waste strict requirements are set for record keeping (Art. 35.1) and such records should be preserved longer than for normal waste (Art. 35.2).

Because the environmental dangers connected to the disposal of waste oils, Directive 75/439 had set specific rules.[26] Rules concerning waste oils are now subsumed in Article 21 of the 2008 Framework Directive. In Article 21(3), the Directive emphasise the processing of waste oils by regeneration rather than by combustion (Art. 21(3).[27]

---

22   OJ 1991 L 377/20, as amended by Directive 94/31, OJ 1994 L 168/28.
23   Originally Decision 94/904, OJ 1994 L 356/14, now replaced by Decision 2001/537, OJ 2001 L 203/18.
24   Art. 41.b contains some transitory amendments to the 'old' Hazardous Waste Directive 91/689/EEC valid from 12 December 2008 till 12 December 2010.
25   Case C-318/98 [2000] ECR I-4785, para. 56.
26   OJ 1975 L 194/31, as amended by Directive 2000/76, OJ 2000 L 332/91; repealed from 12 December 2010.
27   *Cf. also* 'classic' jurisprudence as in Case 240/83, *ADBHU* [1985] ECR 531 and Case 172/82, *Inter-Huiles* [1983] ECR 555.

1 WASTE MANAGEMENT IN EU LEGISLATION: AN INTRODUCTION

1.2.2   Radioactive Waste

Under the Euratom Treaty the EU has a special regime for the management of radioactive waste. Neither the 2006 Waste Framework Directives nor the old Hazardous Waste Directive applied to radioactive waste where the Euratom regime applied.[28] That exclusion was not changed in the 2008 Framework Directive. Where precisely the boundaries lie between the competence of the European Community for the protection of public health and the environment and Euratom powers regarding the safety of sources of ionising radiation remains unclear and is a subject for further research.[29]

In case of a risk of radioactive waste pollution of another Member State, plans for its disposal are governed by Article 37 Euratom, providing the Commission the opportunity to deliver an opinion on the possibility of trans-boundary radioactive contamination.[30] Under the Treaty, the Commission has powers to verify the operation and efficiency of nuclear facilities, including those for storing radioactive waste in the Member States, powers it has not made extensive use of.

This way of regulating such an important matter may no longer be most appropriate. In Directive 2011/70/Euratom[31] a EU framework for the safe management of spent fuel and radioactive waste has now been laid down which is to be transposed before 23 August 2013. It applies Directive 96/29/Euratom which addresses the basic safety standards for the protection against radiation of workers and public, but does not apply to radioactive mining waste which is covered by Directive 2006/21/EC, the Mining Waste Directive (see below, section 1.4). Directive 2011/70 obliges the Member States to adopt a national regulatory framework for the waste substances concerned (Art. 5) and to establish a competent national authority. The sites for radioactive waste are to be subject to licensing. Adequate financing for the often very costly long term management of radioactive waste is to be ensured (Art. 9), which may involve the nuclear industry. Art. 10 foresees a special transparency regime for the sector.

---

28 *See, e.g.,* the Preamble, para. 10 of Directive 2006/21/EC on the management of waste from extractive industries, or, also, the Preamble, para. 10 of Directive 2004/35/EC on environmental liability with regard to the prevention and remedying of environmental damage.

29 *See* ECJ in Case C-29/99, *Commission v. Council* [2002] ECR I-11221, para. 82. *See also* Case C-376/90 where the ECJ rejected the Commission's argument that Member States were not allowed to enact more stringent protective measures than those of the EURATOM regime: *Commission v. Belgium* [1992] ECR I-6153. Moreover, it is also to be seen whether there will be tension between the internal market competence and environmental concerns in respect to the EU energy policy as laid down in Art. 194(2) TFEU (*see* Jans & Vedder, *op. cit.*, p. 86).

30 Art. 37 Euratom has been subject to the Court's scrutiny in the *Catténom* case, Case 187/87 [1988] ECR 5013.

31 OJ 2011 L 1999/48 *ff.*

1.3 Transport of Waste

1.3.1 General

In this area international instruments have had a strong impact, particularly those in respect to the transport of hazardous and radioactive waste. The 1989 Basel Convention on the Control of Trans-boundary Movements of Hazardous Waste and their Disposal, and its 1995 Amendment (Decision II/12) prohibiting all hazardous waste shipment to Non-OECD countries whether for disposal or for recovery, has been the most important international legal and policy instrument.[32] Other OECD decisions including of the Nuclear Energy Agency (NEA), instruments enacted by the IMO and the IAEA, as well as relevant provisions in the EEA and in the Lomé Conventions have also had an impact on Community legislation. In Community law transport of waste is governed by Regulation (EC) 1013/2006[33] on shipments of waste which has replaced Regulation 259/93[34] in order to strengthen and simplify control procedures for waste shipments. It also incorporates into Community legislation subsequent amendments to the waste lists annexed to the Basel Convention. Regulation 1013/2006 distinguishes between shipments into and out of the EU, and shipments between the Member States. Shipments between Member States whether for recovery or for disposal are subject to a procedure of prior notification and consent (PIC). Prior notification is required; grounds for objection against shipments are listed. Shipments destined for disposal are subject to a stricter regime than those for recovery. Possible discrepancy has arisen in respect to the classification of waste and the different treatment as a consequence.[35] The implementation of the principles of proximity, priority for recovery and self-sufficiency may result in a systematic refusal of waste for disposal, whereas systematic refusal of waste for recovery is probably also not to be excluded if a Member State has set high national recovery standards. A considerable jurisprudence exists already on several aspects of the procedure and additional research seems highly relevant at this point.[36]

---

32 But *see also* the 1973 London Convention for the Prevention of Pollution by Ships (MARPOL), as amended by a 1978 Protocol, and the 1998 Rotterdam Convention on the Prior Informed Consent Procedure for Certain Hazardous Chemicals and Pesticides in International Trade. For a useful summary of these international conventions: P. Birnie, A. Boyle & C. Redgwell, *International Law & the Environment*, 3rd edn, Oxford University Press, Oxford, 2009, pp. 473-486, 446-448.
33 OJ 2006 L 190/1.
34 OJ 1993 L 30/1.
35 Case C-192/96, *Beside* [1998] ECR I-4029, and, in paticular, Case C-203/96, *Dusseldorp* [1998] ECR I-4075, where the Court established that unlike other waste and if certain conditions were fulfilled, waste for 'recovery' was to move freely for processing between Member States.
36 *See* for questions raised regarding the PIC procedure: Case C-215/04, *Pedersen* [2006] ECR I-1465, Case C-6/00, *ASA* [2002] ECR I-1961, and Case C-472/02, *Siomab* [2004] ECR I-9971, and on the meaning of Art. 12(1)(c) of the Basel Convention, Case C-227/02, *EU Wood Trading* [2004] ECR I-11957. *Cf. also* Jans & Vedder's discussion and critical remarks on the self-sufficiency and proximity principles, *op. cit.*, p. 495.

Regulation 1013/2006 does not apply to shipments within Member States. The only requirement is that an appropriate system for the control and supervision of such shipments is established which takes the European system into account.

For shipments outside the EU, the Regulation follows the Basel Convention quite closely. The basic rule is Article 34(1) of the Convention prohibiting all waste export for disposal.[37] Exporting waste for recovery to non-OECD countries is prohibited if it concerns hazardous waste or if there is reason to believe that the waste will not be treated in an environmentally sound way at destination. The remaining waste exports to non-OECD countries are subject to the PIC procedure.

Finally, in principle, all imports into the EU for disposal are prohibited. In exceptional cases the regime for intra-EU transports applies.[38]

1.3.2 Transport of Hazardous Waste

As noted above, Regulation (EC) 1013/2006 prohibits the export of hazardous waste to non-OECD countries. In that sense the Regulation implements the Basel Convention (Decision II/12). If for disposal only, the Member States may prohibit the import of all 'Regulation' hazardous waste (conform Art. 11(1)(e), of the Basel Convention). However, if the import is for recovery purposes there is much controversy over the Member States' powers to restrict such imports.

The 2006 Regulation distinguishes 'green' (Annex III) and 'amber' (Annex IV) waste[39]; the 'red' list of the 1993 Regulation has been replaced by a list of wastes (Annex V) for which export is prohibited, including export of mixtures of hazardous and non-hazardous wastes. To non-OECD countries such exports are prohibited whether for disposal or recovery. The composition of these lists in comparison to those of the Basel Convention and other relevant international instruments is an important subject of research.

1.3.3 Transport of Radioactive Waste

The new Directive 2011/70 /Euratom on the management of radioactive waste will also (partly) apply to the transport of such waste. The 1989 Basel Convention and its EC implementing Regulation 1013/2006 do not apply to such transport.[40] For this activity, the

---

37 Export to EFTA (European Free Trade Association) is the exception. To such movements, basically, the EU regime applies.
38 Exceptions can be countries parties to the Basel Convention, countries with which explicit agreements have been concluded and countries subject to war or crisis (*see* further Art. 45).
39 For green list waste a general information requirement is stipulated, for amber waste a PIC procedure.
40 *Cf.* Art. 1(3)(c) of the Basel Regulation.

applicable IAEA and IMO Conventions were applied into Community legislation by way of Directive 92/3/Euratom,[41] replaced by Directive 2006/117/Euratom (transposed since 25/12/2008).[42] In particular, this was the case for the 1997 IAEA Joint Convention on the Safety of Spent Fuel management and on the Safety of Radioactive Waste Management.[43] The 2006 Directive has been modelled on the arrangement for hazardous waste under the Basel Convention (*e.g.*, each transport requires notification and permission), and decisions taken in the context of the OECD (the NEA), the IAEA and the IMO. It maintains the distinction between intra-EU transport and transport outside the EU (as in Regulation 1013/2006 on the Transport of Hazardous waste-see the previous section). Other than under Directive 92/3 Euratom, spent nuclear fuel for reprocessing is now included in the 2006 Directive (under Art. 1(2)). Member States of transit may refuse consent if they consider the shipment contrary to their international, European or national obligations (Art. 9(3)(a)). Member States of destination may also invoke legislation on the management of radio-active waste or spent fuel (Art. 9(3)(b)). In any case conditions attached to the consent must be non-discriminatory, *i.e.*, they may not be more stringent than requirements for similar shipments within that Member State.

1.4 Some Concluding Remarks: Suggestions for Further Research

The previous pages have been on matters of principle and definition, the development of the Community/EU policy and law on the management of various forms of waste management, notably of hazardous including radioactive waste and on the transport of various forms of waste. Waste policy and law has gradually become a real Community concern instead of an area where the Member States' discretion prevails. Lately, the EU approach has become less 'haphazard', evolving, since the adoption in 2005 of the 'Thematic Strategy on the Prevention and Recycling of Waste' into a comprehensive approach for major parts of the subject matter. Also, gradually, the protection of human health and the environment has become the prevailing Community/EU purpose in respect to waste management whereas for a long time the trade in waste (waste as a good and a product) was at least as important. Still, tension between the trade aspects and the prevention of damage to health and environment will undoubtedly remain a characteristic of waste management, notably in respect to its transport. The challenge however, of an adequate and healthy policy regarding waste management remains very considerable and the prolonged Neapolitan

---

41　Council Directive 92/3/Euratom of 3 February 1992 regarding the supervision and control of shipments of radioactive waste between Member States into and out of the Community.
42　OJ 2006 L 337/21.
43　The Convention entered into force on 18 June 2001. Since 2005 Euratom has been a party to the Convention (*see* Decision 2005/84/Euratom, OJ 2005 L 30/10).

waste crisis in Italy is not at all the only indication for its complexity. Proper waste management belongs to the perhaps not so attractive but inevitable and essential activities in modern society.

In terms of further (legal) research areas the preceding pages have pointed at a few of a considerable number. The new 2008 Framework Directive itself brings up various questions, most of them a 'heritage' from the past, *i.e.*:

- Remaining questions of definition, partly resulting from technical development, as in: do the conditions of Article 5 of the Directive adequately define a 'by-product';
- The precise requirements to be fulfilled in order to recover waste as combustion fuel for electricity production (Art. 6 of the Directive);
- What does the rather broad statement mean that waste management be carried out "without endangering human health, without harming the environment" (Art. 13 of the Directive): what obligations follow for the Member States including in terms of their margin of discretion. Has the article direct effect;
- In respect to household waste: how do the proximity and self-sufficiency principles relate to the prohibition of import restrictions on the trade in waste (Art. 16).

Apart from issues more directly related to the Framework Directive, the following seem also interesting further to pursue:

- What remains of the Member State's discretion to organise their own national management of waste, notably regarding the disposal of waste (a matter specifically coming to the fore in the EU's reaction and the ECJ's jurisprudence regarding the Italian waste crisis);
- How do Euratom special powers regarding the safety of sources of ionizing radiation relate to the more general EUresponsibility for public health and the environment (here the new Directive 2011/70/Euratom on the safe management of spent fuel and radioactive waste deserves special attention);
- Do Member States still have the right to refuse hazardous or other waste transports in the light of high national recovery standards;
- How does the hazardous waste list of Regulation 1013/2006 (Annex V) compare with the requirements imposed by the Basel Convention: does the list represent an appropriate and correct implementation of the Basel obligations;
- Do Member States have the right to refuse radioactive waste transport under Article 6 of Directive 2006/117/Euratom?

As said these are only a few issues demanding further consideration, other perhaps more interesting ones will undoubtedly emerge in this highly dynamic and engaging field.

2 WASTE MANAGEMENT IN THE ECHR: AN INTRODUCTION

Ioannis Panoussis

Waste management is a very sensitive issue in many, if not all, European countries. The example of Italy, in the Region of Naples, is extremely relevant but other European countries such as France (especially in the South), Greece and others already had and will have to cope with similar questions in the future. As a consequence we witness the development of national, EU and international norms aiming to safeguard the Environment and to agree on specific policies in order to promote the best possible solutions for the treatment of Waste.

When considering these general elements, we can easily understand that studying waste management policies requires a comparative EU and general international perspective. Aside these specific norms adopted in a national or international context, we can also see that today other branches of law have to take environmental aspects into account. When studying the impact of waste on people's health and life, we can imagine that this subject represents an interesting area of study for Human Rights.

Naturally, international Human Rights norms are not involved in the definition of what waste is or the way each kind of waste is treated. But Human Rights could play a role in order to reaffirm the obligations of States to protect the persons under their jurisdiction. That means that Human Rights are only relevant regarding the actions or inactions of States, not so much for the development of a framework of what public actions should be undertaken. Hence there have been no specific instruments agreed in the Council of Europe dealing with Waste management policies. Therefor the question that arises is, if there is general protection under the European Convention on Human Rights.

In order to answer this question, we need to know if 'environment' is taken into account as a person's right and/or if it corresponds to a State's obligation.[1] If that is the case we should look for specific obligations of States concerning Waste management that a potential victim could use in order to seize the European Court of Human Rights (ECtHR).

---

1 The last twenty years, the Human Rights doctrine has been really interested in the existence of such a right. *See,* among others, D. Shelton, 'Human Rights, Environmental Rights, and the Right to Environment', *Stanford Journal of International Law*, 1991-1992, p. 103; L.E. Rodriguez-Rivera, 'Is the Human Right to Environment Recognized Under International Law – It Depends on the Source', *Colorado Journal of International Environmental Law and Policy*, 2001, p. 1; M. Thorme, 'Establishing Environment as a Human Right', *Denver Journal of International Law and Policy*, 1990-1991, p. 301. For a European approach, *see,* M. Dejeant-Pons, 'Les droits de l'homme à l'environnement dans le cadre du Conseil de l'Europe', *Revue Trimestrielle des Droits de l'Homme*, Vol. 60, 2004, p. 861.

2.1 Protection of the Environment and the European Convention of Human Rights

None of the general instruments of protection of Human Rights, except the African Charter on Human and Peoples Rights,[2] recognizes explicitly the existence of a right to a clean environment. Of course, such rights are recognized in many specific instruments,[3] some of them adopted in the area of Economic, Social and Cultural Rights.[4]

Concerning, especially, the European Convention on Human Rights, there was neither an explicit, nor an implicit approach of this 'right' in the Convention or the additional protocols. That does not mean that 'environment' is totally absent in the work of the Council of Europe. In 1990, the Organization adopted the Dublin Declaration[5] and the Parliamentary Assembly, on three different occasions,[6] adopted recommendations in order to promote a clean and healthy environment. Although this was a good beginning, none of the acts mentioned above was binding and none recognized the existence of a right to such an environment. That is to say that the European Court was the only organ capable of filling the gap by way of its case-law.

2.1.1 Protection of the Environment: A General Approach of the ECtHR Case-Law

Prior to the early 1990s the European Court seemed to ignore Environmental damages as a potential factor of the violation of human rights. Since then, the complexity of some cases and the evolutionary interpretation practiced by the Court gave rise to new case-law where compensations for environmental damages were possible under other rights and freedoms conferred to the victims.

---

[2] Art. 24 of the African on Human and Peoples' Rights, adopted 27 June 1981 reads as follows: "All peoples shall have the right to a general satisfactory environment favorable to their development."

[3] See for example the 1998 Convention on Access to Information, Public Participation and Access to Justice in Environmental Matters, also called the 'Aarhus Convention'.

[4] It is interesting to note that the International Covenant on Economic, Social and Cultural Rights does not guarantee the right to a 'clean' environment as such. Protection of the environment is indirect and we can find some provisions referring to it. For example, the right to health (Art. 12) within the Covenant expressly calls on States parties to take steps for "the improvement of all aspects of environmental and industrial hygiene and the prevention, treatment and control of epidemic, endemic, occupational, and other diseases". At the regional level the San Salvador additional Protocol to the American Convention contains explicitly a provision referring to the environment. Art. 11 is entitled: 'Right to a healthy environment' and proclaims "(1.) Everyone shall have the right to live in a healthy environment and to have access to basic public services and (2.) The States parties shall promote the protection, preservation and improvement of the environment".

[5] The Council of Europe has adopted the 1990 Dublin Declaration on 'The Environmental Imperative' stating that the objective of the Community action for the protection of the environment "must be to guarantee citizens the right to a clean and healthy environment".

[6] The Parliamentary Assembly has officially recommended a 'Human Right to a Healthy and Clean Environment' in the European Convention and made reference to this and other human rights approaches to environmental issues in its Recommendations No. 1130 (1990), No. 1431 (1999) and No. 1614 (2003).

The first important case where the Court explicitly mentions 'environment' as a factor that should be taken into account concerns noise due to aircraft in the *Powell and Rayner* case.[7] Almost the same issue gave rise some years later to the *Hatton* case.[8] In both judgments the Court accepted examination of the potential effect of the Heathrow airport noise on the environment of the applicants under Article 8 of the Convention. Even though a clear link was made between the protection of private and family life and the Environment, the Court refused to recognize the existence of a special right to a 'clean' environment. It considers that "there is no explicit right in the Convention to a clean and quiet environment, but where an individual is directly and seriously affected by noise or other pollution, an issue may arise under Article 8".[9] In both cases, the Court admits the existence of a margin of appreciation for States even though they have a positive obligation to act in favor of the environment. When States proceed to a restriction, they have to respect the conditions imposed by Article 8 §2[10] and they have to especially observe the proportionality between the measures taken and their aim. After balancing the personal interest of the applicants based on environmental considerations and the general interest – economic well-being of the State in those two cases – the Court finally concluded to the non-violation of the Convention.[11]

The leading European cases concerning the environment also include issues about industrial pollution. The well-known *Lopez Ostra*[12] and *Guerra*[13] cases were specifically dealing with this subject pointing out the obligations of States when treating dangerous Waste.

---

7   ECtHR, judgment of the 21st February 1990, *Case of Powell and Rayner v. the United Kingdom*, Series A, 172.
8   ECtHR, Grand Chamber judgment of 8th July 2003, *Hatton and Others v. United Kingdom*.
9   *Ibid.*, §96; earlier, the Chamber had recognized such a right.
10 This paragraph provides for the respect of three conditions: the restriction must be provided by law, it must have a legitimate aim and must be necessary in democratic society. This last condition implies, among others, for the respect of the principle of proportionality. The exact wording used in this article is "There shall be no interference by a public authority with the exercise of this right except such as is in accordance with the law and is necessary in a democratic society in the interests of national security, public safety or the economic well-being of the country, for the prevention of disorder or crime, for the protection of health or morals, or for the protection of the rights and freedoms of others".
11 In §§121-122 of the *Hatton and Others* case, above, the Court expressly observes "that according to the second paragraph of Article 8 restrictions are permitted, inter alia, in the interests of the economic well-being of the country and for the protection of the rights and freedoms of others. It is therefore legitimate for the State to have taken the above economic interests into consideration in the shaping of its policy". And it continues affirming that "the Court must consider whether the State can be said to have struck a fair balance between those interests and the conflicting interests of the persons affected by noise disturbances, including the applicants. Environmental protection should be taken into consideration by States in acting within their margin of appreciation and by the Court in its review of that margin, but it would not be appropriate for the Court to adopt a special approach in this respect by reference to a special status of environmental human rights. In this context the Court must revert to the question of the scope of the margin of appreciation available to the State when taking policy decisions of the kind at issue."
12 ECtHR, judgment of the 9th of December 1994, Case of *Lopez Ostra v. Spain*, Series A, 303-C.
13 ECtHR, Grand Chamber Judgment of the 19th of February 1998, Case of *Guerra and others v. Italy*, Reports 1998-I.

In both cases the applicants were complaining due to the failure of the States to control the effects of industrial pollution. The Court, once again, refuted the existence of a right to environment but took into account the environmental dimension of the cases under Article 8 of the Convention. States have a duty to protect home and private life of persons under their jurisdiction. It considers that "[...] severe environmental pollution may affect individuals' well-being and prevent them from enjoying their homes in such a way as to affect their private and family life adversely [...]".[14] This implies positive obligations in order to protect the rights of individuals, such as taking all necessary measures in order to prevent violations.[15] Naturally the Court recognizes a margin of appreciation in order to safeguard the general interest of the community. States have to proceed to a control of proportionality, to a fair balance between the private interest of the applicants and the general interest of the Community.[16] In both cases this fair balance was inexistent as both States did not take any measures, even worst, did not respect their own national law regarding the protection of persons from environmental pollution.

What is more, in the *Guerra* case, it is interesting to point out the fact that the Court considers that where there are risks of violations of the well-being of persons, States have an obligation to inform individuals about the risks taken when living near a dangerous area. This obligation to inform is even clearer in the *Öneryildiz* case[17] where a number of deaths were caused to the applicant's family because of a methane explosion in a rubbish tip near his house. In this case the facts justified an examination of the case under Article 2 of the Convention which regime is naturally stricter than the one concerning Article 8 as limitations explicitly figure in it and the economic wellbeing of the State is not one of those.[18] The applicant complained that he did not have enough information about the risks related to this domestic area and that the Turkish authorities did not take the necessary active measures to avoid the explosion. It seems by consequence clear that the positive obligations of States are of all kinds and pursue multiple objectives: Human rights violations must be prevented by acting actively (administrative, legislative or operating measures) but also by informing, whenever necessary, in order to provide potential victims the opportunity to act before the worst occurs.[19]

These examples are of course not exhaustive. Actually, the Court has more and more opportunities to take environmental considerations into account under various articles of

---

14 See *Lopez Ostra*, above, §54 and *Guerra and others*, above, §60.
15 See below in the second part of this contribution.
16 See for example *Guerra and others* case, especially §58.
17 ECtHR, Grand chamber judgment of the 30th of November 2004, Case Oneryildiz v. Turkey.
18 The only limitations afforded under the wording of Art. 2 of the Convention are the death penalty (§1) – which is strictly abolished since the adoption of Protocol 13 and the interpretation given by the Court in the *Al-Saadoon and Mufdhi* case in 2010 – and the deaths resulting from a compatible use of force with the theory of absolute necessity (§2).
19 See below, Part II of this contribution.

the Convention. The Strasbourg judges constantly reaffirm that environmental issues are examined under the scope of the Convention if the applicants can prove the existence of a direct and personal negative effect on their private and family life or on another provision of the Convention. For example, in the last few years, it had the opportunity to discuss more complex situations such as the marine pollution in the *Mangouras* case[20] or even the situation of passive smokers in the *Florea* case.[21] The subject of the protection of the environment is constantly moving on. The case-law of the Court is increasingly more protective thanks to the evolutionary interpretation given by the European judges.

Waste management is at the heart of this evolution thanks to the very recent case *Di Sarno v. Italy*. What is really interesting in this case is that the environment seems to gain in autonomy.

2.1.2 Waste Management in the Campania and the 'New' Evolutionary Approach of Environment by the ECtHR

On 10 January 2012, the European Court pronounced a judgment in the *Di Sarno and others v. Italy* case[22] that could be seen as a small revolution. The applicants in this case were 18 Italian nationals, 13 of whom lived in the Campania and 5 who were working there. Due to the extreme situation to which they were exposed, especially at the end of 2007 and the first semester of 2008,[23] they complained against Italy on the basis of Articles 2 and 8 of the Convention. The damage to the environment and by consequence to their lives was due to the bad functioning of the waste management public services in Italy. The Court considered that there was a violation of the Convention.

The way the Court examines the attempts to the well-being of individuals is very interesting in this case. If we proceed to a strict analysis of the previous cases, it seems that the applicant should always prove the existence of a direct and personal effect on each person pretending to be a victim. As there is not a right to a 'clean' environment, which would be general and would not need to be personified, a general effect would not allow an examination of such a case under the Convention. Hopefully or unhopefully, in this case the Court seems to be less restrictive in the appreciation of the situation. A general deterioration of

---

20 ECtHR, Grand Chamber judgment of the 28th of September 2010, Case of *Mangouras v. Spain*.
21 ECtHR, judgment of the 14th of September 2010, *Case of Florea v. Roumania*. This case is also very interesting because of the legal basis under which the Court examines the situation of Mr. Florea. The dangers for her (environment) are examined under Art. 3 of the ECHR.
22 ECtHR, judgment of the 10th of January 2012, Case of *Di Sarno and others v. Italy*. *See* for a detailed analysis of the case Chapter 3.
23 The case concerned the state of emergency lasting for more than 15 years (from 11 February 1994 to 31 December 2009) in relation to waste collection, treatment and disposal in the Campania region of Italy where the applicants lived or worked, including a period of five months in which rubbish piled up in the streets.

the quality of life of the inhabitants and workers in the Campania (especially in Somma Vesuviana) seems to be enough to prove a violation of Article 8 of the Convention and the position of 'victim' of the applicants. The massive impact of the waste crisis seems to justify a more general – and consequently less personal – approach of the rights of the Convention. So general in fact, that we could argue that an autonomous right to a 'clean' environment is now emerging in the Convention.

The consequences here are huge for the status of victims. Even though the Court does not recognize the existence of any *actio popularis*,[24] it holds in §81 that the general effect of the waste crisis affected the hole population of Somma Vesuviana and consequently caused a direct negative effect on the applicants.[25] The Court is not proceeding according to a distinction between inhabitants and workers which also seems remarkable as the consequences for the protection of the homes of the victims under Article 8 is not the same. There is also an element of generalization that shows that the well-being of specific individuals is not at the heart of the reasoning of the Court. Since the first cases concerning the environment, the European judges were always refusing to examine a case if an applicant could not prove the existence of personal damage. Apparently, this is no longer required since the *Di Sarno* judgment.[26]

To conclude this aspect of European case-law, it seems that the protection of the environment is gaining autonomy, although it is not an independent right within the Convention. This autonomy should be understood as the possibility to refer to 'the right to a clean environment' if the factual elements of a specific case, linked directly or indirectly to environmental considerations, fall within the scope of a provision of the Convention. The Court offers a broad approach of what should be considered as directly effecting the well-being of victims, their life, integrity, private life, home or any other related provision of the Convention.

For those who are more skeptical, we will finally consider that this argumentation is only possible in extreme situations like the one in the Campania. The situation in southern Italy was well-known and long-lasting, its effects concerned a large geographical area, elements that explain here the general character of the violation. This could not be the reasoning of the Court in cases like those examined in the 1990s that were related to a limited geographical area.

---

24 *Id.*, §80.
25 The Court affirms specifically that "[…] les requérants dénoncent une situation affectant l'ensemble de la population de la Campanie, à savoir l'atteinte à l'environnement provoquée par le mauvais fonctionnement du système de collecte, de traitement et d'élimination des déchets mis en place par les autorités publiques. Toutefois, elle relève qu'il ressort des documents fournis par les parties que Somma Vesuviana a été frappée par la 'crise des déchets' […] Dans ces conditions, la Cour estime que les dommages à l'environnement dénoncés par les requérants sont de nature à affecter directement leur propre bien-être. Partant, il y a lieu de rejeter l'exception du Gouvernement" [English text not yet published].
26 For a critical approach of this matter, *see* N. Hervieu, 'Protection de l'environnement et impéritie fautive des autorités publiques dans la gestion des déchets', in *Lettre 'Actualités Droits-Libertés' du CREDOF*, 11 January 2012.

The last question that arises is the one concerning the exact obligations assumed by states when the environment is at stake. Generally speaking the European case-law identified specific positive obligations for State Parties.

2.2 STATES OBLIGATIONS IN ENVIRONMENTAL CASES UNDER ECHR LAW

When dealing with the obligations of States under European Human Rights Law, we can easily distinguish between negative obligations and positive obligations. The negative obligation is easy to understand. When a specific case concerns environmental issues, it means that States – through their services or agents – should avoid violations by way of their arbitrary action or interventions in the rights of the individual concerned (life, protection of private and family life, etc.). This negative obligation does not need further explanation. The positive obligations of States are much more interesting. In environmental cases, the Strasbourg Court had the opportunity to identify some specific obligations to take all the reasonable and adequate measures needed in order to protect individuals from a violation that could occur even from the action of a private actor.[27] This obligation finds its origin/foundation in the existence of a risk due to potential or actual environmental damages and in the obligation of States to prevent it. Consequently, what is generally at the origin of the responsibility of a State party is not the arbitrary interference, but the opposite: the inaction, the negligence of the State, its incapacity to be proactive. Naturally this positive obligation exists if the State knows or should have known the existence of the risk. This implies that the violation of an article of the Convention is not automatic and that a case to case analysis is necessary in order to determine if the factual elements at stake prove that the absence of any positive measure is due to negligence or to the impossibility of predicting the risks. It is also important to note that it is not necessary for the individual to prove that the violation occurred. This positive obligation sits on the existence of a risk which means that the Court will take into account the potentiality of a violation. This positive obligation, as mentioned above, corresponds to a duty to prevent and not to repair.

Generally speaking, there are two kinds of obligations: States must take operational measures in order to prevent the realization of the risk and they must inform individuals about the risks. In the former sense, States must act directly by adopting measures that can safeguard the rights of individuals. In the latter sense, States must inform the individuals about the risk in order to offer them the opportunity to take the actions needed in order to avoid the violation of their rights by themselves.

---

27 See, for example, ECtHR, judgment of the 27th of January 2009, *Case of Tătar v. Romania*, §88; Case of Hatton and others, above, §128; ECtHR, judgment of the 10th of November, Case of *Taşkin and others v. Turkey*, §§118, 119.

2.2.1 The Positive Obligations to Take Any Operational Measures

Concerning this first aspect of positive obligations, the European case-law offers some very interesting examples of what a State should do. The case-law concerns either the application of Article 2 (right to life), or the application of Article 8 of the Convention (generally under the protection of privacy and the home).

One of the leading cases concerning that kind of positive obligations, especially when there is a risk of violations of the right to life, is the *Öneryildiz* case.[28] It concerned the treatment of dangerous waste (a rubbish tip) and the possibility of a methane explosion that could cause many deaths. In this specific case, taking into account all the factual elements, the Court considered that it was well known that the activities were dangerous and that the national legislation was not respected. That is why it was easy to establish the responsibility of the Turkish State for its negligence. It could be perceived as a passive violation of the right to life due to the inaction of the national authorities.

Concerning more precisely the nature of the positive obligations that exist upon States under Article 2 of the Convention regarding environmental cases, the Court considers that they are of two kinds. States have a primary duty to put in place a legislative and administrative framework designed to provide effective deterrence against threats to the right to life. That means that States should adapt their legislation and practices in order to positively protect the rights of individuals. The aim of those specific operational measures is to prevent violations of the right to life. The European Court held that when dealing with

> dangerous activities, [...], special emphasis must be placed on regulations geared to the special features of the activity in question, particularly with regard to the level of the potential risk to human lives. They must govern the licensing, setting up, operation, security and supervision of the activity and must make it compulsory for all those concerned to take practical measures to ensure the effective protection of citizens whose lives might be endangered by the inherent risks.[29]

We can easily understand from this extract, that there is not a limitative approach of what national authorities should do. On the contrary, the Court adapts the operational measures to the specific situation examined and addresses the State's obligations which concern not only the authorization but also the exploitation of dangerous sites dealing with waste.

The second aspect of the positive obligations under Article 2 is the obligation to provide a judicial response in case of an alleged infringement of the right to life. This aspect is complementary to the former. The legislative and administrative framework must be properly implemented and any breaches should be redressed and punished. This implies a

---

28 ECtHR, Grand chamber judgment of the 30th of November 2004, Case *Öneryildiz v. Turkey*.
29 *Id.*, §90.

well-known obligation to investigate and to provide an effective judicial system who's aim is to identify those responsible and to punish them. To sum up, the Court considers that

> the judicial system required by Article 2 must make provision for an independent and impartial official investigation procedure that satisfies certain minimum standards as to effectiveness and is capable of ensuring that criminal penalties are applied where lives are lost as a result of a dangerous activity if and to the extent that this is justified by the findings of the investigation.[30]

What is interesting here is that we find the same dual approach as the one that the Court created concerning the positive obligations deriving from the combination of Articles 2 and 3 with Article 1 of the Convention. States have obligations that cover what happens before a violation occurs (prevention) and after a violation occurs (investigation and redressing).[31] Environmental cases are the only ones where the Court proceeds to that interpretation without referring to Article 1.

Dealing now with the positive obligations under Article 8, the European Court applies all the principles related to the operational measures mentioned above. Waste management is a dangerous activity that also needs a proactive approach from national authorities in order to protect private life and especially protect the home.

The *Di Sarno* case is of great interest. Even though the Italian government was not found negligent, it seems that the Court had to deal here with some relevant aspects of what is a necessary operational measure when managing waste in a period of crisis qualified as a situation of 'force majeure'. Is there a duty to provide specific services when the crisis is due to the negligence of a private actor paralyzing a whole Region? Is waste management a dangerous activity that obliges States to act by themselves?

The first interesting aspect of this case concerns the fact that the Court recognizes a wide margin of appreciation in respect to the choices made among the operational measures necessary to respond to the crisis and to the risk of infringement of Human rights. That means by consequence that States can delegate a public service, such as collecting, treatment and eliminating waste to a private actor. But, the fact of delegating this power to a company does not mean that it also transfers the responsibility, in case of bad compliance with the legislative and administrative framework.[32] States still have the obligation to be

---

30 *Id.*, §94.
31 *See* on this specific aspect, I. Panoussis, 'L'obligation générale de protection des droits de l'Homme', *Revue Trimestrielle des Droits de l'Homme*, Vol. 70, 2007, pp. 427-461.
32 *See* especially §110 where the Court reiterates its opinion about the existence of a "marge d'appréciation dont jouissent les Etats dans le choix des mesures concrètes à adopter pour s'acquitter des obligations positives découlant de l'article 8 de la Convention […] La circonstance que les autorités italiennes aient confié à des organismes tiers la gestion d'un service public ne saurait cependant les dispenser des obligations de vigilance leur incombant en vertu de l'article 8 de la Convention" [English text not yet published].

vigilant and they retain their responsibility in case of inaction. That is to say, that States remain the only responsible for the good implementation of the waste management policies adopted in the country. The long-lasting situation in the Campania minimally proves the inefficacity of State but does not justify an exemption of its responsibility.

Should the argument of the existence of a 'force majeure' be taken into account? It seems that the Court has not excluded this possibility. It even refers to general international law in order to define the concept.[33] But States must prove that the event qualified as 'force majeur' is external, unforeseen and impossible to handle by State authorities. Referring to the case-law of the Court of Justice of the EU – and practicing what we can qualify as a 'dialogue between judges' – the Strasbourg judges concluded the absence of such 'force majeure'.[34]

To conclude, it is interesting to note that in the end States have great latitude in taking measures in order to avoid an environmental risk. The European judges consider that national authorities, in applying the principle of subsidiarity, are those that can take the best decisions. What the Court is searching for is not the appreciation of taking one measure instead of another. What the Court will evaluate is the State's capacity to react and the efficacy of the measures.

2.2.2 The Positive Obligation to Inform

Next to this general positive obligation to take any necessary measure in order to avoid the realization of a risk, also is found a procedural obligation to inform. This obligation to inform individuals about the potential risks is absolutely essential in environmental cases. It is important to understand two things before examining this obligation to inform.

First of all, we should avoid any confusion with Article 10 of the ECHR. Article 10 is dealing with freedom of expression and it is well established that this right also contains an aspect of the freedom for individuals to seek and to impart information. Naturally this provision applies in situations where individuals would like to have access to information provided by the media or any other actor that is in possession of relevant information. But this provision does not create a specific obligation upon States to impart any information

---

33 The Court refers to Art. 23 of the Draft Articles of the International Law Commission on Responsibility of States for Internationally Wrongful Acts which defines force majeure as "the occurrence of an irresistible force or of an unforeseen event, beyond the control of the State, making it materially impossible in the circumstances to perform the obligation".

34 It is interesting to notice here the voluntary cooperation between European judges of different systems (or legal orders) that we can call 'dialogue between judges'. The Strasbourg Court refers explicitly to the case-law of the Luxembourg Court on the same facts. See Court of Justice of the European Union, judgment of the 4th of March 2010, *Commission v. Italy*, C-297/08.

in its possession in environmental cases. The Court had the opportunity to affirm that clearly in the *Guerra* case.[35] The obligation to inform when dealing with the Environment is an obligation that derives directly from Articles 2 (right to life) and 8 (right for respect of private and family life – especially home protection) of the Convention. This duty comes from the necessity for individuals to have access to essential information that enables them to assess the risks they and their families might run.[36]

Another interesting aspect is that this obligation to inform is actually well-known and recognized in general international law and is considered as fundamental. This information figures explicitly in Articles 4 and 5 of the Aarhus Convention adopted in 1998.[37] We can also find similar provisions in other specific treaties and regulations such as the Convention on Civil Liabilities for Damage Resulting from Activities Dangerous to the Environment (Lugano, 1993),[38] the United Nations Framework Convention on Climate Change (1992)[39] or, in the EU context, Directive 90/313/EEC on the freedom of access to information on the environment.[40] We could easily argue that all these texts find their source of inspiration in Principle 10 of the Rio Declaration, which declares that each individual shall have appropriate access to information concerning the environment that is

---

35 Case of *Guerra and others*, above, §53. The exact position of the Court consists in affirming that "freedom to receive information, referred to in paragraph 2 of Article 10 of the Convention, 'basically prohibits a government from restricting a person from receiving information that others wish or may be willing to impart to him'. That freedom cannot be construed as imposing on a State, in circumstances such as those of the present case, positive obligations to collect and disseminate information of its own motion".

36 *Id.*, §60.

37 Art. 4, §1 (access to environmental information) reads as follows: "Each Party shall ensure that, subject to the following paragraphs of this article, public authorities, in response to a request for environmental information, make such information available to the public, within the framework of national legislation [...]". Art. 5 (collection and dissemination of environmental information) affirms that "1. Each Party shall ensure that: (a) Public authorities possess and update environmental information which is relevant to their functions; (b) Mandatory systems are established so that there is an adequate flow of information to public authorities about proposed and existing activities which may significantly affect the environment; (c) In the event of any imminent threat to human health or the environment, whether caused by human activities or due to natural causes, all information which could enable the public to take measures to prevent or mitigate harm arising from the threat and is held by a public authority is disseminated immediately and without delay to members of the public who may be affected. 2. Each Party shall ensure that, within the framework of national legislation, the way in which public authorities make environmental information available to the public is transparent and that environmental information is effectively accessible [...]".

38 Chapter 3 of the Lugano Convention refers explicitly in similar terms to the right to information in its Arts. 13-16.

39 Art. 6 (a) (ii) provides with the obligation for States to "promote and facilitate at the national and, as appropriate, subregional and regional levels, and in accordance with national laws and regulations, and within their respective capacities: [...] (ii) Public access to information on climate change and its effects; [...]".

40 Art. 1 describes the aim of this directive by affirming that "The object of this Directive is to ensure freedom of access to, and dissemination of, information on the environment held by public authorities and to set out the basic terms and conditions on which such information should be made available". The other provisions explain the effective measures that States should adapt in their legal order.

held by public authorities, including information on hazardous materials and activities in their communities.[41]

Two more questions still remain unsolved. What kind of environmental information should a State impart and is this obligation absolute?

Concerning the nature of the information, the Court uses very general expressions covering any useful information in order to evaluate the risks. Since the Strasbourg judges refer explicitly to the Aarhus Convention in their case-law,[42] we can try to be more precise on that aspect. Environmental information is defined in Article 2 §3, of the Convention to include the state of the elements of the environment, factors that affect the environment, decision-making processes, and the state of human health and safety.[43] There is no time limit set for that obligation which means that it covers any studies, plans, programs, activities that could be useful before and after the exploitation of a specific geographical zone for example. What matters is that individuals must have available a complete analysis of the potential risks and accordingly adapt their actions.

Naturally, in some specific circumstances, States are not willing to deliver any information in their possession. Is this in conflict with the positive obligation to inform? Not necessarily. The crucial question here is whether §2 of Article 8 concerning the possible interferences of a State in the exercise of the right to respect for one's private and family life can apply when dealing with positive obligations? The European Court seems to adopt a position which promotes the existence of a fair balance between the interests of the Community and those of individuals.[44] States consequently enjoy a certain margin

---

41 The 1992 Rio Declaration on Environment and Development defines the rights of the people to be involved in the development of their economies, and the responsibilities of human beings to safeguard the common environment. The declaration builds upon the basic ideas concerning the attitudes of individuals and Nations towards the environment and development. The exact wording of Principle 10 affirms that "Environmental issues are best handled with the participation of all concerned citizens, at the relevant level. At the national level, each individual shall have appropriate access to information concerning the environment that is held by public authorities, including information on hazardous materials and activities in their communities, and the opportunity to participate in decision-making processes. States shall facilitate and encourage public awareness and participation by making information widely available. Effective access to judicial and administrative proceedings, including redress and remedy, shall be provided".

42 See for instance, Case of *Di Sarno and others*, above, §107.

43 Environmental information is defined as follows: "'Environmental information' means any information in written, visual, aural, electronic or any other material form on: (a) The state of elements of the environment, such as air and atmosphere, water, soil, land, landscape and natural sites, biological diversity and its components, including genetically modified organisms, and the interaction among these elements; (b) Factors, such as substances, energy, noise and radiation, and activities or measures, including administrative measures, environmental agreements, policies, legislation, plans and programmes, affecting or likely to affect the elements of the environment within the scope of subparagraph (a) above, and cost-benefit and other economic analyses and assumptions used in environmental decision-making; (c) The state of human health and safety, conditions of human life, cultural sites and built structures, inasmuch as they are or may be affected by the state of the elements of the environment or, through these elements, by the factors, activities or measures referred to in subparagraph (b) above."

44 Case of *Powell and Rayner*, above, §41.

of appreciation in applying the Convention. That is why the Court clearly affirms that "even in relation to the positive obligations flowing from the first paragraph of Article 8 (art. 8 §1), in striking [the required] balance the aims mentioned in the second paragraph (art. 8 §2) may be of a certain relevance".[45]

Even though the case-law is not very precise concerning the reasons that could reasonably justify the absence or incomplete information, once again we can refer directly to the Aarhus Convention which explicitly identifies what could be understood as a 'legitimate aim' permitting restrictions in the exercise of this right in environmental cases. Naturally these aims are very close to those found in Article 8 §2[46] but are adapted to the specific situation. Article 4, §§3 and 4, of the Aarhus Convention gives two kinds of 'legitimate aims'. Either they affect certain specific interests (§4), or the authorities don't (yet) have the information or the applicant addressed a manifestly unreasonable or too general query (§3). The first situation is the one that can be seen as similar to the reason's provided in Article 8 §2. They address the protection of the interests of the Community which must be taken into account when searching for a fair balance with those of the individuals concerned. These 'legitimate aims' that can justify restrictions to the right to be informed are the preservation of: proceedings of public authorities, international relations, national defense or public security, the course of justice, commercial and industrial confidentiality, intellectual property rights, personal data, the interests of people delivering voluntarily some crucial information, the protection of the environment.[47]

---

45 *Id.*, §41.
46 The legitimate aims that can justify interference within the context of Art. 8 ECHR are national security, public safety or the economic well-being of the country, the prevention of disorder or crime, the protection of health or morals, or the protection of the rights and freedoms of others.
47 This provision reads as follows: "4. A request for environmental information may be refused if the disclosure would adversely affect:
  (a) The confidentiality of the proceedings of public authorities, where such confidentiality is provided for under national law;
  (b) International relations, national defence or public security;
  (c) The course of justice, the ability of a person to receive a fair trial or the ability of a public authority to conduct an enquiry of a criminal or disciplinary nature;
  (d) The confidentiality of commercial and industrial information, where such confidentiality is protected by law in order to protect a legitimate economic interest. Within this framework, information on emissions which is relevant for the protection of the environment shall be disclosed;
  (e) Intellectual property rights;
  (f) The confidentiality of personal data and/or files relating to a natural person where that person has not consented to the disclosure of the information to the public, where such confidentiality is provided for in national law;
  (g) The interests of a third party which has supplied the information requested without that party being under or capable of being put under a legal obligation to do so, and where that party does not consent to the release of the material; or
  (h) The environment to which the information relates, such as the breeding sites of rare species.
  The aforementioned grounds for refusal shall be interpreted in a restrictive way, taking into account the public interest served by disclosure and taking into account whether the information requested relates to emissions into the environment."

In order to conclude, it is important to understand that it is up to States to prove the existence of a negative impact on one of those elements in order to justify a restriction. The wording used in Article 4 §4 of the Aarhus Convention (*would adversely affect* instead of *may adversely affect*) is such that a certain degree of certainty must be provided concerning the *adverse effect* of the information given to individuals. In any case, it is by consequence, impossible to presume the negative impact.

All these elements examined above naturally apply to any form of environmental damage. Hence, management of hazardous waste also enters into consideration. The recent *Di Sarno* case also proves that it is necessary to adapt some elements under specific exceptional circumstances such as experienced in the Region of Naples.

Part II
Jurisprudence

3 THE 'WASTE CRISIS' IN CAMPANIA BEFORE THE EUROPEAN COURT OF HUMAN RIGHTS: SOME REMARKS ON THE CASE *DI SARNO* AND OTHERS V. ITALY

Mario Odoni

3.1 INTRODUCTION

The case under consideration originated in an application of 9 January 2008 lodged with the European Court of Human Rights against the Italian Republic by 18 Italian nationals. Thirteen of them lived in the municipality of Somma Vesuviana (Campania) while five others worked there.

The applicants complained that the State's bad management of the public waste collection, treatment and disposal service in Campania, likewise its failed due diligence in prosecuting those responsible for such a situation, had affected some of their rights under the European Convention of Human Rights.

In particular, relying on Articles 2 (right to life) and 8 (right to respect for private and family life), the applicants first submitted that Italy had failed to take appropriate measures to secure the proper functioning of the public waste collection, treatment and disposal service and had implemented inappropriate legislative and administrative policies. As a result the State had caused serious damage to the environment in their region and placed their lives and health, likewise those of the whole local population, at risk. Furthermore they complained that Italian authorities had failed to inform those concerned of the risks involved in living in a polluted area.[1]

Relying on Articles 6 (right to a fair hearing) and 13 (right to an effective remedy), the applicants alleged that the authorities had taken no initiatives to safeguard the inhabitants' rights and had delayed in the prosecution of those responsible for the bad 'waste management'.[2]

With regard to the complaint concerning the opening of criminal proceedings, the Court observed that neither Articles 6 and 13 nor any other provision of the Convention

---

1 ECtHR, *Di Sarno and Others v. Italy*, Application No. 30765/08, Judgement of 10 January 2012, para. 94.
2 *Di Sarno, op. cit.*, para. 114.

guaranteed an applicant a right to secure the prosecution and conviction of a third party or a right to 'private revenge'. On the other hand, the Court declared admissible the remainder of the complaint under Article 13, since it was related to the absence of effective remedies in the Italian legal system by which redress for the damage could be obtained.[3] With regard to the other complaints, the Court held that the facts alleged by the applicants had to be considered under Article 8, in relation to their right to respect for private and family life and home, but not under Article 2 as they had further submitted.[4]

3.2 The Circumstances of the Case

At the outset of its lengthy and detailed report on the circumstances of the case, the Court summed up the incredible story of the state of emergency in the region of Campania, which was declared by the Prime Minister on 11 February 1994 under Law n. 225 of 1992 on the establishment of the National Service of civil protection and formally ended on 31 December 2009. The state of emergency was declared owing to serious problems with the disposal of urban waste.

It must be noted that the management of the state of emergency was entrusted to ten different 'deputy commissioners' appointed by the Prime Minister. Among them were the head of the National Service of civil protection as well as the President of the Region Campania.[5]

During the long period of time indicated above the deputy commissioners, exercising the extraordinary powers they were endowed with, made a number of attempts to solve the 'waste problem' in the region, first of all by planning the construction of several landfill sites, facilities for sorting waste and conversion into refuse-derived fuel (RDF) and incinerators. The set up of an electric power plant using RDF was also planned by 31 December 2000.[6]

Unfortunately, unlike the Italy's Northern Regions, Campania did not have any municipal enterprise or other public utility endowed with the indispensable waste management know-how to carry out all related activities. For this reason, the deputy commissioners in office had to entrust the waste collection, treatment and disposal service to some private companies by a tendering procedure.[7] Such a procedure was applied both for the concession concerning the waste disposal service in Campania and for the concession to operate

---

3 *Di Sarno, op. cit.*, paras. 115, 116.
4 *Di Sarno, op. cit.*, para. 96.
5 *Di Sarno, op. cit.*, paras. 7 *ff.*
6 *Di Sarno, op. cit.*, paras. 11 *ff.*
7 See S. Marotta, 'L'emergenza rifiuti in Campania tra pubblico e privato', *in* A. Lucarelli & A. Pierobon (eds.), *Governo e gestione dei rifiuti. Idee, percorsi, proposte*, Edizioni Scientifiche Italiane, Naples, 2009, p. 426.

3 THE 'WASTE CRISIS' IN CAMPANIA BEFORE THE EUROPEAN COURT OF HUMAN RIGHTS: SOME REMARKS ON THE CASE DI SARNO AND OTHERS V. ITALY

in the Province of Naples. Then, owing to grave breaches of the respective concession agreements by the bidders, some criminal proceedings were begun in 2003 and in 2006 against the directors, managers and employees of the companies involved. Even a deputy commissioner was among those accused.[8]

In the meantime, as a consequence of the delays caused by these contractual breaches and of the closure of the Tufino landfill site in January 2001, the waste disposal services had been suspended in the Province of Naples. In order to face the problem of the accumulation of rubbish on public roads, the other municipalities of the Province authorized the storage of the waste in their landfill sites on a temporary basis.[9]

However, a further crisis occurred in 2007, when tonnes of waste piled up in the streets of Naples and several other towns, including the municipality of Somma Vesuviana, where the applicants live (and/or work).[10]

All the extraordinary measures, taken by the several Governments following one after another during the long period of time under consideration, cannot be reported here in detail. For the purposes of the present brief comment, suffice it to observe that unhappily the Italian authorities' action concerning the waste issue in Campania was in every circumstance inspired by the imperative of the 'emergency', instead of pursuing the preventive policies that the subject matter required.

This pathological 'emergency approach' sometimes brought about very astonishing measures. One might refer, for example, to the singular Government's decision to rescind by a decree the unfulfilled concession contracts.[11]

Quite paradoxically, even the two infringement procedures started by the European Commission against Italy, both concluded by a ECJ judgement declaring the Italian Republic's failure to fulfil its obligations under EU law,[12] seem to have been exploited as an excuse to persist in adopting an 'emergency approach' to waste management in Campania. They were put forward to the public opinion as further grounds for justifying the continuation of an 'emergency system' based on monocratic organs, endowed with *extra ordinem* powers, as a substitute for the legitimate local administrations.

Anyway, the facts showed how the 'emergency approach' to waste management was short-sighted and caused even greater damage, instead of solving the crisis.

---

8 *Di Sarno*, op. cit., paras. 20 *ff.*, 48 *ff.*
9 *Di Sarno*, op. cit., para. 17.
10 *Di Sarno*, op. cit., para. 36.
11 Law Decree No. 245 of 30 November 2005; *cf. Di Sarno*, op. cit., para. 26. On the legal problems arising from the cancellation of the concession contracts by the Law Decree No. 245, see C. Iannello, 'Profili giuridici dell'emergenza rifiuti nella Regione Campania', *in* Lucarelli & Pierobon, op. cit., p. 406, n. 3.
12 *See* respectively, ECJ, C-135/05, Judgement of 26 April 2007 and C-297/08, Judgement of 4 March 2010; *see also Di Sarno*, op. cit., paras. 52 *ff.*

3.3 The Way the Court Rejected the Government's Preliminary Objection Concerning the Applicant's 'Victim' Status and Some Anomalies of the Case under Consideration

The Italian 'emergency system' under consideration was ultimately condemned by the European Court of Human Rights in the *Di Sarno* case. But this criticism to the respondent Government's inappropriate policies on waste management may only be read 'between the lines' of the reasoning by which the Court concluded that the State had violated the applicants' rights under Articles 8 and 13 of the Convention. Accordingly, one must carefully examine the whole text of the judgement. First of all, it is important to point out how the Court rejected the Government's preliminary objections, because actually that was the way it decided on the merits too.

The Government maintained that the applicants could not claim to be 'victim' of a violation of the Convention within the meaning of Article 34. In particular, they had not proved to live or work near landfill sites or streets where the rubbish piled up might have seriously affected their health or well-being.[13] Indeed, according to well-known case-law, in order to raise an issue under Article 8 of the Convention the crucial element is the existence of a harmful effect on a person's private or family life and not simply the general deterioration of the environment.

Moreover, the Government argued that actually the applicants complained about the Italian legislative and administrative policies on 'waste management', thus bringing a sort of *actio popularis*, which is not allowed under the ECHR system.[14]

In view of the Government's contention, the Court first confirmed that an *actio popularis* would not be allowed under the ECHR and that the mere general deterioration of the environment could not be considered a violation of Article 8.[15] Then, quite astonishingly, it concluded that the environmental damage complained of by the applicants had been such as to directly affect their own well-being. The Court observed that the municipality of Somma Vesuviana, where they lived or worked, had been affected by the 'waste crisis', as it emerged from the documents produced by the parties. In particular, referring to several Government's documents and apart from the situation affecting the whole of the Campania's population, the Court pointed out that, during the acute phase of the crisis – from the end of 2007 until May 2008 – the inhabitants of Somma Vesuviana had been subjected to living in an environment polluted by the continual piling-up of rubbish on the streets.[16]

Thus, simply having regard to these public circumstances, the Court decided to reject the objection concerning the applicant's 'victim' status. In other words, while considering

---

13 *Di Sarno, op. cit.*, para. 78.
14 *Di Sarno, op. cit.*, para. 78.
15 *Di Sarno, op. cit.*, para. 80.
16 *Di Sarno, op. cit.*, para. 81.

irrelevant the 'large scale' state of emergency in Campania, the Court held that the 'smaller scale' situation in Somma Vesuviana fell within the scope of Article 8. The ultimate result seems to amount to a 'smaller' *actio popularis* granted to the inhabitants of Somma Vesuviana.[17]

Whatever one could think about such an interpretation, it is evident that, when the Court was arguing to reject the 'victim' status preliminary objection, actually it was already paving the way for its assessment on the merits of the case. Indeed, despite the Government's contention on the point, the Court took for granted that the public situation in Somma Vesuviana interfered with the applicant's rights under Article 8. This simple presumption in the Court's reasoning may sound strange, if one considers its opinion that

> in order to fall within the scope of Article 8, complaints relating to environmental nuisances have to show, firstly, that there was an actual interference with the applicant's private sphere, and, secondly, that a level of severity was attained.[18]

But this is not the only anomaly that one can point out in the case under consideration. Differently from previous cases in which environmental questions gave rise to violations of Article 8, the Court did not have to assess whether the interference with the rights protected by the first paragraph of this rule was 'justifiable' within the meaning of its paragraph 2.

Just to make a comparison, think for instance about the *Giacomelli v. Italy* case: here the applicant complained of the persistent noise and harmful emissions from a plant for the storage and treatment of 'special waste', a plant located only 30 metres away from her house.[19] In such a case the interference with the rights protected by the first paragraph of Article 8 was not disputed, nonetheless the Court had to determine whether it was necessary for achieving one of the aims mentioned in the second paragraph (like the public safety or the economic well-being of the country, for example).[20] In the Court's opinion, even admitting the State's wide margin of appreciation in making the initial assessment of the 'necessity' for the interference, "regard must be had to the fair balance that has to be struck between the competing interests of the individual and of the community as a whole",[21] namely the applicant's effective enjoyment of her right to respect for her home and her private and family life and the interest of the community in having a plant for the treatment of waste.[22]

---

17 *See* N. Hervieu, 'Droit au respect de la vie privée et du domicile (Art. 8 CEDH): Protection de l'environnement et impéritie fautive des autorités publiques dans la gestion des déchets', *La Revue des Droits de l'Homme*, <http://revdh.org/2012/01/11/droit-au-respect-de-la-vie-privee-et-du-domicile-art-8-protection-de-lenvironnement-et-imperitie-fautive-des-autorites-publiques-dans-la-gestion-des-dechets/>, who regarded the Court's decision above mentioned as an "acceptation implicite d'une sorte d'*actio popularis* à dimension locale et à teneur environnementale".
18 ECtHR, *Fadeyeva v. Russia*, Application No. 55723/00, Judgement of 9 June 2005, para. 70.
19 ECtHR, *Giacomelli v. Italy*, Application No. 59909/00, Judgement of 2 November 2006, paras. 68 *ff.*
20 *Giacomelli, op. cit.*, para. 72.
21 *Giacomelli, op. cit.*, para. 78.
22 *Giacomelli, op. cit.*, para. 97.

Turning to the particular circumstances of the *Di Sarno* case, it is clear that there was no need to determine whether the State had struck a 'fair balance' between the interest of the applicants and that of the community as a whole, as required by paragraph 2 of Article 8, simply because the interests at stake were not 'competing' but coincident. Indeed, it is self-evident that the piling-up of rubbish on the streets could not be justifiable for achieving one of the aims mentioned in the second paragraph. One could rather assert that such a situation can only be a hindrance to any of those aims.

3.4 The Way the Court Applied in the Present Case the Criterion 'in Accordance with the Law' Provided in Paragraph 2 of Article 8 of the Convention and Held that the State Violated the Applicants' Rights to Respect for Their Private Lives and Their Homes

As in other previous cases, the Court reiterated that whatever approach to the question is adopted – namely either an analysis in terms of a positive duty of the State to take reasonable and appropriate measures to secure the individuals' rights under paragraph 1 of Article 8, or in terms of a public authority's interference to be justified in accordance with paragraph 2 – *the applicable principles are broadly similar*.[23] But, considering the circumstances pointed out above, the scope of this Court's statement is not very clear in the present case. As argued above, here the applicability of the 'fair balance' criterion is excluded. Did the Court perhaps refer to the other criterion one can deduce from paragraph 2 of Article 8, namely that to be justified the 'interference' must be 'in accordance with the law'?[24]

In this respect, firstly it must be taken into account that the Court considered the case relating to the alleged State's failure to take the appropriate measures to secure the proper functioning of the public waste collection, treatment and disposal service. In other words, it acknowledged that the question to be analysed was in terms of positive obligations on the State.[25] Secondly, the Court's opinion must also be taken into account that

> where the State is required to take positive measures, […] even if the State has failed to apply one particular measure provided by domestic law, it may still fulfil its positive duty by other means. Therefore, in those cases the criterion "in accordance with the law" of the justification test cannot be applied in the same way as in cases of direct interference by the State. […] Thus […] domestic legality should be approached not as a separate and conclusive test, but rather as one of many aspects which should be taken into account in assessing whether the State has struck a "fair balance" in accordance with Article 8 § 2.[26]

---

23 *Di Sarno, op. cit.,* para. 105.
24 Cf. *Fadeyeva, op. cit.,* paras. 95 ff.
25 *Di Sarno, op. cit.,* para. 106.
26 *Fadeyeva, op. cit.,* paras. 96, 98.

3 THE 'WASTE CRISIS' IN CAMPANIA BEFORE THE EUROPEAN COURT OF HUMAN RIGHTS: SOME REMARKS ON THE CASE DI SARNO AND OTHERS V. ITALY

Now, one could wonder whether the criterion 'in accordance with the law' might still be of a certain relevance in the present case, where actually no 'fair balance' had to be struck between the interests of the applicants and of the community as a whole, since those interests could not be regarded as 'competing'. The Court did not consider expressly such a problem, nor did it exclude the relevance of the criterion. However, it seems that a positive replay on the point might be read within its reasoning.

In order to determine the nature of the State's positive obligations in the case under consideration, the Court stressed that the waste collection, treatment and disposal is without doubt a hazardous activity.[27] Even if it did not accept examining the case under Article 2 of the Convention (right to life), the Court described in terms of *preventive* measures the steps the State was expected to adopt, by expressly citing[28] a previous case[29] related to positive obligations drawn from Article 2.[30] Indeed, it stated that, especially in the context of a dangerous activity, States had first and foremost a positive obligation to put in place regulations geared to the special features of the activity in question, particularly with regard to the level of potential risk. This obligation must govern the licensing, setting up, operation, security and supervision of the activity and must make it compulsory for all those concerned to take practical measures to ensure the effective protection of citizens whose lives might be endangered by the inherent risks.[31]

Accordingly, the State was required to take reasonable and appropriate measures capable of safeguarding the individuals' rights to respect their home and for their private and family life and more in general to the enjoyment of a healthy and protected environment.[32] Furthermore, admitting that the choice to entrust the waste collection, treatment and disposal service to private companies fell within the State's margin of appreciation, the Court pointed out that under Article 8 of the Convention the State had a positive obligation to supervise those private companies entrusted with the public service.[33]

The emphasis on the *preventive* nature of the State's positive obligations seems to anticipate the definitive Court's assessment on the subject matter. It is here that one may understand, even if 'reading between the lines' as said, the way it applied the above mentioned criterion 'in accordance with the law' in the present case. In particular, one may realize

---

27 Di Sarno, op. cit., para. 110.
28 Di Sarno, op. cit., para. 106.
29 ECtHR, Öneryildiz v. Turkey, Application No. 48939/99, Judgement of 30 November 2004, para. 90.
30 On the Court's tendency, in its recent case-law relating to environmental issues, to standardize the parameters according to which it determines the State's positive obligations both under Art. 2 and under Art. 8, with the result of extending to its assessment under Art. 8 the stricter criteria normally applied under Art. 2, see A. Sironi, 'La tutela della persona in conseguenza di danni all'ambiente nella giurisprudenza della Corte europea dei diritti umani. Tra diritto al rispetto della vita privata e diritto alla vita', *Diritti umani e diritto internazionale*, Vol. 5, 2011, pp. 30 ff.
31 Di Sarno, op. cit., para. 106.
32 Di Sarno, op. cit., para. 110.
33 Ibid.

that, describing the circumstances of the case by a very lengthy and detailed report on the disastrous waste management in Campania and in the municipality of Somma Vesuviana – from the second half of the nineties until 2010 – actually the Court did not only intend to point out the State's violations of its own domestic law[34] (and of EU law, which must be regarded as falling within the notion of 'law' of Art. 8, para. 2). It rather intended to highlight the *origin* of those violations: the inadequacy of the State's whole approach to the issue, namely the pathological 'emergency management' of the 'waste situation' in Campania. In particular, considering how the Court stressed the aspect of potential risks inherent in waste management activity, one could argue that it ultimately held Italy had first and foremost violated the very 'precautionary approach' that nowadays inspires all the main rules governing the subject matter, especially under EU law.[35]

In this sense, it seems significant how the Court rejected another Government's argument. Italy had maintained that the state of crisis was attributable to certain circumstances, which it claimed to constitute a situation of *force majeure*. Contributing factors were the presence of organized crime in the region, the failure by the waste collection service bidders to meet their contractual obligations and secure the proper functioning of the service and the opposition of the local inhabitants to the establishment of landfills and refuse-derived fuel production facilities.[36] In this respect, the Court merely observed that, under Article 23 of the United Nations International Law Commission's Draft Articles on Responsibility of States for Internationally Wrongful Act, *force majeure* is "[…] an irresistible force

---

34 Perhaps, it would be going too far to claim that the Court might have taken into account some issues that the 'emergency management' of the 'waste situation' in Campania raises under Italian constitutional law. In this regard, one could refer to the use and in many respects the abuse of extraordinary normative and administrative *extra ordinem* powers, which the Government justified on the grounds of the emergency situation (*see* D. Mone, 'L'abuso del potere di ordinanza e la violazione dei diritti fondamentali', *in* Lucarelli & Pierobon, *op. cit.*, pp. 396 *ff.*). These extraordinary powers were conferred, again and again, for a very lengthy period, on monocratic organs, the 'deputy commissioners' appointed by the Prime Minister. Derogating many laws on the several matters involved, the *extra ordinem* powers of the 'deputy commissioners' ended by creating an actual 'special legal system' in force only in the Region of Campania (*see* A. Lucarelli, 'Governare e gestire la raccolta differenziata dal regime emergenziale al regime ordinario: verso il ritorno delle responsabilità politiche', *in* Lucarelli & Pierobon, *op. cit.*, pp. 461 *ff.* and L. Colella, 'La governance dei rifiuti in Campania tra tutela dell'ambiente e pianificazione del territorio. Dalla "crisi dell'emergenza rifiuti" alla "società europea del riciclaggio"', *Rivista giuridica dell'ambiente*, 2010, p. 524. Moreover, in this way the Government deprived local authorities of their legitimate competences, with the negative effect of relieving them also from their responsibilities (*see* Mone, *op. cit.*, p. 398 and Iannello, *op. cit.*, p. 407).

However, one could wonder whether this reiterated and prolonged system of extraordinary powers is compatible with *the rule of law*, which is expressly mentioned in the preamble of the Convention. To answer this question would imply, for instance, an in-depth analysis of the powers conferred on the deputy commissioners, particularly in order to verify whether they are not expressed in terms of *unfettered* powers (*cf.*, for instance, *mutatis mutandis*, ECtHR, *Amann v. Switzerland* [GC] Application No. 27798/95, Judgement of 16 February 2000, para. 56). Obviously, such an analysis could not be carried out here.

35 One could refer, for instance, to the new Framework Directive on waste management 2008/98/EC, expressly aimed at "preventing and reducing the adverse impacts of the generation and management of waste" (Art. 1), regarding which *see* Chapter 1.

36 *Di Sarno, op. cit.*, para. 99.

or [...] an unforeseen event, beyond the control of the State, making it materially impossible in the circumstances to perform [an international] obligation".[37]

A detail must not be overlooked, namely that the Court also referred to the foregoing paragraph 77 of its own judgement, where it reported the whole text of the mentioned Article 23, whose paragraph 2 *a)* provides that a State may not invoke the *force majeure* if "the situation [...] is due, either alone or in combination with other factors, *to the conduct of the State invoking it*".[38] Thus, by an indirect reference to Article 23, paragraph 2 *a)* of the ILC Draft *and also by referring to the EU Court's conclusions* in the Case C-297/08,[39] where the exercise of *all due diligence* by the State is mentioned as a condition to claim *force majeure*,[40] the Strasbourg Court ultimately intended to blame the State's failure to take a *preventive* and *precautionary* approach to the 'waste management' matter, as required by its own domestic law and EU law.[41] Accordingly, it concluded that, despite the wide margin of appreciation left to the respondent State, one is obliged to observe that the Italian authorities' prolonged inability to secure the proper functioning of the public waste collection, treatment and disposal service affected the applicants' rights to respect for their private lives and their homes in violation of Article 8 of the Convention.[42]

3.5 THE DISMISSAL OF THE GOVERNMENT'S PRELIMINARY OBJECTION BASED ON APPLICANTS' FAILURE TO EXHAUST DOMESTIC REMEDIES AND THE FINDING THAT THE STATE VIOLATED ARTICLE 13 OF THE CONVENTION

The same line of reasoning pointed out above, namely that the respondent State failed to fulfil its positive obligations under the Convention owing to a pathological 'emergency approach', which ultimately resulted in its failure to comply with its own domestic law and EU law, also seems to have inspired the Court when it decided to accept the applicants'

---

37 *Di Sarno, op. cit.*, para. 111.
38 *Di Sarno, op. cit.*, para. 77, emphasis added.
39 *Di Sarno, op. cit.*, paras. 111 and 56.
40 *See* C-297/08, Judgement of 4 March 2010, para. 85: "[...] with regard to the non-performance of contractual obligations by the undertakings entrusted with the construction of certain waste disposal infrastructures, it need only be stated that, although the notion of *force majeure* is not predicated on absolute impossibility, it nevertheless requires the non-performance of the act in question to be attributable to circumstances, beyond the control of the party claiming *force majeure*, which are abnormal and unforeseeable and the consequences of which could not have been avoided *despite the exercise of all due diligence*" (emphasis added).
41 In its detailed report on the circumstances of the case (*Di Sarno, op. cit.*, para. 56), the Court also referred to the ECJ finding of the existence of a "*structural* deficit in terms of the installations necessary for the disposal of the urban waste produced in Campania, as evidenced by the considerable quantities of waste which have accumulated along the public roads in the region" (C-297/08, Judgement of 4 March 2010, para. 75, emphasis added).
42 *Di Sarno, op. cit.*, para. 112. Otherwise, the Court concluded that there had been no violation of Art. 8 with regard to the obligation to inform the population and the applicants themselves of the risks involved in living in the polluted areas of Campania (*ibid.*, para. 113).

complaint, which relied upon Article 13 of the Convention. Indeed, it stated that, since the applicants complained of the absence of effective remedies in the Italian legal system, by which to obtain redress for their damage, such a complaint was closely connected with the one already examined under Article 8.[43] Accordingly, the Court simply referred to its foregoing reasoning.[44]

In addition to this, once again one must point out that, also with respect to the complaint under Article 13, the merits were actually decided by the Court at the same time when it rejected the Government's preliminary objections, in particular that one based on applicants' failure to exhaust domestic remedies. According to the Government, the applicants could have brought an action for compensation against the agencies responsible for the malfunctioning of the waste collection, treatment and disposal service, in order to seek redress for the damage resulted from this malfunction, as other inhabitants of the Campania region had done. Moreover, they could have asked the Environment Ministry to bring an action against the same agencies above mentioned, to seek compensation for environmental damage.[45]

But the Court's negative assessment of Italy's prolonged 'emergency management' of the waste issue reflected upon the way it rejected this Government's objection. First, it observed that the purpose of the rule of exhaustion of domestic remedies (Art. 35 §1) is to afford the Contracting States the opportunity of preventing or putting right the violations alleged against them before those allegations are submitted to the Court itself. Then it pointed out that the same rule is based on the assumption, reflected in Article 13 of the Convention – with which it has close affinity – that there is an effective remedy available in the domestic system in respect of the alleged breach.[46]

With regard to the particular circumstances of the case, the Court's remark that the Government had not produced any civil court decision awarding damages for the piling-up of rubbish on the streets to the inhabitants of the areas concerned, sounds like a pleonastic observation.[47] And it even sounds didactic the way the Court pointed out that the Italian Court of Cassation had established that claims for damages related to the 'waste crisis' fall under the competence of administrative jurisdictions, likewise the remark that the rule concerning the possibility of requesting the Environment Ministry to bring an action for environmental damage had been repealed.[48]

Actually, the conclusive Court's answer with respect to the preliminary objection under consideration – an answer that also makes clear what the Court meant by 'effective remedy'

---

43 Di Sarno, op. cit., paras. 93-111.
44 Di Sarno, op. cit., para. 116.
45 Di Sarno, op. cit., paras. 82, 83.
46 Di Sarno, op. cit., para. 85.
47 Di Sarno, op. cit., para. 87.
48 Di Sarno, op. cit., paras. 87, 89.

under Article 13 in the present case – was that an applicants' action for damages might theoretically have resulted in compensation for those concerned but would not have led to the removal of the rubbish from the streets and other public places.[49] In this 'sharp' way the Court rejected the Government's objection based on applicants' failure to exhaust domestic remedies and disclosed its assessment on the complaint under Article 13 at the same time. Indeed, when it concluded that there had been a violation of Article 13, it simply referred to its foregoing considerations on the non-exhaustion of domestic remedies objection of the Government.[50]

3.6 Conclusions

As the Court itself hinted, one could doubt that a compensation for damages would be a suitable way of putting right the violations of the Convention alleged in the present case.[51] Perhaps, one could say the same with regard to the applicants' choice to make an application to the European Court of Human Rights. Then, what was the actual purpose of their application?

Obviously, recovering damages could not be the applicants' main purpose: it would be very difficult to assess the damage in a case such as the present one and otherwise they had not complained of any health problem related to their exposure to the waste. One might rather think that the kind of satisfaction they actually above all were demanding was for a declaratory judgement that the State failed to fulfil its obligations and had violated their rights. In this respect, one must admit that the first Government's contention on the case was right: it is true that actually the applicants complained of the Italian legislative and administrative policies on 'waste management'. The 'emergency approach' taken by the State in the waste management was the real 'accused' before the European Court of Human Rights. The applicants complained of a permanent *extra ordinem* system of management, which did not solve their problems and left them with an intolerable sense of injustice. This was also the real reason behind the complaint under Article 13 of the Convention.

The Court seems to have understood the actual applicants' main purpose. Apart from all the foregoing considerations, this also seems to be confirmed by the way the Court rejected another Government's preliminary objection, namely that under Article 35 §1 of the Convention, which provides that it may only deal with the facts that occur within the six months preceding the application. The Court simply observed that the applicants did

---

49 *Di Sarno, op. cit.*, para. 87. On the notion of 'effective remedy' under Art. 13, *see* A. Pertici & R. Romboli, 'Art. 13 – Diritto ad un ricorso effettivo', *in* S. Bartole, B. Conforti & G. Raimondi, *Commentario alla Convenzione europea per la tutela dei diritti dell'uomo e delle libertà fondamentali*, CEDAM, Padua, 2001, pp. 394 ff.
50 *Di Sarno, op. cit.*, para. 118.
51 *Ibid.*

not complain of an 'instantaneous breach' (a breach not having continuing character) and when the alleged violation is a 'continuous situation' the six months period may only start from the end of such a situation.[52]

Then the Court gave the applicants exactly what they actually were demanding: an authoritative declaratory judgement that the Italian authorities had for a lengthy period been unable to ensure the proper functioning of the waste collection, treatment and disposal service, owing to their disastrous legislative and administrative policies on 'waste management' in Campania. In this light, the Court's conclusion that, in the particular circumstances, its findings of the Convention's violations constituted an adequate reparation for the non-pecuniary damage does not sound like just lip service.[53]

---

52 *Di Sarno, op. cit.*, para. 93.
53 *Di Sarno, op. cit.*, para. 122.

4 EU CASE-LAW AND WASTE MANAGEMENT IN CAMPANIA

Leonardo Massai

The issue of waste management in Campania, Italy, emerged in the nineties and is one of the current major problems in the field of waste management in Europe. This case is therefore embracing a big variety of legislation both at the European and the national level. The failure by the Italian authorities to comply with European legislation on waste management gave rise to several legal concerns and judicial actions. In this chapter, the case-law of the European Court of Justice (ECJ) particularly relevant for the problems with the management of waste in Campania will have central stage.

4.1 THE PROBLEM OF WASTE MANAGEMENT IN CAMPANIA

As clearly highlighted in the motion of censure of the European Parliament of 26 January 2011,[1]

> the waste crisis in the province of Campania is the most complex chapter of a history of problematic waste management in many parts of Italy, a waste emergency was declared in the 1990s, and where Government Commissioners with special powers and funds were nominated.

In terms of waste mangament, the difficulties encountered by the province of Naples concerning the waste cycle relates with the density of population in this area, roughly 52% of total population of Campania, and the volume of waste produced. In 2009 the Italian authorities ended the state of emergency in the Campania and decided to delegate to the Provincial Authorities the management of the waste cycle.[2] Two main crisis have to be highlighted: one in the summer of 2007 and another in the spring of 2010, shortly after the adoption of the report on the fact-finding mission to Campania by the Petitions Committee of the European Parliament. Measures adopted by the local authorities to solve the waste problem caused several protests by the population. The initial solution of producing 'Ecolabels' and organic waste turned out to be a failure, simply because of the

---
1 European Parliament, 26 January 2011, Motion for a Resolution, further to Questions for Oral Answer B7-0667/2010, B7-0801/2010, B7-0805/2010 and B7-0806/2010 pursuant to Rule 115(5) of the Rules of Procedure on the waste crisis in Campania.
2 Italian Decree No. 195 of 31st December 2009.

impossibility of disposing of them properly. The first incinerator in Acerra was opened in March 2010 but its operation has suffered from the lack of appropriate infrastructure for separation and treatment of waste. Concerns remain over the fate of toxic ashes resulting from the incineration. Exceptional measures such as the opening of new landfills were subject to protests by the local population. Furthermore, legal concerns were raised regarding the operation of such landfills. Firstly, many landfills are privately run without the required licence or permit and therefore in non compliance with the national legislation. Secondly, the access to information by citizens and local authorities to the landfills and to the Acerra incinerator was limited. Many landfills were declared areas of strategic interest and under strict army control. As a consequence, both the Aarhus Convention (citizens have the right to be informed of the situation in their own territory and it is the duty of the authorities to provide information and to motivate citizens to develop a responsible attitude and behaviour) and Directive 2003/35/EC (Member States shall ensure that the public is given early and effective opportunities to participate in the preparation and modification or review of the plans or programmes required to be drawn up) were violated.

The above mentioned motion of censure identified that public discontent is increasing in the region, that progress in waste reduction and recycling is minimal and that the funding from the European Commission to waste-related projects is stopped. In terms of public health, the quality of household waste is low and illegal dumping of waste is very frequent and also the geological and hydrological factors have not been given appropriate consideration when deciding on the location of landfills sites. As a consequence soil and ground water sources pollution is a serious threat in the region.

Furthermore, EU legislation and principles are also not respected with the waste cycle still relying mainly on landfill, where waste is mixed with different types of industrial waste, and incineration, contrary to the new Waste Framework Directive 2008/98/EC. There is no coherent plan for waste management.

4.2 Relevant EU Legislation on Waste Management

EU legislation on the protection of the environment is very advanced and represents one of the biggest and relevant parts of the Acquis Communautaire. Currently in the EU, there are more than 300 pieces of legislation on environmental matters and environmental law. It is historically one of the more challenging fields of application of EU law by the Member States. Consequently, the failure to implement EU environmental legislation correctly is one of the major causes of infringement procedures initiated by the European Courts against the Member States. In accordance with Article 190 of the TFEU, the EU main objectives in the field of environmental protection are:
- preserving, protecting and improving the quality of the environment;
- protecting human health;

- prudent and rational utilisation of natural resources;
- promoting measures at international level to deal with regional or worldwide environmental problems, and in particular combating climate change.

Furthermore, EU policy on environment

> shall aim at a high level of protection taking into account the diversity of situations in the various regions of the Union. It shall be based on the precautionary principle and on the principles that preventive action should be taken, that environmental damage should as a priority be rectified at source and that the polluter should pay.

Having said that, within EU environmental legislation, waste can be considered one of the key sectors where European legislators have always been very active.

EU policy on waste management is based on three basic principles:

- Prevention: reduction of waste generation and presence of dangerous substances, improvement of manufacturing methods and increasing greener production;
- Recycling and reuse: collection, reuse, recycling and disposal for packaging waste, end-of-life vehicles, batteries, electrical and electronic waste;
- Improving disposal and monitoring: safe incineration for waste that cannot be recycled or reused, with landfill only used as a last resort.

Below follows a list of major EU legislation currently in force in the field of waste management.[3]

4.2.1 Framework Waste Legislation

Waste Framework Directive, or Directive 2008/98/EC of the European Parliament and of the Council of 19 November 2008 on waste and repealing certain Directives. This Directive repealed Directive 2006/12/EC of the European Parliament and of the Council of 5 April 2006 on waste (the codified version of Directive 75/442/EEC as amended), the hazardous waste Directive 91/689/EEC, and the Waste Oils Directive 75/439/EEC. The directive provides for a general framework of waste management requirements and sets the basic waste management definitions for the EU. Under Article 4 is stipulated that

> Member States shall take the necessary measures to ensure that waste is disposed of without endangering human health and without harming the environment, and in particular:
> - without risk to water, air, soil and plants and animals,
> - without causing a nuisance through noise or odours,
> - without adversely affecting the countryside or places of special interest.

---

3   *See* Chapter 1.

- Commission Decision of 3 May 2000 (2000/532/EC) replacing Decision 94/3/EC establishing a list of wastes pursuant to Article 1(a) of Council Directive 75/442/EEC on waste and Council Decision 94/904/EC establishing a list of hazardous waste pursuant to Article 1(4) of Council Directive 91/689/EEC on hazardous waste. This Decision identifies the classification system for wastes, including a distinction between hazardous and non-hazardous wastes, and it is closely linked to the list of the main characteristics which render waste hazardous contained in Annex III to the Waste Framework Directive above.
- Regulation (EC) No. 1013/2006 of the European Parliament and of the Council of 14 June 2006 on shipments of waste. This Regulation specifies under which conditions waste can be shipped between countries.

4.2.2   Relevant Legislation on Waste Management Operations

- Council Directive 1999/31/EC of 26 April 1999 on the landfill of waste. The objective of the Directive is to prevent or reduce environmental damages caused by the landfilling of waste, by introducing stringent technical requirements for waste and landfills.
  - Ancillary legislation relating to landfill of waste;
  - Commission Decision of 17 November 2000 concerning a questionnaire for Member States reports on the implementation of Directive 1999/31/EC on the landfill of waste.
- Council Directive 91/689/EEC of 12 December 1991 on hazardous waste introducing a uniform definition of hazardous waste and aiming at ensuring ecologically sound management of hazardous waste.
- Directive 2000/76/EC of the European Parliament and of the Council on the incineration of waste repealing former directives on the incineration of hazardous waste (Directive 94/67/EC) and household waste (Directives 89/369/EEC and 89/429/EEC). The aim of this directive is to prevent or to reduce the environmental harms caused by the incineration and co-incineration of waste. In particular, it should reduce pollution caused by emissions into the air, soil, surface water and groundwater, and the risks posed to human health.
- Directive 2000/59/EC of the European Parliament and of the Council of 27 November 2000 on port reception facilities for ship-generated waste and cargo residues.
- Directive 99/31/EC on landfill of waste provides for specific waste acceptance procedures under Article 11 and Annex II:

  1. Member States shall take measures in order that prior to accepting the waste at the landfill site:
  (a) before or at the time of delivery, or of the first in a series of deliveries, provided the type of waste remains unchanged, the holder or the

operator can show, by means of the appropraite documentation, that the waste in question can be accepted at that site according to the conditions set in the permit, and that it fulfils the acceptance criteria set out in Annex II;

(b) the following reception procedures are respected by the operator:
- checking of the waste documentation;
- visual inspection of the waste at the entrance and at the point of deposit and, as appropriate, verification of conformity with the description provided in the documentation submitted by the holder;
- keeping a register of the quantities and characteristics of the waste deposited, indicating origin, date of delivery, identity of the producer or collector in the case of municipal waste, and, in the case of hazardous waste, the precise location on the site;

(c) the operator of the landfill shall always provide written acknowledgement of receipt of each delivery acepted on the site;

(d) without prejudice to the provisions of Regulation (EEC) No 259/93, if waste is not accepted at a landfill the operator shall notify without delay the competent authority of the non-acceptance of the waste.

In accordance with Article 3(4) and (5) of Directive 99/31/EC landfill sites for non-hazardous or inert wastes with a low capacity or in isolated sites are exempted from the above mentioned provisions. However, Member States shall

> [...] take the necessary measures to provide for:
> - regular visual inspection of the waste at the point of deposit in order to ensure that only non-hazardous waste from the island or the isolated settlement is accepted at the site; and
> - a register on the quantities of waste that are deposited at the site be kept.

Member States shall ensure that information on the quantities and, where possible, the type of waste going to such exempted sites forms part of the regular reports to the Commission on the implementation of the Directive.

Additional EU legislation relevant in the field of waste management are Directive 2008/99 on the protection of the environment through criminal law and Directive 2003/35/EC providing for public participation in respect of the drawing up of certain plans and programmes relating to the environment (Art. 2).

As to the implementation of EU legislation on waste management, on 17 January 2013 the European Commission released a Report on the performance of the Member States

in the period 2007-2009.[4] All major EU directives on waste management are addressed in the report:
- Waste Framework Directive 2008/98/EC: several Member States still depending on landfilling, many difficulties in the new Member States, Austria and Germany with the highest rate about recycling;
- Directive 91/689/EEC on Hazardous Waste (now repealed as the subjectmatter is covered by the Framework Directive): results are not completely satisfactory, with problems in the implementation, in particular on the enforcement of the mixing ban, the relevant exemptions and periodic inspections;
- Directive 75/439/EEC on waste oils (also now repealed and covered by the Framework Directive): oil waste combustion or regeneration are reduced;
- Directive 86/27/EEC on sewage sludge: the usage of sewage sludge in agriculture is increased (goal set by the directive over achieved) with some Member States imposing even stricter rules;
- Directive 94/62/EC on packaging prevention, re-use and recycling: generation of packaging waste remaining stable, rate of recovery and recycling differing among Member States;
- Landfill Directive 1999/31/EC: Belgium, Denmark, The Netherlands, Austria, Germany and Sweden with less than 5% of landfill sites, the rest of the Member States are far from this level;
- WEEE Directive 2002/96/EC on waste electrical and electronic equipment: only Slovenia and Italy have not yet reached the target set by the directive.

4.3 Breaches of EU Waste Law (General)

A perfect example of the difficulties encountered by the Member States in the compliance with EU waste law is provided by the implementation of Directive 1999/31/EC on landfill of waste, subject to many petitions on the subject submitted to the European Parliament by various actors. The directive has 34 recitals, which constitute its aims and objectives, together with Article 1 concerning the overall objective. Member States have been required to apply this Directive since April 2001, for all previously existing landfills the rules became binding eight years after. The parameters set by the directive include:
- landfills should be adequately monitored, including visual inspection at entry, and managed to prevent or reduce potential adverse effects on the environment and risks to public health;

---

4 Report from the Commission to the European Parliament, the Council, the European Economic and Social Committee and the Commettee of the Regions on the implementation of the EU waste legislation Directive 2006/12/EC on waste, Directive 91/689/EEC on hazardous waste, Directive 75/439/EEC on waste oils, Directive 86/278/EEC on sewage sludge, Directive 94/62/EC on packaging and packaging waste, Directive 1999/31/EC on the landfill of waste, and Directive 2002/96/EC on waste electrical and electronic equipment for the period 2007 – 2009, Brussels, 17 January 2013, COM(2013) 6 final.

- requirements with which landfill sites must comply as regards location, conditioning, management, control, closure and preventive and protective measures to be taken against any threat to the environment in the short and long-term perspective;
- stringent operational and technical requirements on the waste and landfills, to provide measures, procedures and guidance to prevent or reduce, as far as possible, negative effects on the environment in particular the pollution of surface water, groundwater, soil and air, and on the global environment, including greenhouse effect, as well as any resulting risk to human health from the landfilling of waste during the whole life-cycle of the landfill.

Finally, in accordance with Annex 1 of the directive, landfills must be located far away "from the boundary of the site to residential or recreational areas, waterways, water bodies or other agricultural or urban sites" and the existence of groundwater, coastal water or nature protection zones in the area should be taken under consideration.

The following points have been identified by the Parliament's fact-finding mission to Campania, as to the implementation of the Landfill waste Directive[5]:
- the progress in waste reduction and recycling of household waste is minimal and the current waste cycle still heavily relies on landfill and incineration, in contrast with the guidelines of the Waste Framework Directive (2008/98/EC);
- a coherent plan for waste management in the region is still missing, in breach of EU principles on waste legislation;
- general safe use of landfills or incineration is lacking, waste has continued to be brought to landfills indiscriminately, in some cases apparently mixed with different types of industrial waste;
- the quality of household waste and the dumping of hazardous waste in illegal dumping sites are not verified (violation Arts. 17 and 18 of the Waste Framework Directive, and also the Landfill Directive);
- high risks of contamination of surrounding soil and ground water sources increased, due to scarce consideration of geological and hydrological factors when deciding on the location of landfills (*i.e.* sites such as Chiaiano).

4.4 Infringement Procedure under EU Law

The Treaty on the Functioning of the European Union defines under Articles 258 to 260 the so-called infringement procedure, a law enforcement tool in the hands of the European Commission. The Commission has the power to initiate such a procdure, but it provides

---

5   European Parliament, 14 September 2010, Working Document on the fact-finding mission to Campania, Italy, from 28 to 30 April 2010 Committee on Petitions, Rapporteur: Judith A. Merkies.

also a channel for individuals to complain to the Commission about any potential failure to implement EU law correctly by the Member States.

The infringement procedure is a procedure vis-à-vis the Member States, in particular those who fail to fulfil an obligation under the EU treaties, *i.e.* it concerns the correct implementation of a directive or a breach of a fundamental principle of EU law. The European Commission is the institution which historically has the power to initiate such a procedure. To be precise the TFEU also foresees the possibility for Member States and, lately after the revision of the Treaty of Lisbon, also for European citizens, to initiate the procedure.

However, the Commission is the ultimate institution which decides whether or not to bring a matter before the European Court of Justice. The procedure can be divided in two rounds: a prelitigation phase where the Commission makes use of all of its diplomatic powers to facilitate the compliance of the Member States with EU law and a judicial phase where the European Court of Justice enters the procedure. The first official document which can be produced by the Commission in the event of a Member State being in breach of EU law is the 'reasoned opinion', a letter of formal notice where a time limit is officially specified. In terms of defence, Member States can claim force majeure arguments like a bomb attack. Problems with parliamentary procedures or difficulties arising from the separation of powers are justifications claimed by States that have been always refused by the Court, similarily the lack of intentional wrongdoing by a Member State, as the admissibility of an infringement action by the Commission depends on objective considerations. The infringement procedure can be triggered on the initiative of the Commission (Art. 258 TFEU) or by the Member States (Art. 259 TFEU). In the event of persistence of non compliance by a Member State Article 260 TFEU foresees the possibility of a lump sum or penalty payments to be imposed either by the Commission (simplified sanctions procedure) or by the Court of Justice.

The effects of a conviction in an infringement procedure can be:
- Declaratory, such as a non constitutory decision:
  - Effect *Ex tunc*;
  - Decision not necessary for successfully invoking other remedies;
- Member States must take appropriate measures to comply with the judgment (Art. 260 TFEU)[6];
- The Commission can specify a lump sum or penalty payment.

---

6   1. If the Court of Justice of the European Union finds that a Member State has failed to fulfil an obligation under the Treaties, the State shall be required to take the necessary measures to comply with the judgment of the Court.
    2. If the Commission considers that the Member State concerned has not taken the necessary measures to comply with the judgment of the Court, it may bring the case before the Court after giving that State the opportunity to submit its observations. It shall specify the amount of the lump sum or penalty payment to be paid by the Member State concerned which it considers appropriate in the circumstances. If the Court finds that the Member State concerned has not complied with its judgment it may impose a lump sum or penalty payment on it.

4.5 Case-Law Relevant for the Problems in Campania

In this section, a few cases directly related with the case of waste management in Campania are highlighted.

4.5.1 Case 135/05 European Commission v. Italy

In this case the European Court of Justice declared that by failing to adopt all the necessary measures to ensure that waste is recovered or disposed of without endangering human health and without using processes or methods which could harm the environment, and to prohibit the abandonment, dumping or uncontrolled disposal of waste, the Italian Republic had failed to fulfil its obligations under Community law.

The relevant paragraphs of the judgement (here emphasized), which concludes that Italy has breached Directive 75/442, Directive 91/689 and Directive 1999/31 go from 37 to 45:

- (para. 37) Article 4 of Directive 75/442 provides that *Member States are to take the necessary measures to ensure that waste is recovered or disposed of without endangering human health and without using processes or methods which could harm the environment, without however specifying the actual content of the measures which must be taken in order to ensure that such objective is attained*. It is none the less true that the provision is binding on the Member States as to the objective to be achieved, whilst leaving to the Member States a *margin of discretion* in assessing the need for such measures (Case C365/97 *Commission v. Italy* ('San Rocco') [1999] ECR I-7773, paragraph 67). It cannot, therefore, in principle, be directly inferred from the fact that a situation is not in conformity with the objectives laid down in Article 4 of Directive 75/442 that the Member State concerned has necessarily failed to fulfil its obligations under that provision. Nevertheless, it is established that if that situation persists and leads in particular to *a significant deterioration in the environment over a protracted period without any action being taken by the competent authorities, it may be an indication that the Member States have exceeded the discretion conferred on them by that provision* (San Rocco, paragraphs 67 and 68).
- (para. 38) In that regard, it must be stated that the *validity of the complaints against the Italian Republic is clearly apparent from the case-file*. While the information provided by its government has established that compliance in Italy with the objectives of the provisions of Community law which are the subject of the failure to fulfil obligations has improved over the course of time. However that information reveals that the general non-compliance

of the tips in the light of those provisions was persisting at the expiry of the period laid down in the reasoned opinion.
- (para. 39) As regards the complaint alleging infringement of Article 4 of Directive 75/442, it is common ground that, at the expiry of the period laid down in the reasoned opinion, *there was, throughout Italy, a considerable number of tips, the operators of which had not ensured the recovery or disposal of waste in such a way as not to endanger human health and not to use processes or methods which could harm the environment, as well as of sites of uncontrolled waste disposal.* By way of example, as is clear from Annex 1 to the Italian Government's rejoinder, *it admitted the existence, in the Abruzzo region, of 92 sites affected by abandoned waste*, established during a check at the local level, following the survey carried out by the CFS.
- (para. 40) The existence of such a situation over a prolonged period necessarily brings about a *significant deterioration in the environment.*
- (para. 41) As regards the complaint alleging infringement of Article 8 of Directive 75/442, it is established that, *at the expiry of the prescribed period, the Italian authorities had not ensured that holders of waste either recover or dispose of it themselves or have it handled by an undertaking which carries out the operations of recovery or disposal, in accordance with the provisions of Directive 75/442.* In that regard, it is clear from Annex 3 to the Italian Government's rejoinder that the Italian authorities counted at least *nine sites with such characteristics* in the Umbria region and 31 in the Puglia region (province of Bari).
- (para. 42) So far as concerns the complaint alleging infringement of Article 9 of Directive 75/442, it is not disputed that, when the period laid down by the reasoned opinion expired, *numerous tips were operating without a permit having been obtained from the competent authorities.* That is particularly evidenced, as is clear from Annex 3 to the Italian Government's rejoinder, by the cases of abandoned waste already mentioned in paragraphs 39 and 41 of the present judgment, but also by the presence of at least 14 illegal tips in the Puglia region (province of Lecce).
- (para. 43) As regards the complaint alleging that the Italian authorities did not ensure the recording or identification of hazardous waste on every site where the tipping or discharge thereof takes place, that is the allegation of infringement of Article 2 of Directive 91/689, it is sufficient to observe that the *government of that Member State presented no arguments or specific evidence to contradict the Commission's allegations.* In particular, it does not dispute the existence in Italy, when the period laid down by the reasoned opinion expired, of at least 700 illegal tips containing hazardous waste. As such they are therefore not subject to any control measures. It follows that the Italian authorities were not aware of the deposits of hazardous waste

discharged at those tips, and therefore the obligation to record and identify them has not been complied with.
- (para. 44) Finally, the same applies to the complaint alleging infringement of Article 14 of Directive 1999/31. In this instance, the Italian Government itself stated that 747 landfills in Italian territory should have been the subject of conditioning plans. Examination of all the documents annexed to the government's rejoinder reveals that, *when the prescribed period expired, such plans had been presented for only 551 landfills and that only 131 plans had been approved by the competent authorities.* In addition, as the Commission correctly points out, the government has not made clear what action was taken as regards the landfills for which the conditioning plans had not been approved.
- (para. 45) It follows that the Italian Republic has, generally and persistently, failed to fulfil its obligations under Articles 4, 8 and 9 of Directive 75/442, Article 2(1) of Directive 91/689 and Article 14(a) to (c) of Directive 1999/31. Consequently, the Commission's action is well founded.

4.5.2 C 297/08 Commission v. Italy

In this case, the European Court of Justice declared that, by failing to adopt all the necessary measures for the region of Campania, the Italian Republic failed to fulfil its obligations under Articles 4 and 5 of Directive 2006/12 (now repelead by Directive 2008/98/EC). The relevant paragraphs are the following (emphasis added):

- (para. 68) Consequently, in such a national network as defined by a Member State, if *one of the regions lacks, in telling measure and for a significant length of time, infrastructure sufficient to meet its waste disposal needs, it is legitimate to conclude that such serious deficiencies at regional level are likely to compromise the national network of waste disposal installations, which will then no longer be integrated and adequate, as required under Directive 2006/12, or capable of meeting the obligation to enable the Member State concerned to move individually towards the aim of self-sufficiency as defined in Article 5(1) of that directive.*
- (para. 69) In the present case, it should be noted that – as the Commission observed – the Italian Republic itself opted for waste management at the level of the region of Campania as an 'Optimal Territorial Ambit'. As it is clear from the regional law of 1993 and the 1997 regional waste management plan, as amended by the 2007 plan, the decision was taken, with a view to achieving regional self-sufficiency, to require the municipalities of Campania to deliver the waste collected in their territory to the regional service, an

obligation which can be justified, moreover, by the need to ensure that operations are maintained at the level of activity necessary for the treatment installations to remain viable and, in that way, to preserve a treatment capacity sufficient to enable the principle of self-sufficiency to be put into practice at national level (see Case C-324/99 *Daimler Chrysler* [2001] ECR I-9897, paragraph 62).

- (para. 70) Furthermore, according to the statements made by the Italian Republic, the production of urban waste in Campania accounts for 7% of urban waste production nationwide (that is to say, a significant portion). Secondly, the population of that region represents approximately 9% of the national population, a major deficiency in Campania's capacity to dispose of its waste is likely seriously to compromise the ability of the Italian Republic to move towards the aim of self-sufficiency at national level.
- (para. 71) In those circumstances, it is appropriate to consider whether, within the Italian national network of waste disposal installations, Campania has sufficient installations enabling urban waste to be disposed of near to the place where it is produced.
- (para. 72) In that regard, the Italian Republic has recognised that the installations in operation, whether landfills, incinerators or thermal recovery plants, were not sufficient in number to meet the waste disposal requirements of the region of Campania.
- (para. 73) *The Italian Republic has in fact acknowledged that, on the expiry of the deadline set in the reasoned opinion, only one landfill was in operation for the entire region of Campania; the CMW production plants for Campania could not ensure the final disposal of waste; and the incinerators planned for Acerra and Santa Maria La Fossa were still not operational.*
- (para. 74) As emerging from the regional waste management plan approved in 1997 and from subsequent plans adopted by the Italian authorities to deal with the waste crisis, *those authorities considered, inter alia, that in order to meet the urban waste disposal needs of Campania, other landfills would have to be brought on stream*, such as those at Savignano Irpino and Sant'Arcangelo Trimonte; two more incinerators would have to be provided in addition to those at Acerra and Santa Maria La Fossa; and the CMW production plants should have been made genuinely operational.
- (para. 75) Although Article 5 of Directive 2006/12 allows inter-regional cooperation in the management and disposal of waste, and even cooperation between Member States, *the fact remains that, in the present case, even with the assistance of other Italian regions and the German authorities, it has not*

been possible to remedy the structural deficit in terms of the installations necessary for the disposal of the urban waste produced in Campania, as evidenced by the considerable quantities of waste which have accumulated along the public roads in the region.

- (para. 80) *The Italian Republic further argues that it cannot be held responsible for the alleged failure to fulfil obligations, which is attributable, rather, to certain events which constitute force majeure, such as the opposition of the local inhabitants to the establishment of landfills in their municipalities, the presence of organised criminal activity in the region and the failure by public contractors to meet their contractual obligations to construct certain essential installations in the region.*
- (para. 81) It should be stated in that regard that the procedure provided for in Article 258 TFEU presupposes an objective finding that a Member State has failed to fulfil its obligations under the Treaty or secondary legislation (see Case-301/81 Commission v Belgium [1983] ECR 467, paragraph 8, and Case C-508/03 Commission v United Kingdom [2006] ECR I 3969, paragraph 67).
- (para. 82) *Where such a finding has been made, as in the present case, it is irrelevant whether the failure to fulfil obligations is the result of intention or negligence on the part of the Member State responsible, or of technical difficulties encountered* by it (Case C-17/97 Commission v Spain [1998] ECR I 5991, paragraph 15).
- (para. 99) *The consequences of non-compliance with the obligation under Article 4(1) of Directive 2006/12 are likely, given the very nature of that obligation, to endanger human health and harm the environment, even in a small part of the territory of a Member State* (Case C- 365/97 Commission v Italy, paragraph 70), as it was also recognized in the judgment in Case C- 45/91 Commission v Greece.
- (para. 103) It should be noted, first of all, that *the Italian Republic does not dispute that, when the deadline set in the reasoned opinion expired, the waste littering the public roads totalled 55,000 tonnes, adding to the 110,000 tonnes to 120,000 tonnes of waste awaiting treatment at municipal storage sites.* In any event, that information emerges from the memorandum of the *Commissario delegato* of 2 March 2008, attached to the reply of the Italian Republic to the reasoned opinion. Furthermore, according to the statements made by the Italian Republic, the local inhabitants, protesting such accumulation, have taken the initiative of igniting fires in the piles of refuse, which is harmful both for the environment and for their own health.

- (para. 104) It is therefore clear from the above that, in the region of Campania, *the Italian Republic has not succeeded in complying with its obligation under Article 4(2) of Directive 2006/12* to take the necessary measures to prohibit the abandonment, dumping or uncontrolled disposal of waste.
- (para. 113) In the light of the above, it must be held that, *by failing to adopt, for the region of Campania, all the measures necessary to ensure that waste is recovered and disposed of without endangering human health and without harming the environment and, in particular, by failing to establish an integrated and adequate network of disposal installations, the Italian Republic has failed to fulfil its obligations under Articles 4 and 5 of Directive 2006/12.*

4.5.3   *Case 374/11* European Commission v. Ireland

In October 2009, Ireland was convicted of violating EU waste law. After the end of the preliminary phase, and the impossibility of Ireland to remedy all shortcomings, and in accordance with Article 260 TFEU the Commission asked the European Court of Justice (ECJ) to impose to Ireland to pay a lump sum of over €5 million, and a daily penalty payment of €26,173 until the country complied with the earlier judgment. The ECJ recognized that Ireland was still violating EU environmental law, but imposed a lower fine than the Commission demanded, while rejecting the country's complaint that it should have been given more time to remedy the situation.

In Case C-188/08 of 2009 the Court found Irish law in violation of the former Waste Framework Directive (WFD) 75/442/EC (nowadays Directive 2008/98/EC), notably where that directive prescribes that waste is to be disposed of without endangering human health and the environment (Art. 4), and that waste disposal establishments are to be subjected to appropriate periodic inspections (Art. 8). In particular, Ireland was breaching EU law as to the disposal of domestic waste waters in the countryside through several septic tanks and other individual waste water treatment systems. Furthermore, national legislation in Ireland was still not in line with the requirements of the directive, notably not all secondary law was in place and an inspection plan was missing.

In the Case C-374/11, Ireland had claimed that the action of the Commission was premature and more time was needed to comply with the 2009 judgment. Although Article 260(1) TFEU does not specify the amount of time needed by the State to satisfy a judgement of the Court, the ECJ referred to an 'immediate and uniform application of European Union law'. This means that after a conviction, the compliance process is to be initiated 'at once', and completed 'as soon as possible'. It judged that in casu, the Commission was entitled to lodge an application 21 months after the delivery of the judgement in Case C-188/08, even where implementation of that judgment involved complex operations.

In identifying the amount of the lump sum the ECJ used all its discretionary power, notably taking into consideration the circumstances and proportionality regarding the infringement established and the ability to pay of the Member State concerned. It took into account the duration and the degree of seriousness of the infringement and the public and private interests involved. In addition the Court noted that the waste framework directive was due to be respected by 1993 and that considering the objectives of the protection of human health and the environment, the matter is of 'indisputable gravity'.

The issue of waste management in Europe, and in particular in Italy is of enormous gravity. This is confirmed by the fact that on 15 March 2013 the European Commission announced to defer Italy to the Court of Justice, again for matters related with the bad implementation and non compliance with EU law. The decision concerned the treatment of waste in the Region of Lazio (Rome), in particular in light of the initiative of the region against the decree of the Ministry of Environment of 3 January 2013. The Region believes that this decree is putting the landfill of Malagrotta and the disposal of waste at serious risk. The Italian Minister of Environment considered the decision of the Commissions as inevitable but has decided to convene a meeting with stakeholders and interested companies to prepare a binding action plan to solve the problem.

4.6 NEXT STEPS

Since Italy did not notify the transposition of Directive 2008/99/EC on the protection of the environment through criminal law within the deadline of 26 December 2010, Italy is still expected to fully comply with the directive and to apply sanctions accordingly to the waste related offences listed in the directive including to legal persons when the conditions therefore are fulfilled.

In addition, the Commission will monitor that the Campania authorities comply fully with the infringement procedures that are initiated and decide, on a case by case basis, whether new legal actions may be required, in accordance with the procedure inscribed in Article 260 TFEU.

Part III
Assessment and Evaluation

5   Implementation of EU Waste Law: Just as Difficult as Enforcement of EU Law in Other Domains?

Marc Clément

Implementation of EU waste law – particularly in the Naples context – has highlighted the role the Commission plays in this field. However, it would be a mistake to believe that the Campania region situation is so specific that it does not fit within the more general picture of the implementation of EU law. On the contrary, the Campania waste crisis should be placed in the wider context of enforcement of EU law in the 27 Member States. Therefore difficulties in implementation as identified in the context of the Naples waste crisis are to be understood as pathological cases demonstrating the weaknesses of a legal system: the EU legal system relies on good faith and co-operation between EU institutions and Member States and is not designed for emergency situations.

Before discussing the implementation means that are in the hands of the Commission, it is essential to clearly include these implementation powers in a broader picture. The infringement procedure managed by the Commission results from the Articles 258 and 260 of the Treaty on the Functioning of the European Union. It should be kept in mind that this specific means of enforcing European law is an alternative to the regular way of enforcement which remains the integration of EU law in the legal system of each individual Member State. With limited resources, the Commission is not – and is not expected to be – the policeman in charge of monitoring implementation of EU law for 500 million citizens.

5.1   Implementation of EU Law and the Role of National Judges

From the famous *Van Gent and Loos* and *Costa* cases, all European judges are directly due to take into consideration EU Regulations and Directives when they rule a case. That is to say: EU law is bundled into each Member State's legal order and no difference is to be made between national and European sources of law. Moreover, Regulations and Directives have a form of supremacy over national rules.

As a consequence, conflicts between EU legal texts and national laws are to be solved by giving priority to EU laws over national legal sources, including under the hypothesis that the former are of superior rank. Of course, in practice, these conflicts are 'diluted' by the so-called dialogue of judges. But one should notice that, as the example of the decisions of the German constitutional Court shows, judges at the national level cannot avoid highly prudent analysis of potential conflicts between National and EU laws. They may refer to some kind of independence of legal orders and claim that in theory there is not subordination of national legal orders to the EU legal order, but, at the same time they will have to find creative legal approaches for making both levels compatible… Therefore it is very important not to take too seriously statements adopted by national courts claiming that they could potentially rule against the European Court of Justice. In practice national decisions tend to be fully compatible with the case-law of the EU Court. There is indeed a kind of legal fiction maintaining full sovereignty of national judges which can only survive because of the absence of the exercise of this sovereignty! It should also be stressed that the Court of Justice of the European Union develops its case-law by taking inspiration from national legal systems.

Furthermore, Article 6 of the Treaty on the European Union[1] reflects the interactions between European and national constitutional traditions. Finally, one should not forget that the ECJ is composed of 27 Judges from the 27 Member States: although they do not represent their country, they provide a direct link with all EU legal traditions.

In this context of dialogue between national judges and EU judges, the Court of Justice and national jurisdictions of EU Member States have developed a solid corpus of case-law establishing that EU laws are to be fully applied by national judges: national judges must take into account EU law in the same way as they use national laws, which means that they should for instance, invoke EU laws *ex officio* if that is what they would do for national laws; national judges must read national laws in a way which is compatible with EU laws, that is to say that if they are faced with a difficulty in interpretation of national law they should refer to EU Directives for solving this difficulty; national judges have to discard national laws that are not in line with EU laws; national judges in case of difficulties interpreting EU laws can refer their case to the Court of Justice by using the mechanism of preliminary questions. National supreme courts are obliged to refer their case if they face difficulties of interpretation. These rules which emerged progressively from the first cases ruled by the ECJ in the sixties have now been fully integrated by national judges of Member States. One should stress that this integration was not straight forward and some needed more or less time depending on each Member State; one could still identify in

---

[1] Art. 6 of the Treaty of the European Union, para. 3: "Fundamental rights, as guaranteed by the European Convention for the Protection of Human Rights and Fundamental Freedoms and as they result from the constitutional traditions common to the Member States, shall constitute general principles of the Union's law."

some Member States' Supreme Courts a reluctance to consider their sovereignty as limited by the ECJ, but such attitudes are now rare.

5.2 Implementation of EU Law and the Commission

The Commission is traditionally said to be the 'Guardian of the Treaties'. Indeed, the Commission mainly has a double role: mastering the legislative process in the EU by having the monopoly of legislative initiatives and being in charge of verifying that implementation of EU law is correctly done by Member States. In the views of the Founding Fathers of the EU, the need of a supranational body representing the interests of Europe opposed to Member States driven by national considerations was paramount. One might notice, for instance, that in the Memoirs of Jean Monnet, the Commission is presented as the institution avoiding intergovernmental bargaining. It is interesting to note that the Court of Justice and its essential role developed in the sixties is not mentioned by Jean Monnet. For him, the Commission is in charge of ensuring that the European spirit prevails; this role may fade once integration is well underway.

It is why from the very beginning of the EU (the 1957 Treaty), the Commission is granted the power to open infringement proceedings against Member States if the Commission believes that a Member State does not fulfilled its obligations under the Treaty and other related EU laws. These powers have been reinforced constantly in the adoption of the new treaties, but the principles remain the same.

The Commission must first allow Member States to provide observations. This takes the form of a Letter of Formal Notice addressed to the Member State and inviting the Member State to reply in 2 months. After the reply of the Member State – or in absence of reply – the Commission may start the next step in the procedure which is to send a Reasoned Opinion. The Member State has again 2 months to reply. Between the Letter of Formal Notice and a Reasoned Opinion, discussions may take place. This could be due to the fact that the Member State would like to present measures correcting the issues raised by the Commission. For instance, in the case of the need to adopt national legislation to correct a bad transposition of an EU Directive, Member States may want to consult the Commission on drafting more appropriate legislation. It could also be that the Commission would like to have more information on the situation. This may be the case regarding issues related to concrete results which should have been obtained by Member States. For instance, if a species is to be protected, the number of animals might have to be checked and the impact of measures taken by the Member State has to be assessed. From these examples, it follows that the level of difficulty in identifying and proving a breach of EU law is much greater in cases where 'bad application' is at stake than in 'non-conformity' cases. The latter ones refer to cases regarding purely legal issues: national law is not in conformity with EU law and legislative action is needed by the Member State. The former relate to cases where the EU legislation is correctly transposed but its application is poor.

One should take into account that the burden of proof is to be borne by the Commission. This is a particularly significant problem in a context as the Commission does not have inspection services. This point is not an obstacle to develop an action in the context of purely legal cases. In such cases, the Commission analyses the legal texts and presents to the Court its interpretation. But when the Commission needs to rely on a set of facts corresponding for instance to illegal landfills, lack of control or lack of species protection, then the case is likely to be decided by the ECJ on the basis of showing that the Member State failed to enforce EU law correctly as illustrated by factual evidence. This is not an impossible task and numerous judgements illustrate this situation. However, the collection of facts and situations is likely to depend on the activities of, *e.g.*, an NGO informing the Commission of the real situation. It will also require time to ensure the quality of the facts reported.

This explains that the preliminary process of a Letter of Formal Notice followed by a Reasoned Opinion may take time, generally more than a year. If after the reply of the Member State which following the Reasoned Opinion, the Commission is still not satisfied with the situation, then it may decide to bring a case at the ECJ.

It is obvious that this long process with intensive dialogue with the Member States is not addressing 'small claims': it aims at solving implementation issues which represents significant problems. There is of course an obvious need to allocate the limited resources of the Commission to substantial breaches of EU law. Until 2007, the official policy of the Commission did not take these strategic aspects into consideration: on the contrary, following the turmoil of the Santer Commission, the Commission issued a Communication in 2002 (COM(2002)141) indicating that all complaints will be assessed and addressed by the Commission. This meant that potentially each time a complainant informed the Commission of a bad application of EU law, a new infringement case was opened . . . in environmental matters this led to a substantial increase in the number of cases which culminated in 2005. In parallel the resources allocated to the management of infringement cases remained more or less the same. As a consequence, the duration for the treatment of these cases tend to increase steadily. It became necessary to react and to define a new strategy. This was done in 2007.

A first 'horizontal' Communication of the Commission addressed these points (COM(2007)502 A Europe of results – Applying Community law). The Communication develops two lines: on the one hand it stresses the need to find alternatives to infringements proceedings and on the other hand it tries to increase the efficiency of the actions of the Commission. The direct effect of the Communication is the development of an

5   Implementation of EU Waste Law: Just as Difficult as Enforcement of EU Law in Other Domains?

extension of the Solvit approach (developed in the context of the Internal Market) which is called EU Pilot. This IT tool aims at reinforcing the exchanges between the Commission and the Member States. Once a complaint is filed by the Commission, if clarifications are needed, the Commission services will enter questions related to the issue raised in the complaint in EU Pilot. The Member State will then have ten weeks to reply. It is expected that this pre-infringement phase will help in solving the simplest cases. In this context, the Commission recently updated the 2002 Communication on the management of complaints (COM(2012)154)[2] maintaining the main aspects of complaint management but referring to IT tools developed after 2002.

Another consequence of the 2007 Communication is the increase of the number of 'College' meetings dedicated to infringements: it should be borne in mind that addressing a Letter of Formal Notice, a Reasoned Opinion or referring the case to the ECJ corresponds to decisions of the Commission, *i.e.* a decision taken by all Commissioners (the College). Before 2007, only 4 meetings were dedicated to infringements, the Commission now holds 9 meetings on this matter (one each month, except in the summer and in December). In addition the Communication makes clear that there are benchmarks to follow in terms of time spent on cases (between opening a case and referring it to the ECJ). The priorities of the Commission – cases related to transposition and cases related to execution of previous ECJ rulings – are to be managed swiftly.

It is remarkable that the only Directorate-General which developed an explicit policy in the infringement domain – by producing Communications – is the Directorate-General Environment. Two specific communications have been issued successively: in 2008 the Communication COM(2008)773 on implementing European Community Environmental Law and in 2012 the Communication COM(2012)95 Improving the delivery of benefits from EU environment measures: building confidence through better knowledge and responsiveness. The first Communication develops more specifically priorities for the environmental sectors giving examples of more structural actions. For instance, instead of dealing in one infringement case with a specific landfill, one should address more widely a structural lack of implementation at the scale of the Member State or to include in a single infringement procedure a number of urban waste water treatment facilities which do not comply with the Directive.

Both Communications focus on correct transposition which is the priority of the Commission: without correct legal transposition, correct application is not possible. Both Communications – in line with the 2007 general Communication – stress the role of co-operation between the Commission and the Member States: guidelines, implementation plans are to be developed to accompany the transposition of the Directives.

---

2   European Commission, *Updating the Handling of Relations with the Complainant in Respect of the Application of Union Law*, Brussels, 2 April 2012, COM(2012)154 final.

The 2012 Communication introduces a new dimension in the implementation picture. In order to address the challenges related to the correct application of EU law (assuming that transposition is correct), it is necessary to develop knowledge and possibilities to monitor the environmental impact as well as compliance with permits (inspections). The Communication is not very precise on the expected developments in these domains. The environmental inspections are not regulated by EU law so far. The European Parliament has called several times for more stringent rules. However, reluctance from Member States is also clear. Although the Commission indicates some potential paths towards reinforced EU legislation, it has not yet decided the level of detail and the legal instruments which will be chosen in this field. The main difficulty is that it is again a domain which is closely linked with enforcement and which depends heavily on the administrative structures of each Member State.

The implementation and enforcement of EU environmental law will require closer co-operation between the Commission and Member States but this co-operation will not develop without 'incentives'. In the context of financial turmoil and budgetary limits, the main driving force remains involvement of non-governmental organisations (NGOs). Complaints and petitions[3] are playing a key-role in maintaining some pressure on EU institutions and Member States. But again, it wouldn't make sense – and would not be desirable – to expect the Commission to play a role other than in structural or high priority issues. The daily application of EU environmental law is to be managed at the national level.

This is the reason why access to justice in environmental matters is essential. The Aarhus Convention signed in 1998 and integrated in the EU legal framework through the decision of the EU to be a party to the Convention in 2005, is the main legal instrument related to public information, public participation and access to justice in environmental matters. These issues are certainly highly complex in particular as they have a strong impact on the procedures and the very basic legal concepts of Member States. It suffices to say that the third pillar of the Convention (access to justice) is still not fully implemented for the EU. The recent case-law of the ECJ indicates that no direct effect is to be expected from the provisions of Article 9 paragraph 3 of the Convention although the Court clearly indicates some need to facilitate access to justice for NGOs (C-240/09 *Lesoochranárske zoskupenie VLK*[4]).

---

3   COM(2008) 773: "As co-legislator, the European Parliament has a clear interest in effective implementation. The environment accounts for about 10% of all parliamentary questions put to the Commission. The Environment Committee has periodic sessions on the implementation of EC environmental law, and the environment is currently the main subject in 35% of the petitions handled by the Petitions Committee."

4   C-240/09, 8 March 2011, Lesoochranárske zoskupenie VLK, "Article 9(3) of the Convention on access to information, public participation in decision-making and access to justice in environmental matters approved on behalf of the European Community by Council Decision 2005/370/EC of 17 February 2005 does not have direct effect in European Union law. It is, however, for the referring court to interpret, to the fullest extent possible, the procedural rules relating to the conditions to be met in order to bring administrative or judicial proceedings in accordance with the objectives of Article 9(3) of that convention and the objective of effective judicial protection of the rights conferred by European Union law, in order to enable an environmental protection organisation, such as the Lesoochranárske zoskupenie, to challenge before a court a decision taken following administrative proceedings liable to be contrary to European Union environmental law."

5 IMPLEMENTATION OF EU WASTE LAW: JUST AS DIFFICULT AS ENFORCEMENT OF EU LAW IN OTHER DOMAINS?

The 2012 Communication indicates that the Commission intends to reinitiate considerations regarding the implementation of the access to justice pillar of the Aarhus Convention. The 2003 proposal for a Directive in this domain was opposed by the Council: it was considered that in view of subsidiarity the matter should be regulated at EU level. However, after the rejection of the 2003 proposal, considerable work has been done by the Commission (studies, expert groups, conferences) and the need for more harmonisation among Member States seems obvious.[5]

The overall picture is clear: very recent initiatives of the Commission are strongly pushing the issue of implementation of EU environmental law to the top of political priorities. The initiative is comprehensive as it covers the Commission's specific powers in the context of infringement proceedings but it also specifically targets the role of the Member States. This is certainly the most important shift: before 2007 the action of the Commission regarding implementation was more conceived as a traditional enforcement activity *per se*. The implementation process was mainly driven by complaints and was primarily a reactive top-down process. From 2007 onwards a new culture emerged which has a tendency to combine preventive and punitive features of enforcement procedure. Amongst the most novel aspects of this approach, are the active efforts of the Commission to develop a dialogue with national judges. Also the development and organisation of seminars[6] dedicated to EU environmental law involving judges from different Member States illustrate this new approach. The Commission now considers that its task of *Guardian of the Treaties* may not be performed in an isolated way.

5.3   AND WHAT ABOUT EU WASTE LAW?

EU waste legislation should not be fundamentally seen as a singular case among the implementation challenges which the Commission has to face. The number of cases in environmental matters is generally equally divided among sectors (nature, water, waste). Nature cases – Birds and Habitats Directives – have frequently been the most controversial cases, in particular with regard to hunting activities or large infrastructure projects. For instance, spring hunting in Malta is still an important political issue, the *Via Baltica* project between Poland and Lithuania triggered a conflict between the Commission and Poland which had to be settled – in favour of the Commission – by the Court of Justice. EU waste legislation was not the sole sector where difficulties in respect to implementation emerged. Although it is true that EU waste legislation is one of the most demanding

---

5   See for instance the 2007 study 'Inventory of EU Member States' Measures on Access to Justice in Environmental Matters' and the 2012 study on access to justice in environmental matters on the website of the Commission, <http://ec.europa.eu/environment/aarhus/studies.htm>.
6   See <http://ec.europa.eu/environment/legal/law/judges.htm> and the detailed materials available.

environmental sectors as it requires building infrastructures and the setup of collection and treatment systems. It is also true that the lack of implementation of legislation in the waste sector has led to a high impact on environmental values and has also consequences for human health. It is remarkable that the Court of Justice in its case-law very often links both consequences closely – environment and human health – in order to decide whether EU waste legislation should be applied, taking into account the precautionary principle. The definition of waste (C-1/03 *Van de Walle*[7]) is seen by the Court as a broad definition precisely on the basis of arguments including the precautionary principle: a definition of waste that is too restrictive would lead to increasing risks for the environment and the population would be exposed to risks resulting from the lack of appropriate treatment of harmful substances.

This is why the EU waste legislation and the related case-law constitute a solid set of demanding and precise rules ensuring that planning, development and management of waste facilities is done in a correct way by Member States.

As explained above, the lack of correct implementation of this legislation can only be addressed if national judges are able to take a significant part of the burden: for instance in the cases C-423/05 *Commission v. France* and C-135/05 *Commission v. Italy*, the Commission obtained a general condemnation of the Member States with regard to illegal landfills. However, it required a collection of facts, which in the French case relied on the official management plans communicated by France to the Commission. These facts referred to existing non-compliant landfills. In the case of Italy they concerned official reports evaluating the situation of illegal landfills. These cases illustrate the complexity of proving the mere existence of these landfills. In the absence of official reports which can hardly be challenged by national authorities, it is extremely difficult for the Commission to address any structural problems regarding waste facilities.

Therefore, a substantial role for the implementation is to be played by citizens and associations who can gather enough information to submit their cases to national judges. National judges in this context are the most appropriate means by which to obtain rapid solutions as the Commission is now more inclined to address structural problems (see above, on the Communications on infringement policy). Collecting sufficient evidence

---

[7] C-1/03, 7 September 2004, Van de Walle, para. 45, "First, as the Court has held, the verb 'to discard' must be interpreted in the light of the aim of Directive 75/442, which, in the wording of the third recital in the preamble, is the protection of human health and the environment against harmful effects caused by the collection, transport, treatment, storage and tipping of waste, and that of Article 174(2) EC, which states that Community policy on the environment is to aim at a high level of protection and is to be based, in particular, on the precautionary principle and the principle that preventive action should be taken. The verb 'to discard', which determines the scope of 'waste', therefore cannot be interpreted restrictively (*see* to that effect Joined Cases C-418/97 and C-419/97 *ARCO Chemie Nederland and Others* [2000] ECR I-4475, paragraphs 36 to 40)."

5 Implementation of EU Waste Law: Just as Difficult as Enforcement of EU Law in Other Domains?

on structural problems takes time. Therefore, direct submission to national courts is certainly the most appropriate and efficient enforcement path.

However this scheme may only work under the condition that access to justice is granted easier than before. This would entail the absence of legal and practical barriers, the admissibility of claims and costs for complainants, efficiency of justice, possibilities of injunctive relief, and decisions taken in a reasonable time-frame.

6   The Legal Paradox of EU Waste Management

Aurélien Raccah

Nowadays the environment must be economically profitable. According to the *Europe 2020 Strategy*, the objective is to promote 'a resource efficient, greener and more competitive economy'.[1] Thus, the EU environmental ambitions shall be balanced with their profitability. At least, this global strategy shall focus on energy, especially on the reduction of greenhouse gas emissions by 20% compared to 1990 levels. At most, applying it to waste policy is another challenge if one takes into consideration that the European Union generates 2,501 million tonnes of waste each year,[2] including 220 million from households *i.e.* almost half a ton per inhabitant. This pollution has a double effect. Disposing it in a landfill affects seriously the environment. Recycling every waste costs too much for the society. The challenge is to turn the waste into a business.

The sixth environment action programme (EAP) for 2002-2012 set up waste management as a key priority, aiming to decrease the disposal of waste, to increase their re-use through adapted treatments and to minimise their risk to the environment.[3] In 2005, the European Commission argued that

> waste is an opportunity – Europe's drive to deal with waste in environmentally sound ways has generated jobs and business opportunities. The waste management and recycling sector has a high growth rate and has an estimated turnover of over €100 billion for EU-25. It is labour intensive and provides between 1.2 and 1.5 million jobs.[4]

An impact assessment mentioned a turnover between €75 and €95 billion for EU-25, providing between 500,000 and 1.5 million jobs.[5] Another study foresaw an estimate of environmental employment of around 4 million jobs, plus 770,000 in the new EU Member

---

1   European Commission, *Europe 2020, A Strategy for Smart, Sustainable and Inclusive Growth*, Brussels, 3 March 2010, COM(2010) 2020 final, pp. 14-16.
2   Eurostat, *Total Amount of Waste Generated by Waste Category (Households and Businesses)*, 2010 (last data available in 2014). Cf. <http://epp.eurostat.ec.europa.eu/statistics_explained/index.php/Waste_statistics>.
3   Art. 8 of the Decision No. 1600/2002/EC of 22 July 2002 laying down the Sixth Community Environment Action Programme, OJ 2002 L 242/1.
4   European Commission, *Taking Sustainable Use of Resources Forward: A Thematic Strategy on the Prevention and Recycling of Waste*, Brussels, 21 December 2005, COM(2005) 666 final, p. 3.
5   European Commission, *Impact Assessment on the Thematic Strategy on the Prevention and Recycling of Waste and the Immediate Implementing Measures*, Brussels, 21 December 2005, SEC(2005) 1681, pp. 6, 15-16.

States.[6] A more recent one demonstrates that full implementation of EU waste law would save €72 billion a year, increase the annual turnover in this sector by €42 billion and create over 400 thousand jobs by 2020.[7] The aim is to "use waste as a resource"[8] to counterbalance the economic paradox.

From 1975, EU law widely defines the concept of waste as "any substance or object which the holder discards or intends or is required to discard".[9] Benefitting from waste remains however a difficult challenge. By definition, a product becomes waste because it does not serve the holder anymore. If it is still re-useable, it is qualified as 'by-products',[10] even if it is not the end product that the manufacturing process directly seeks to produce.[11] By-products do not fall into the waste qualification as long as they can be directly reused.

Despite this distinction, Member States shall ensure the collection, treatment and recycling or re-use of approximately eighteen categories of waste (batteries, electrical and electronic equipment, end-of-life vehicles, packaging, sewage sludge, shipment of waste, waste oils . . .). The targets range from 50 to 100% according to the matter. Since few waste policies commenced between the 1970's and 1990's, many deadlines have already been attained; others are still running until 2020 or later. We are today in a transition period for almost all EU waste law. However, the starting statement is that many current objectives are not achieved. Huge differences are observed between the Member States. We can easily see that Nordic States are often close to the 100% objectives while Latin, Southern and Eastern States often fail in implementing directives. However there are counterexamples explained below.

EU waste policy contains a legal paradox: it shall render effective objectives which are unachievable in many national legal systems. The EU waste directives set up targets, sometimes with a specific percentage, to be achieved by a certain date. These objectives legally bind the Member states but most of them cannot be fully reached because they are too high, complex or costly. Therefore, how to ensure an effective implementation of

---

[6] Ecotech, *Analysis of the EU Eco-Industries, Their Employment and Export Potential*, 2002, p. 95.

[7] European Commission, *Implementing EU Waste Legislation for Green Growth*, final report of 29 November 2011, p. 11.

[8] European Commission, *Report on the Thematic Strategy on the Prevention and Recycling of Waste*, Brussels, 19 January 2011, COM(2011) 13 final, p. 6.

[9] Art. 3, §1, Directive 2008/98/EC; Ex. Art. 1(a), Directive 75/442/EEC of 15 July 1975 on waste; Case C-1/03, *Paul Van de Walle e.a.* [2004] ECR I-7632, §§42-48; Case C-129/96, *Inter-Environnement Wallonie* [1997] ECR I-7411, §26, and Case C-9/00, *Palin Granit and Vehmassalon kansanterveystyön kuntayhtymän hallitus* [2002] ECR I-3533, §22. See, a recent case-law presentation by M. Clement, *Droit européen de l'environnement*, Larcier, Brussels, 2013, pp. 439-540.

[10] European Commission, *On the Interpretative of Waste and By-products*, Brussels, 21 February 2007, COM(2007) 59 final.

[11] Case C-9/00, *Palin Granit* [2002]; Case C-418/97, *ARCO* [2000] ECR I-04475.

the EU law on waste if its objectives can only be partially achieved? The present study points out the legal problems which arise from the directives on waste law. The first part focuses on the unavoidable partiality of the EU law in waste matters (section 6.1). This partiality results from the crossing of political objectives with legal insecurity. The second part identifies two major reasons for this legal paradox consisting which provide legally unattainable objectives (section 6.2).

6.1 A Partial EU Waste Policy

EU environmental law, including waste law is by definition, partial. Recycling 100% of all waste is not possible. That explains why most of the EU directives fix transition stages with partial targets, such as recycling 50% of household wastes by 2020. Politically, they are very ambitious and have positive effects on the environment (A). However, these partial objectives included in EU law introduce too much confusion in legal terms. The number of infringements of EU waste law is so high that the Commission cannot sue for most of them (B).

6.1.1 Quantitative Targets of Achievement in EU Waste Policy

In 2002, the 6th EAP invited the European Commission to continue the development "of quantitative and qualitative reduction targets covering all relevant waste" for the ten next years.[12] Ten years later, the review is quantitatively positive, legally controversial. The eighteen categories of waste do all contain very high collection, treatment, recycling or re-use targets (1) which have already reversed the negative impact of wastes on the environment (2).

6.1.1.1 Ambitious Objectives to be Reached within the EU Waste Law

The general approach in the EU waste policy is nowadays regulated by the Waste Framework Directive of 2008 (gathering household waste, construction and demolition waste, by-products, hazardous waste, waste oils, bio-waste). A five-step waste hierarchy has been chosen for waste management: prevention, preparing for re-use, recycling, recovery and disposal.[13] This corresponds to a gradual scale of taking measures protecting the environment. By 2020, the general objective for the Member States is to take any measures to increase the re-use or recycling of household wastes to a minimum of overall 50% and 70%

---

12 Art. 8, §2 (ii) (a) of the Decision 1600/2002/EC.
13 Art. 4, §1 of the Directive 2008/98/EC of 19 November 2008 on waste and repealing certain directives, OJ 2008 L 312/3. Adopted in 1975 and revised many times, substantially in 1991 and in 2006 (Directive 2006/12/EC), the waste framework directive codifies the main objectives in this field.

of non-hazardous construction and demolition waste (all measured by weight).[14] This is the most ambitious objective of waste management set in the world.

More specifically, every directive contains very high objectives against pollution from waste. From the nineteen seventies on, we count approximately eighteen categories of waste policies with such ambitious objectives.

Directive 86/278/EEC on sewage sludge belongs to the good examples of quasi complete implementation.[15] It aims at encouraging the use of sewage sludge in agriculture, preventing its negative effects on soil, vegetation, animals and human health and limiting heavy metals in soils.[16] This approach has then been enlarged to the sewage sludge from municipal waste waters.

Since 31 December 2005, all agglomerations of more than 2,000 inhabitants should be equipped with modernised collection and water treatment systems (some deadlines have been extended to 2015 for EU-12). More than 22,000 agglomerations in the European Union are subject to the requirements of Directive 91/271/EEC of 21 May 1991 concerning urban waste water. This directive concerns the collection, treatment and disposal of waste and the treatment and discharge of waste water from certain industrial sectors of urban water and protects the environment against the adverse effects of discharging wastewater. It provides, on the one hand, that all the agglomerations are equipped with collection systems for urban waste water and, on the other hand, that urban waste water entering collection systems shall be subject to secondary treatment before discharge. It implicitly means that 100% of the objectives shall be reached.

In the follow-up to the Basel Convention 1989,[17] a regulation on shipment of waste within the European Union has been adopted,[18] later approved by the OECD.[19] It aims to regulate the supervision and control of shipments of waste within the EU, but applies also to any waste imported into, exported from or in transit through the EU. Almost all wastes are concerned, except shipments of radioactive waste which are subject to a specific Euratom procedure.[20]

---

14 Art. 11, §2, of the Directive 2008/98/EC.
15 Council Directive 86/278/EEC of 12 June 1986 on the protection of the environment, and in particular of the soil, when sewage sludge is used in agriculture, OJ 1986 L 181, pp. 6-12.
16 European Commission, *Report on the Implementation of the EU Waste Legislation*, Brussels, 17 January 2013, COM(2013) 6 final, p. 5.
17 Basel Convention of 22 March 1989 on the control of trans-boundary movements of hazardous wastes and their disposal.
18 Originally based on Council Regulation (EEC) No. 259/93 of 1 February 1993 on the supervision and control of shipments of waste within, into and out of the European Community, now ruled by Regulation (EC) No. 1013/2006 of the European Parliament and of the Council of 14 June 2006 on shipments of waste [amended].
19 Decision C(2001)107/Final of the OECD Council concerning the revision of Decision C(92)39/Final on the control of trans-boundary movements of wastes destined for recovery operations (OECD Decision).
20 Council Directive 2006/117/Euratom of 20 November 2006 on the supervision and control of shipments of radioactive waste and spent fuel (*see,* above, Chapter 1, Sections 1.2.2 and 1.3.3).

By the end of 2008, the Packaging Directive[21] sets that Member States had to meet more ambitious recycling and recovery rates, including material-specific recycling levels.

The Landfill Directive 1999/31/EC[22] obliges Member States to reduce the amount of biodegradable municipal waste that they landfill to 35% of 1995 levels by 2016 (for some countries by 2020) which will significantly reduce this problem.

The Directive on end-of-life vehicles (ELV) requires that the Member States take the necessary measures towards economic operators to ensure that 'no later than 1 January 2006' the reuse and recovery of end-of-life vehicles shall be increased to a minimum of 85% by an average weight per vehicle and year and the recycling to 80% (passing respectively to 95% and 85% from 2015 on).[23] Moreover materials in end-of-life vehicles may also be covered by the directives on waste of electrical and electronic equipment (WEEE), on restrictions of the use of certain hazardous substances (RoHS) and the REACH regulation concerning chemical substances.

Concerning batteries, Directive 2006/66/EC limits the use of mercury and cadmium in batteries and accumulators.[24] The Member States shall organise a collection scheme, achieving 25% of it by 26 September 2012 and 45% by 26 September 2016.[25] Moreover, they shall ensure that the producers set up schemes 'using the best techniques available', no later than 26 September 2009. On 26 March 2012, the European Commission proposed a new amendment to enlarge the application of this directive to emergency and alarm systems, medical equipment and cordless power tools (CPT) which are currently exempted.[26]

Concerning the Directive on WEEE, since August 13, 2005, consumers, households and professionals must be able to dispose of WEEE free of charge, distributors of a new product must recover the older products of the same type and producers must organise recovery systems individual or collective. WEEE treatment then gives rise to the extraction of various fluids. Producers must ensure compliance with quality standards annexed to Directive 2002/96/EC. Institutions responsible for processing must obtain a permit from the competent authorities. Finally, the Directive has set 31 December 2006 as the deadline for achieving recovery rates, average weight per appliance, between 65 and 80% depending on the categories of EEE.

---

21 Directive 94/62/EC on packaging and packaging waste, OJ 1994 L 365, p. 10.
22 Council Directive 1999/31/EC of 26 April 1999 on the landfill of waste.
23 Art. 7, Directive 2000/53/EC on end-of-life vehicles, amended by Directive 2011/37/EC.
24 Directive 2006/66/EC on batteries and accumulators and waste batteries of 6 September 2006.
25 Art. 10 of the Directive 2006/66/EC.
26 Proposal for a directive amending Directive 2006/66/EC on batteries and accumulators and waste batteries, 26 March 2012, COM(2012) 136 final. *See also* Impact assessment accompanying the proposal for a Directive amending Directive 2006/66/EC on batteries and accumulators and waste batteries and accumulators as regards the placing on the market of portable batteries and accumulators containing cadmium intended for use in cordless power tools, 26 March 2012, COM(2012) 136 final.

Our first statement is that environmental policy is politically positive and exhaustive in the area of waste. Since 1975, the European Commission has progressively pressed the Member States to change the increase of pollution. The European Union takes undoubtedly the lead in the world as far as legislation protecting the environment is concerned and serves as model for many countries.[27]

6.1.1.2 The Statements in the Report on EU Waste Law Implementation

In 2005, the European Commission stated that "the complexity of EU and Member State legislation tends to discourage recycling and recovery activities"and that "EU waste law often remains unclear".[28] It recognised that the statistics on waste are of poor quality, even if Eurostat provides regular data.[29] In 2011[30] and in 2013,[31] the statement remains the same for the reporting period 2007-2009 (reports not provided on time, unclear, imprecise and incomplete answers, lack of clarity...) for most of the areas nowadays covered by the 2008 Waste Framework Directive (management plans, hazardous waste, waste oils). Small developments are significant (most Member States submitted on time). Controlling the implementation of the whole waste legislation in 27 Member States on very specific environmental norms requires common methods. The European Commission is still working on that point. A questionnaire for Member States reports has been recently published.[32]

A general statement shows that the EU waste directives are well transposed into national law, but they remain partially ineffective in many Member States.

For the period 2007-2009, all reporting Member States applied the Waste Framework Directive, drew up national waste management plans and introduced an obligation to obtain a permit for waste handling.[33] However the methods differ between States. Many of them are still landfilling household waste (Bulgaria, Romania, Malta, Lithuania and

---

27 R.J. Konz, 'The End-of-Life Vehicle (ELV) Directive: The Road to Responsible Disposal', *Minn. J. Int'l L.*, Vol. 18, 2009, p. 431.
28 European Commission, *Impact Assessment*, SEC(2005) 1681, p. 14.
29 Legal bases for the waste statistics: Regulation (EC) No. 2150/2002 of 25 November 2002 on waste statistics as amended by Regulation (EU) No. 849/2010 of 27 September 2010; Regulation (EC) No. 782/2005 of 24 May 2005 setting out the format for the transmission of results on waste statistics; Regulation (EC) No. 1445/2005 of 5 September 2005 defining the proper quality evaluation criteria and the contents of the quality reports for waste statistics.
30 European Commission, *Implementing EU Waste Legislation for Green Growth*, final report of 29 November 2011, p. 14.
31 European Commission, *Report on the Implementation*, COM(2013) 6 final, p. 2. The European Commission points out France, Greece, Malta, the Belgian regions of Brussels and Wallonia for not reporting on time for the period 2007-2009.
32 European Commission, *Commission Implementing Decision of 18.4.2012 Establishing a Questionnaire for Member States Reports on the Implementation of Directive 2008/98/EC of the European Parliament and of the Council on Waste*, Brussels, 18 April 2012, COM(2012) 2384 final.
33 European Commission, *Report on the Implementation*, COM(2013) 6 final, p. 3.

Latvia landfilling over 90% of their waste) while others landfill less than 5% (Belgium, Denmark, Germany, the Netherlands, Austria and Sweden). Austria, Germany, Belgium, the Netherlands and Sweden recycle more than 50% of their municipal waste. Sweden, Denmark, the Netherlands, Luxembourg, Belgium, Germany and France incinerate them largely.

The deadline for the transposition of Directive 86/278/EEC on sewage sludge was June 18th, 1989. However, the European Commission received less than half of the national reports on time.[34] A new directive has thus been adopted to standardise the questionnaire for drawing up these reports.[35] Eleven years after the deadline, the Commission was finally able to report that this directive was well transposed with a positive impact on soils.[36]

The Directive on waste water had to be fully applied in more than 22,000 agglomerations before 2005. However, the objectives are not completely achieved. In 2009 the following was achieved: 93% of these agglomerations had a waste water collection system, 78% of those required secondary treatment and 65% of those qualified as 'sensitive' areas required a more rigorous treatment. In 2011,[37] collection systems finally reached 99% of the total polluting load of EU-15 (Italy and Greece still have only 93% and 87% of their generated load collected in collecting systems) but only 65% of the total generated load in the EU-12 (Member States joining the EU after 2004) end up in collection systems. Secondary treatment was in place for 96% of the load of EU-15, but for only 48% of the load of EU-12. Finally, more stringent treatment was in place for 89% of the load of EU-15 but for only 27% of the generated load of EU-12. Even if the evolution is positive, thousands of cities do not meet the requirements of Directive 91/271/EEC.

Directive 91/689/EEC on hazardous waste now repealed and replaced by the relevant provisions of Framework Directive 2008/98/EC- banned part of such waste and imposed traceability requirements, but it suffered of a lack of reporting information. Hazardous waste may now cease to be waste in the meaning of Directive 2008/98/EC if a recovery operation enables it to be made usable without endangering human health and without harming the environment.[38]

---

34 Commission Communication to the Council and the European Parliament of 27 February 1997 concerning the application of Directives 75/439/EEC, 75/442/EEC, 78/319/EEC and 86/278/EEC on waste management [COM(97) 23 final].
35 Council Directive 91/692/EEC of 23 December 1991 standardizing and rationalizing reports on the implementation of certain Directives relating to the environment.
36 Report from the Commission to the Council and the European Parliament of 10 January 2000 on the implementation of Community waste legislation for the period 1995-1997 (Directives 75/442/EEC, 91/689/EEC, 75/439/EEC and 86/278/EEC) [COM(1999) 752 final]; Report from the Commission of 20 November 2009 on implementation of the community waste legislation [among others] Directive 86/278/EEC on sewage sludge for the period 2004-2006 [COM(2009) 633 final].
37 European Commission, *6th Commission Summary on the Implementation of the Urban Waste Water Treatment Directive*, Brussels, 7 December 2011, SEC(2011) 1561 final.
38 Case 358/11, *Lapin elinkeino* [2013].

The waste oil Directive,[39] aiming to ensure the safe collection, storage, disposal and eventual recycling of waste oils, was still not completely applied after three decades.[40] The collection rate is increasing but attained only 81% and the regeneration rate only 65% in 2003.[41] In this field, the Member States shall give priority to the processing of waste oils by regeneration over their combustion and landfilling, but the treatment methods differ again significantly between the States.

The Commission lastly concluded that Directive 91/157/EEC on batteries "failed to adequately address the risks posed by waste batteries and to create a uniform system for collecting and recycling batteries".[42] For example, in 2002, more than 45% of all portable batteries sold in the EU (*i.e.* 72,155 tons) went to landfilling or incineration. Waste batteries collected were disposed of in this way instead of being recycled. The deadline for the transposition of Directive 2006/66/EC into national law was 26 September 2008 and since 26 September 2008 producers have had to comply with it. No report has been produced as yet.

The Directive on the end-of-life vehicles obliges Member States to report to the Commission every three years.[43] The two first reports[44] have been unsatisfactory. By 21 April 2002, all Member States had failed to communicate their national measure to the Commission.[45] After this deadline, few of them continued not to comply with the directive, others did not send information on time, "many responses were missing, incomplete or unclear [. . .] timeliness of reporting was poor, and the quality of the reporting methodologies made the received figures questionable in some cases".[46] Current Eurostat statistics also show that many Member States do not reach the 85% reuse, recycling and recovery targets.[47]

---

39 Council Directive 75/439/EEC of 16 June 1975 on the disposal of waste oils, OJ 1975 L 194, pp. 23-25, as amended by Council Directive 87/101/EEC of 22 December 1986 (OJ 1987 L 42, p. 43), repealed from 10 December 2010 and nowadays incorporated in Directive 2008/98/EC.
40 Case C-92/03, *Commission v. Portugal* [2005] ECR I-870; Case C-15/03, *Commission v. Austria* [2005] ECR I-851; Case C-424/02, *Commission v. UK* [2004] ECR I-7262. *Cf.* European Commission, *Impact Assessment*, SEC(2005) 1681, p. 15; *Critical Review of Existing Studies and Life Cycle Analysis on the Regeneration and Incineration of Waste Oils*, December 2001.
41 European Commission, *Impact Assessment*, SEC(2005) 1681, p. 23.
42 Commission Services document, March 2011 (published in November 2012), p. 4.
43 Art. 9 of Directive 2000/53/EC. A questionnaire on the implementation of this directive has been established by Commission Decision 2001/753/EC and the procedure refers to Art. 6 of Directive 91/692/EEC.
44 Report for 2002-2005, COM/2007/0618 final; Report from the Commission to the Council, the European Parliament, the European Economic and Social Committee, and the Committee of Regions on the implementation of Directive 2000/53/EC on end-of-life vehicles for the period 2005-2008, COM/2009/0635 final.
45 European Commission, Directive 200/53/EC, Guidance document, January 2005, p. 32.
46 COM/2009/0635 final.
47 Eurostat, *Reuse, Recycling and Recovery of ELVs, by Country and Year, in Percent (%)*, <http://epp.eurostat.ec.europa.eu/portal/page/portal/waste/key_waste_streams/end_of_life_vehicles_elvs>.

Concerning the waste electrical and electronic equipment (WEEE), there are several legal problems introduced by Directive 2002/95/EC. Firstly, there is confusion between policy objectives and normative obligations in the directive, so it is almost impossible to sanction the competent authorities. Directive 2002/95/EC indicates only that Member States "shall ensure that, by 31 December 2006 at the latest, an annual average rate of separate collection of WEEE from households with at least four kilograms per capita is reached".[48] Beside the fact that this goal has only been partially achieved, studies suggest that only a third of WEEE have undergone adequate treatment, the remaining two thirds being landfilled.[49] Secondly, the administrative procedures established against companies vary considerably from one country to another and may as well, as the German and British litigation revealed, create distortions in competition between manufacturers according to their country of origin.

Our overview shows that the objectives chosen for the directives are often unrealistic. From the beginning of the legislative initiatives, almost no waste policy was effectively applied by the competent authorities. The provisions of the directives are ambitious political objectives disconnected from the law. Not reaching 100% of implementation is called, in law, an infringement. This situation naturally leads to important case-law.

6.1.2 Some Important EU Case-Law on Waste

The important number of infringements of the EU waste directives exceeds the capacity of the European Commission to sue regarding all of them.[50] Waste still represents on average 20% of all EU environmental infringement cases.[51] In the light of this considerable number, the selection of case-law does not always seem to be transparent (1). Moreover, the penalties for non-compliance with the EU waste directives depend on national measures, which create disparities between Member States for the same violations (2).

6.1.2.1 Non-Transparent European Case-Law on Waste

The legal proceedings in matter of waste are mostly actions for failure to fulfil EU obligations initiated by the European Commission against Member States which do not comply with the EU law.[52] However, according to the important number of infringements to EU waste law which are based on the Commission's reports itself, the Commission should

---

48 Art. 5, §5 of Directive 2002/95/EC.
49 Report of the Commission on the implementation of waste in 2004-2006, COM(2009) 633 final, p. 7.
50 *See* infringement cases on the Commission's website, <http://ec.europa.eu/environment/legal/law/press_en.htm>.
51 European Commission, *Report on the Thematic Strategy*, COM(2011) 13 final, p. 3.
52 Arts. 258-260 TFEU.

begin many more procedures. We count approximately 200 cases relating to waste law from the early eighties, *i.e.* less than ten cases a year, to ensure the implementation of instruments on eighteen categories of wastes. Even if the implementation assessment would include procedures before national bodies and national courts,[53] the result remains weak.

Directive 75/442/EEC and Directive 91/689/EEC have led to the largest number of cases. That has been the case for France[54] and for the UK[55] by failing to draw up waste management plans for certain regions; for Italy by not forwarding to the Commission information concerning plans for the management and disposal of waste and hazardous waste, as well as information concerning plans for the management of packaging waste in the entire country[56]; for Spain by failing to ensure the application of EU obligations regarding incineration facilities on the island of La Palma,[57] as well as to draw up management plans in other regions[58]; for Greece by failing to draw up management plan for hazardous waste[59] and the existence of unlawful deposits of waste[60]; for Luxemburg for specific aspects of the national waste management plan[61]; for Ireland for not providing a waste management plan in respect of Directive 75/442/EEC.[62]

The case *Commission v. Italy*, C-297/08, of 2010 relating to the waste crisis in Campania became particularly well known because of the specific case of Naples.[63] Italy has been found as failing to fulfil its obligations under Articles 4 and 5 of Directive 2006/12/EC on waste[64] to adopt, for the region of Campania, the measures necessary to ensure the recovery and the disposal of waste without endangering human health and without harming the environment. In particular, Italy has failed to establish an integrated and adequate network of disposal installations.

As seen above, Directive 2006/12 provides that Member States shall ensure that waste is recovered or disposed and shall establish an integrated and adequate network of disposal installations. For that purpose, the competent authorities shall draw up a waste

---

[53] *See* for example Case C-97/11, *Amia SpA v. Provincia Regionale di Palermo* [2012].
[54] Case C-292/99, *Commission v. France* [2002].
[55] Case C-35/00, *Commission v. UK* [2002].
[56] Case C-466/99, *Commission v. Italy* [2002]; Case C-46/01, *Commission v. Italy* [2002]; Case C-135/05, *Commission v. Italy* [2007]; Cases C-194/05 & C-195/05, *Commission v. Italy* [2007]; Case C-263/05, *Commission v. Italy* [2007].
[57] Case C-139/00, *Commission v. Spain* [2002].
[58] Case C-446/01, *Commission v. Spain* [2003]; Case C-121/03, *Commission v. Spain* [2005].
[59] Case C-33/01, *Commission v. Greece* [2002]; Case C-83/02, *Commission v. Greece* [2003].
[60] Case C-420/02, *Commission v. Greece* [2004].
[61] Case C-174/01, *Commission v. Luxemburg* [2002]; Case C-196/01, *Commission v. Luxemburg* [2003].
[62] Case C-494/01, *Commission v. Ireland* [2005]; Case C-248/05, *Commission v. Ireland* [2007].
[63] Case 297/08, *Commission v. Italy* [2010]; *see*, above, Chapter 4, Section 4.5.2.
[64] Substituting Directive 75/442/EEC and today substituted by Directive 2008/98/EC.

management plan (type, quantity and origin of waste, technical requirements, special arrangements, suitable disposal sites or installations) which may, in particular, provide "appropriate measures to encourage rationalisation of the collection, sorting and treatment of waste".[65] This Directive has been well transposed at the national level in Italy, but from 1994 the region of Campania, comprising 551 municipalities, including Naples, was faced with management and disposal problems of its urban waste. The installations, whether landfills, incinerators or thermal recovery plants, were not sufficient to meet the waste disposal requirements of the region of Campania. The Italian Republic deployed considerable administrative, financial (€400 million between 2003 and 2008) and military resources. An agreement concerning additional shipments has been recently signed with other Italian regions and Germany to evacuate many tons of waste. However, the Court stated that even with this assistance, considerable quantities of waste remain along the public roads in the region. From 2007, the European Commission sued in an action for failure. The Commission stated that "only 10.6% of the waste produced is sorted at the time of collection, as compared with a Community average of 33%". The location criteria of waste disposal sites (principle of proximity) require the existence of an infrastructure which is adequate and nearby, well connected to transport networks within the framework of inter-regional or even cross-border cooperation and outside of any sensitive area.[66]

Under Article 258 TFEU, a Member State remains responsible for any failure to fulfil its obligations under the Treaty or secondary legislation,[67] irrelevant of whether it is the result of intention, negligence or of technical difficulties encountered by it.[68] Internal situations or presence of criminal activity may not be pleaded.[69] Member States have a "large margin of discretion in assessing the need for such measures"[70] and are thus responsible to sue their competent authorities. This is a way to decentralise the control to the Member States.

The Court holds that "the Commission is entitled to decide, in its discretion, on what date it may be appropriate to bring an action and it is not for the Court to review the exercise of that discretion".[71] The Court finally answers to our previous question: in proceedings brought for failure to fulfil an obligation,

---

65 Case C-480/06, *Commission v. Germany* [2009] §37.
66 Joined Cases C-53/02 and C-217/02, *Commune de Braine-le-Château and Others* [2004] §34.
67 Case 301/81, *Commission v. Belgium* [1983] §8; Case C-508/03, *Commission v. United Kingdom* [2006] §67.
68 Case C-71/97, *Commission v. Spain* [1998] §15.
69 Case C-45/91, *Commission v. Greece* [1992] §§20, 21; Case C-121/07, *Commission v. France* [2008] §72.
70 §96; Case C-365/97, *Commission v. Italy* [1999] §67; Case C-420/02, *Commission v. Greece* [2004] §21.
71 Case C-422/92, *Commission v. Germany* [1995] §18.

> [...] it is incumbent upon the Commission to prove the infringement alleged by providing the Court with the evidence necessary to enable it to establish that the obligation has not been fulfilled, without being able to rely on any presumption for those purposes.[72]

and

> [...] account should be taken of the fact that, where it is a question of checking that the national provisions intended to ensure effective implementation of Directive 2006/12 are applied correctly in practice, the Commission, which does not have investigative powers of its own in this area, is largely reliant on the information provided by complainants, by public or private bodies, by the press or by the Member State concerned.[73]

Once the Commission collected enough evidence concerning a Member State, "it is for that Member State to challenge in substance and in detail the data produced and the inferences drawn".[74] To sum up, the European Union is not able to assess all the situations on its own but once it points out a case, the Member State better be well prepared.

As mentioned above, the Directive on sewage sludge required eleven years to be well reported. In the meantime, the Commission stated that several Member States failed in its implementation. Only one proceeding has been initiated, against Belgium.[75] No measure has been taken against Member States not reporting.

Concerning the end-of-life vehicles, even if the implementation reports state that objectives are not completely reached by many Member States, only few of them have been finally tried for failure to transpose the directive correctly.[76] For instance, in the case *Commission v. France* of 2010,[77] the Court reminds that the objective of the directive on end-of-life vehicles is to minimise their impact on the environment, but does not prevent Member States from adopting more stringent protective measures if they are compatible with the EU obligations. The Court focuses first of all on the 'certificate of destruction' ensuring a better traceability of the vehicles, which was confused in the French system with the

---

72 Case C-297/08, *European Commission v. Italy* [2010] §101; *see also* Case C-150/07, *Commission v. Portugal* [2009] para. 65.
73 Case C-494/01, *Commission v. Ireland* [2005] ECR I-3331, §43; Case C-135/05, *Commission v. Italy* [2007] §28.
74 Case C-365/97, *Commission v. Italy* [1999] §§84, 86; *see also* Case C-189/07, *Commission v. Spain* [2008] §82.
75 Case C-260/93, *Commission v. Belgium* [1994].
76 Case C-277/03, *Commission v. UK* [2004]; Case C-292/03, *Commission v. Finland* [2004]; Case C-331/03, *Commission v. France* [2004]; Case C-460/03, *Commission v. Ireland* [2004]; Case C-394/05, *Commission v. Italy* [2007]; Case C-64/09, *Commission v. France* [2010].
77 Case C-64/09, *Commission v. France* [2010].

'receipt of acceptance for destruction'. Then the Court holds that Directive 2000/53 provides that the delivery of an ELV to an authorised treatment facility must be free of charge, the related costs being borne by the manufacturers, which is not the case in France. Other cases are still pending.[78] None of the States which do not respect the re-use, recycling and recovery targets has been charged by the Commission.

Regarding Directive 2006/66/EC on batteries, no review has been undertaken yet. However some failures to apply the old Directive 91/157/EEC on batteries and accumulators containing certain dangerous substances have been declared by the Court.[79] The Directive 2006/66/EC substituted the previous one considered as failing to reach the objective.

Shipment of waste has been a matter tried before the ECJ.[80] In 1995, Germany was declared as failing to fulfil its obligations to establish a system of control of trans-frontier shipments of dangerous waste by excluding certain categories of recyclable waste from the scope of its legislation on the disposal of waste.[81] No action for failure under the legislation on shipment of waste led to penalty payments.

The objectives of Directive 1999/31/EC on the landfill of waste are foreseen to be realised in 2016 and 2020. The Member States had to transpose the directive properly. Two Member States partially failed. The UK first did not transpose on time[82] and Italy did not transpose correctly.[83] The other cases relating to Directive 1999/31/EC are references for a preliminary ruling.[84]

Waste packaging has been also been subject to important case-law. Some Member States failed to comply with their obligations[85] and the interpretation of Directive 94/62/EC on waste packaging led to references for preliminary ruling.[86] The most important case

---

78 European Commission, Reasoned opinions concerning Romania and Slovakia (IP/12/540 on 31 May 2012), Poland (IP/12/293 on 22 March 2012), Italy (IP/11/731, 16 June 2011).
79 Case C-298/97, *Commission v. Spain* [1998]; Case C-298/97, *Commission v. UK* [1998]; Case C-215/98, *Commission v. Greece* [1999]; Case C-178/98, *Commission v. France* [1999]; Case C-347/97, *Commission v. Spain* [1999].
80 Ex-Directives 75/442 and 78/319, nowadays substituted by Regulation (EC) No. 1013/2006 of the European Parliament and of the Council of 14 June 2006 on shipments of waste.
81 Case C-422/92, *Commission v. Germany* [1995].
82 Case C-423/02, *Commission v. UK* [2003].
83 Case C-442/06, *Commission v. Italy* [2008].
84 Case C-6/03, *Deponiezweckverband Eiterköpfe v. Land Rheinland-Pfalz* [2005]; Case C-172/08, *Pontina Ambiente Srl v. Regione Lazio* [2010]; Case C-121/11, *Pro-Braine ASBL e.a. v. The Commune of Braine-le-Château* [2012]; Case C-97/11, *Amia SpA, in liquidation v. Provincia Regionale di Palermo* [2012].
85 Case C-123/99, *Commission v. Greece* [2000]; Case C-292/99, *Commission v. France* [2002]; Case C-466/99, *Commisssion v. Italy* [2002]; Case C-35/00, *Commission v. UK* [2002]; Case C-270/03, *Commission v. Italy* [2005]; Case C-263/05, *Commission v. Italy* [2007].
86 Case C-444/00, *Mayer Parry Recycling Ltd* [2003]; Case C-341/01, *Plato Plastik Robert Frank GmbH and Caropack Handelsgesellschaft mbH* [2004].

opposed Germany to the Commission. The Commission was supported by France and the UK.[87] The Commission contested the German rules. By introducing deposit and return obligations for non-re-usable packaging that depend on the proportion of re-usable packaging on the German market, this German system imposes a particular burden on producers of natural mineral water that comes from other Member States. Re-usable packaging results in additional costs for producers of natural mineral water established in other Member States and may therefore constitute a measure having equivalent effect to a quantitative restriction within the meaning of ex-Article 28 EC. The German Government argued that these rules do not serve to protect national interests unilaterally but are intended merely to implement the obligations arising from another Directive, 80/777/EEC of 15 July 1980 on the exploitation and marketing of natural mineral waters in creating a system seeking the re-use of packaging for products which must be bottled at source. However, the Court declared that Germany has failed to fulfill its obligations under Directive 94/62/EC in conjunction with Article 28 EC. The German re-use system has eventually been then approved by the Court.[88]

The other cases judged by the ECJ concern asked for a preliminary ruling under Article 267 TFEU. The Court has defined the concept of 'waste',[89] the qualification of 'hazardous waste',[90] the access to justice in waste matters,[91] the concept of 'consent' regarding the landfill of waste,[92] the assessment of the effects of certain plans and programmes on the environment[93] ... All this case-law aims at ensuring a common interpretation in the national legal orders.

6.1.2.2 Few Legal Sanctions for Failure to Fulfil EU Obligations

Most of the EU waste legislation does not contain direct legal sanctions. There is a clear devolution of sanctioning from EU law to national law. According to Article 4 EU, the latter depends on the national legislation which means that the same infringement does not endorse the same sanction everywhere. This is mostly addressed in the Waste Framework Directive 2008/98/EC. Member States shall take the responsibility of the complete waste management in their territory in taking necessary measures "to ensure that any original waste producer or other holder carries out the treatment of waste himself".[94] Any individual or professional, private or public actor in charge of waste collection, treatment or recycling shall fall into the national legislation.

---

87 Case C-463/01, *Commission v. Germany* [2004].
88 Case C-309/02, *Radlberger Getränkegesellschaft mbH & Co., S. Spitz KG v. Land Baden-Württemberg* [2004].
89 Case C-1/03, *Paul Van de Walle e.a.* [2004]; Case C-457/02, *Antonio Niselli* [2004].
90 Case C-358/11, *Lapin elinkeino* [2013]; Case C-318/98, *Giancarlo Fornasar e.a.* [2000].
91 Case C-260/11, *David Edwards e.a.* [2013].
92 Case C-121/11, *Pro-Braine ASBL e.a. v. The Commune de Braine-le-Château* [2012].
93 Case C-41/11, *Inter-Environnement Wallonie ASBL, Terre wallonne ASBL v. Région wallonne* [2012].
94 Art. 15, Directive 2008/98/EC.

Enforcement and penalties are explicitly devolved to the national legal orders. The Directive provides that

> Member States shall take the necessary measures to prohibit the abandonment, dumping or uncontrolled management of waste [and they] shall lay down provisions on the penalties applicable to infringements of the provisions of this Directive and shall take all measures necessary to ensure that they are implemented. The penalties shall be effective, proportionate and dissuasive.[95]

Directive 2006/66/EC on batteries obliges the Member States to "lay down rules on penalties". Directive 2000/53/EC on ELV provides that "Member States shall bring into force the laws, regulations and administrative provisions necessary to comply with this Directive".[96] At the EU level, most of the cases lead to a simple declaration of failure to fulfil obligations from the ECJ. Only few cases led to financial sanctions. In 2000, Greece has been blamed with €20,000 of penalty payment each day of delay for failure to the obligations relating to wastes elimination in the province of the Canee, in Crete.[97] The Court already declared that Greece failed to take the necessary measures to comply with a preceding judgement.[98] It concerned the implementation of the plans necessary for the disposal of waste and of toxic and dangerous waste for the area concerned without endangering human health and without harming the environment. Six years after the first judgment, the waste disposal plans were still at a preliminary stage and the river Kouroupitos continued to serve as a site for the uncontrolled disposal of waste.

6.2 Main Reasons of the Problems Faced by the EU Waste Law

This study on waste management leads to two main arguments explaining the problems of legality. The division of competences in what is called the 'multilevel governance' affects the effectiveness of the EU law (A). The European representatives (overall from the European Commission and the Council of the European Union) seem mostly to be pressed by ambitious political objectives which cannot be achieved in the allowed time. The main reason is an economic one: the EU waste law is very costly for many local authorities which simply do not have the financial capacity to support the European objectives (B).

---

95   Art. 36, Directive 2008/98/EC.
96   Art. 10, Directive 2000/53/EC.
97   Case C-387/97, *Commission v. Greece* [2000].
98   Case C-45/91, *Commission v. Greece* [1992].

6.2.1   Competent Authorities in Waste Management

Waste law, as part of environmental law, is a shared competence between the EU and the Member States[99] and within the latter, national, regional and local bodies also have their share. Moreover private operators are involved as producers, distributors, collectors, insurance companies, dismantlers, shredders, 'recoverers', recyclers and other treatment operators.[100] As is the case with many EU legal instruments, the variety of actors complicates the implementation process. The determination of liability is done case-by-case according to the national division of competences (1). EU law suffers of a lack of direct European control, as long as the control is decentralised to the Member States themselves (2).

6.2.1.1   Division of Competence in the Member States

In a case *Commission v. Belgium* relating to the Directive on the end-of-life vehicles, the Court has recently reiterated the principle of national institutional autonomy, under which Member States are free to distribute their competence in their own legal system and to implement any directive by means of measures taken by regional or local authorities. This division of powers does not, however, exempt from the obligation to ensure that the provisions of the directive are implemented in national law.[101] In the present case, the European Court argued that a different definition of the notion of producer between the Belgium regions-especially the one in Wallonia differs-may affect the interpretation of the directive and would create a legal uncertainty for the last owner of vehicle who must be able to transfer it freely to the authorised treatment facilities. However, the Court considers that the Commission has not demonstrated how this difference would lead to legal uncertainty likely to invalidate the regional definition at issue. It is a consequence of the Belgium federal structure that the regions are entitled to define the relevant connecting criterion to establish their competence. For once, Belgium won the case against the Commission.

Twenty eight Member States, gathering around 450 regions and 100,000 local authorities[102] represents a challenge for EU law effectiveness. In any of these regional and local authorities, waste should comply with the same objectives of collection, treatment and recycling. In the case relating to the waste management in Campania, the Court stated

---

99   Arts. 4(e) & 191-193 TFEU.
100 *See* Arts. 2, 10 Directive 2000/53/EC on the definition of 'economic operators'.
101 Case C-391/11, *Commission v. Belgium* [2012] §31; Case C-417/99, *Commission v. Spain* [2001] §37; Cases 227/85 to 230/85, *Commission v. Belgium* [1988] §9; Case 97/81, *Commission v. Netherlands* [1982] §12.
102 No precise number can be give as long as one may define differently the concept of regional and local authorities. According to the NUTS nomenclature, subdividing the economic territory of the European Union, there are 97 regions at NUTS 1 level, 271 regions at NUTS 2 level and 1303 regions at NUTS 3 level and at lower LAU level around 120,000 municipalities or equivalent units in the 27 Member States.

that even if the Member State is responsible for the implementation of the EU law, it remains the specific responsibility "for each region, municipality or other local authority to take appropriate steps to ensure that its own waste is collected, treated and disposed of".[103] This articulation can also be illustrated with the implementation of the Directive 2002/96/EC on waste electrical and electronic equipment (WEEE), which asks Member States to take all necessary legislative, regulatory and administrative measures for the collection, treatment and recycling of WEEE. This directive concerns primarily the responsibility of manufacturers, but also urban waste management. Member States transpose at national level and then local governments shall ensure the existence of free recovery systems of WEEE on their territory.

In Germany, waste management belongs to the shared competence between the Bund and the Länder.[104] In the specific matter of waste of electrical and electronic equipment, the Federation has used its competence to transpose Directive 2002/96/EC in the act on the circulation, the recovery and removal of environmental electrical and electronic equipment (*Gesetz über das Inverkehrbringen, die Rücknahme und die umweltverträgliche Entsorgung von Elektro- und Elektronikgeräten*, here *Elektro-G*) of 16 March 2005[105] The act transcribes in particular the obligations for companies and determines the role of federal institutions. However, the designation of 'public authorities responsible for waste removal' (*öffentlich-rechtlicher Entsorgungsträger*), corresponding implicitly to municipalities and their groups, refers to the territorial organisation of each Land.[106] The federal law does not have the competence to appoint them explicitly.[107] However the federal list, like the framework law on waste, contains a series of obligations to local authorities. In addition, the German manufacturers fulfil their obligations to federal registration with the *Stiftung Elektro-Altgeräte Register* (EAR).[108] This is the only German eco-organisation with public service missions on behalf of the Federal Ministry for the Environment. The EAR coordinates the implementation of collection systems by the German local authorities. This single system at the federal level avoids disparities between the Länder.

In 2007, the United Kingdom had not yet transposed Directive 2002/96/EC. This gave rise to an infringement ruling.[109] The Directive came into force in July 2007, instead of

---

103 Case C-297/08, *European Commission v. Italy* [2010] §67; Case C-155/91, *Commission v. Council* [1993] ECR I-939, §13.
104 Art. 74, §1, Ab. 24 GG.
105 Published on 23 March 2005, into force on 24 March 2005, *Elektro- und Elektronikgerätegesetz vom 16. März 2005* (BGBl. I S. 762), abbr. *ElektroG*, as amended by Art. 3 of the *Gesetz vom 19. Juli 2007* (BGBl. I S. 1462). *See also, Elektro- und Elektronikgerätegesetz-Kostenverordnung vom 6. Juli 2005* (BGBl. I S. 2020) as amended by the *Verordnung vom 5. Dezember 2007* (BGBl. I S. 2825).
106 §9 des *Elektro-G*.
107 *Kreislaufwirtschafts- und Abfallgesetz*.
108 §17 *ElektroG*.
109 Case C-139/06, *Commission v. Royaume-Uni* [2007].

on August 13, 2005 as required. The transposition carried out by national regulations (statutory instrument) is entitled Waste Electrical and Electronic Equipment Regulations 2006.[110] It refers and interprets the Directive especially to make it intelligible to the enforcement agencies. The system developed is based mainly on producers and distributors that ensure both the implementation and the funding.[111] The public authorities are designated by region: the Environment Agency (Environment Agency) for England and Wales, the Scottish Environment Protection Agency (SEPA) for Scotland and the Department of the Environment for Northern Ireland. Regional administrative centralism within a single agency clarifies the system. It gathers the registration of manufacturers, the relations with both eco-coordinating bodies (Valpak, COIN) and the organisation of the territorial waste collection. The distinction is made around the approval procedures of organisms 'approved authorised treatment facility',[112] 'authorised treatment facility' and 'approved exporter' issued by the regional authorities in the various companies involved in the collection and recycling of WEEE. The administrative costs for these vary can be up to 12,174 pounds depending on the region and the turnover of the company.[113] In 2009, the United Kingdom had managed 36.6% of WEEE recycling.

In France, the Decree on the composition of electrical and electronic equipment and the disposal of waste from these facilities, of 20 July 2005,[114] sets the framework for the implementation of selective collection and appropriate treatment. It transcribed the terms of the Directive and determines the appropriate authorities. As of 1 January 2006, the domestic producers of EEE are required to provide, individually or collectively, collection, removal and treatment of waste, regardless of their date of marketing.[115] It also specifies that the costs incurred by local authorities are offset by a coordinating body which approved the reverse equivalent fraction of the financial contribution received from producers. On the basis of the decree, four eco-coordinating bodies (Ecologic, Eco-systems and ERP for WEEE outside lamps, Récylum for used lamps) have been accredited for a period of six years, by joint order of the Ministers responsible for the environment, industry and local communities. They are in charge of the supply chain management

---

110 *The Waste Electrical and Electronic Equipment Regulations 2006*, No. 3289, 11 December 2006 – UK WEEE Regulations (SI 2006 No. 3289) – modifiée par *The Waste Electrical and Electronic Equipment (Amendment) Regulations 2007*, No. 3454, 6 December 2007.
111 Arts. 8-35 WEEE Regulations 2006.
112 Arts. 46-53 WEEE Regulations 2006.
113 Arts. 45, 51 WEEE Regulations 2006.
114 Décret No. 2005-829 du 20 juillet 2005, JO 22 July 2005. Ce décret a été codifié aux articles R. 543-172 à R. 543-206 du code de l'environnement et abrogé par le décret No. 2007-1467 du 12 octobre 2007 relatif au livre V de la partie réglementaire du code de l'environnement et modifiant certaines autres dispositions de ce code, JORF No. 240 du 16 October 2007, p. 17002.
115 Art. L. 541-10-2 du code de l'environnement.

of WEEE. In addition, a coordinating body, the non-profit society OCAD3E, has been approved by Ministerial Decree of 22 September 2006 in order to offset the costs of the collection of WEEE supported by local communities, who are bound to OCAD3E by contract. In early 2010, the Ministry of Ecology presented positive results, arguing that most producers (3,800 registered with the ADEME) joined one of these eco-organisations, more than 18,600 collection points of distributors are now operational across the country and even that "nearly 1,000 local authorities, representatives of about 3,400 collection points covering nearly 55 million people in mid-2009" have developed WEEE recycling collection centres in the cities.[116]

6.2.1.2 Lack of European Controllers

In principle, the European Commission "shall oversee the application of Union law under the control of the Court of Justice of the European Union".[117] In practice, approximately 650 civil servants work within the DG Environment for 6 directorates, the directorate C.2 on waste management has not many personnel. The European Commission cannot control the implementation of the eighteen waste policies (incineration, landfill, batteries, biodegradable waste . . .). That explains why EU law and the Commission tend to decentralise the compliance control.

The Waste Framework Directive 2008/98/EC provides that appropriate periodic inspections shall be done by the national competent authorities in any establishments or undertakings which carry out waste treatment operations.[118] These inspections shall cover the origin, nature, quantity and destination of the waste collected and transported. For this purpose, they shall also be subject to chronological record of all useful information relating to the waste (quantity, nature, origin, destination, frequency of collection, mode of transport and treatment method).[119] Moreover most of the directives in the area of waste provide a regular Member State report.

As the Court stated in 2010 in *Commission versus Italy*, the European Commission does not have investigative powers under Directive 2006/12. Thus an action for failure to fulfil an obligation "is largely reliant on the information provided by complainants, by public or private bodies, by the press or by the Member States concerned".[120]

---

116 Ministère de l'Ecologie, de l'Energie, du Développement durable et de la Mer, Bilan de la filière DEEE pour la période 2006-2009 et les nouveaux défis fixés pour 2010-2014.
117 Art. 17, §1 TEU.
118 Art. 34, Directive 2008/98/EC.
119 Art. 35, Directive 2008/98/EC.
120 Case C-297/08, *European Commission v. Italy* [2010] §101; Case C-494/01, *Commission v. Ireland* [2005] ECR I-3331, §43; Case C-135/05, *Commission v. Italy* [2007] §28.

6.2.2   Cost of the EU Waste Policy

Waste law requires the creation of heavy collection, treatment and recycling facilities to achieve the announced targets (1). The determination of the financial liabilities is never easy. EU waste law however charges, firstly, the public authorities as regards the regulation, the creation of networks and the control and, secondly, the economic operators under the polluter-pays principle (2).

6.2.2.1   The Cost of Appropriate Infrastructures

The impact assessments of the European Commission on waste are irregular. Most of them are delegated to external offices.

Directive 2008/98/CE provides that "the costs of waste management shall be borne by the original waste producer or by the current or previous waste holders".[121] This principle is very close to the polluter-pays principle. Member States are free to decide whether the costs of waste management are to be borne partly or wholly by the producer of the product from which the waste came. In most of the Member States, the system of collecting, treating, recycling or disposing of the waste is mostly devolved to the regional and local authorities. For instance, in the case *Futura Immobiliare srl Hotel Futura*,[122] the applicants argued that the local waste tax was calculated on the basis of an estimated volume of waste they may generate rather than on the basis of the proper quantity of waste they have produced. The Court confirms "that for the purposes of financing an urban waste management and disposal service", such a tax calculated on the basis of an estimate of the volume of waste generated by users of that service is compatible to EU law, as long as it respects the proportionality principle. In that specific case, the costs were manifestly disproportionate to the volumes of the waste.

KPMG apparently wrote a first impact assessment on the directive on the end-of-life vehicles in 2003. The only one available impact assessment has however been published by the European Commission seven years after the directive.[123] It identified at least two scenarios to implement the directive. A low technology development scenario would create a net added value (difference between the value of metals that can be obtained from 2015 ELVs and the recycling process cost) between €80 and €55 per ELV, *i.e.* €760 million per year for the estimated number of ELVs arising in 2015. A high technology development scenario, involving a greater share of recycled plastics, would represent an added value between €120 and €90, *i.e.* approximately €1.6 billion per year. "This value would

---

121   Art. 14, Directive 2008/98/EC.
122   Case C-254/08, *Futura Immobiliare srl Hotel Futura v. Comune di Casoria* [2009].
123   European Commission, Impact Assessment, Document accompanying the report on the targets contained in Art. 7(2)(b) of Directive 2000/53/EC on end-of-life vehicle, COM(2007) 5 final, 16 January 2007.

be shared in profit between the operators involved in the ELV process, with, most likely, some payment to the last owner".[124] However, as other studies underlined there are other costs implied by the required facilities. The impact assessments in the Member states do not focus on the gain, but mostly on the cost of such a law. In Ireland, a national impact assessment estimates that a national network of 43 contracted authorised treatment facilities up to the standards required by the directive could cost in the range of €1.7 million.[125] In France, the Agency for environment also tried to analyse the economic impact of the end-of-life vehicle treatment.[126] It stated that important financial investments are required to employ the necessary workforce (between 8€ and 11€/ELV), to comply with the administrative monitoring (between 5€ and 15€/ELV) and overall with the facility standards (between 8€ and 17€/ELV). Moreover buying an ELV costs on average of 100€, shredder residues represent around 55€/ELV, technology enhancement 120€/ELV, the carcass 35€/ELV. Finally, the sale of used auto parts may represent up to 500€/ELV. Most of these points have not been taken into consideration by the impact assessment of the European Commission. The different reports on the ELV directive demonstrate that the recycling process is valuable only on a case-by-case study, *i.e.* according to the Member States, the competent authorities, the companies involved in the process . . . Once again, producing a more global impact assessment does not justify an added value. Moreover the Court of justice of the European Union recently confirmed that the obligation to assess the effects of certain public and private projects on the environment does not include the effects on the value of material assets.[127] The national courts are free to determine the requirements of European Union law applicable to the right to compensation in case of damages to a private property.

Concerning the WEEE Directive, the first legal issues generated considerable financial burden. The European Commission itself observed that

> the experience of the first years of implementation of the WEEE Directive has helped to highlight the technical, legal and administrative barriers resulting in unnecessary costs for market actors and administrations perpetuating the damage to the environment and result in a low level of innovation in the areas of collection and treatment of waste, by unequal conditions of competition or a distortion of competition and unnecessary administrative burden.[128]

---

124 I.A., pp. 27, 77-79.
125 Statement on Regulatory Impact, Waste Management (end-of-life vehicles) Regulations 2006, SI No. 282 of 2006, p. 7.
126 Etude économique sur la filière de traitement des véhicules hors d'usage, septembre 2003. *Cf.* Décret No. 2011-153 du 4 février 2011 portant diverses dispositions d'adaptation au droit communautaire en matière de gestion des véhicules hors d'usage et des déchets d'équipements électriques et électroniques.
127 Case 420/11, *Jutta Leth v. Republik Österreich, Land Niederösterreich* [2013].
128 European Commission, Proposal of Directive WEEE, COM(2008) 610 final, p. 2.

6.2.2.2 The Polluter Pays Principle

From the 1970s, the EU legislation on the protection of environment ruled under the polluter-pays principle. Producers are mostly concerned.[129] However the determination of the polluter may also concern the customer or the last consumer. In any case and in contradiction to the present principle, the latter pay directly or indirectly the bill by way on the price of the product. Based on Article 191, §2 TFEU, the polluter pays principle is nowadays a key principle of the EU waste law. According to the Waste Framework Directive 2008/98/EC,[130] any original waste producer or any other holder carrying out the treatment of waste shall be responsible of the waste management. However, as mentioned above, the Member States are free to organise polluter responsibility.[131]

One of the major cases, in 1999, relates to the Erika shipwreck, an oil tanker flying the Maltese flag and chartered by Total International Ltd, causing pollution on the French Atlantic coast. The Italian company ENEL concluded a contract with Total International Ltd for the delivery of heavy fuel oil to be used as fuel for electricity production. Total France SA sold the heavy fuel oil to Total International Ltd, which chartered the vessel Erika to carry it from Dunkirk (France) to Milazzo (Italy). The *Commune de Mesquer* brought proceedings against the Total companies in the French courts, seeking to incur the liability of Total for the consequences of the damage caused by the waste spread on the territory of the municipality. The French *Court de cassation* asked the Court of justice of the European Union whether heavy fuel oil, as the product of a refining process, meeting the user's specifications and intended by the producer to be sold as a combustible fuel, may be qualified as waste.[132]

First of all, the Court recalls that under the Directive 75/442, "any substance or object [...] which the holder discards or intends or is required to discard is to be regarded as waste". The scope of the term 'waste' turns on the meaning of the term 'discard',[133] which should be interpreted in the light of the aim of the directive,[134] which consists in the protection of human health and the environment against harmful effects caused by waste management (precautionary principle and prevention principle).[135] It also recalls that the concept of waste cannot be interpreted restrictively[136] and it may cover all objects and substances discarded by their owner.[137] In comparison to the *Palin Granit* case, the Court said that

---

129 See P. Thieffry, *La responsabilité du producteur du fait des déchets*, Bruylant, Brussels, 2013.
130 Art. 15, Directive 2008/98/EC.
131 Case C-254/08, *Futura Immobiliare srl Hotel Futura v. Comune di Casoria* [2009].
132 Case C-188/07, *Commune de Mesquer v. Total France SA* [2008].
133 Case C-129/96, *Inter-Environnement Wallonie* [1997] §26; Case C-1/03, *Van de Walle and Others* [2004].
134 Joined Cases C-418/97 and C-419/97, *ARCO Chemie Nederland and Others* [2000] §37.
135 Case C-457/02, *Niselli* [2004] §33.
136 Joined Cases C-418/97 and C-419/97, *ARCO Chemie Nederland and Others* [2000] §37.
137 Case C-9/00, *Palin Granit and Vehmassalon kansanterveystyön kuntayhtymän hallitus* [2002] §29.

leftover stone from extraction processes of a granite quarry constitutes waste.[138] They may therefore constitute a by-product if the goods are re-used. Consequently, heavy fuel oil sold as a combustible fuel, does not constitute waste where it is exploited or marketed on economically advantageous terms. Secondly, an accidental spillage of hydrocarbons is an act by which the holder discards them and the holder cannot re-use on economically advantageous terms. It must be regarded as a burden which the holder 'discards'. The Court decided that

> [...] hydrocarbons accidentally spilled at sea following a shipwreck, mixed with water and sediment and drifting along the coast of a Member State until being washed up on that coast, constitute waste within the meaning of Directive 75/442.

Thirdly, in accordance with the 'polluter pays' principle, the cost of disposing of the waste is to be borne by the previous holders or the producer of the product from which the waste came. For this purpose, the national court may regard the seller of those hydrocarbons and charterer of the ship carrying them as a producer of that waste and thereby as a 'previous holder', if that court reaches the conclusion that that seller-charterer contributed to the risk that the pollution caused by the shipwreck would occur. In other cases, the Court confirmed that a causal link is required to incur the liability of the producer according to the polluter pays principle.[139]

The Directive on end-of-life vehicles also introduced the principle of producer responsibility. Car manufacturers are responsible for significant part of the costs of treating end-of-life vehicles and they shall allow the last owner to return the car to authorised treatment facilities. In Belgium, for instance, each region has adopted a regulatory measure to transpose the directive. Public authorities organise the monitoring of ELV, the facility licenses, the national procedural standards and the report to the European Commission. Producers and importers shall take care of the dismantling operations already during the car design; the last owner is obliged to bring his car to an authorised treatment facility; dealer, mechanic and destroyer shall take in charge of any ELV and issue a certificate of acceptance.[140]

Producer responsibility is also the original feature created by Directive 2002/96/EC of 27 January 2003 on waste electrical and electronic equipment (WEEE) and by Directive 2002/95/EC of 27 January 2003 on the restriction of the use of certain hazardous

---

138 Case C-9/00, §§32, 33.
139 Case C-378/08, *Raffinerie Mediterranee (ERG) SpA* [2010].
140 The action brought on 25 July 2011, *European Commission v. Kingdom of Belgium* (Case C-391/11), has been dismissed.

substances in electrical and electronic equipment.[141] It provided relief to local authorities who are not solely responsible for the system operation of the collection, disposal and treatment. The Commission estimates the total cost of €5.6 billion euros per year by 2020.

The Member States had also to ensure that, no later than 26 September 2009, producers set up schemes using best available techniques to provide for the treatment and recycling of waste batteries and accumulators.[142] In addition, producers shall 'finance any net costs' arising from the collection, treatment and recycling of all waste portable batteries and accumulators collected and of all waste industrial and automotive batteries and accumulators.[143] To this purpose, each producer shall be registered to ensure they comply with the objectives of the directive.[144]

The European Commission should publish soon a study to assist Member States in improving waste management based on an assessment of their waste policy performance.[145] It will in particularly identify the 10 Member States with the largest implementation gaps in order to issue concrete policy recommendations to solve the implementation problems in waste law. That will be very useful, in particular for the 13 Member States which joined the EU since 2007 as most reports and case-law on EU waste law still ignore them.

---

141 Directive 2002/96/EC of 27 January 2003 relating to WEEE amending by Directive 2008/34/EC of 11 March 2008 and Directive 2003/108/EC of 8 December 2003; Directive 2002/95/EC of 27 January 2003 relating to limitation of use of certain hazardous substances in WEEE, as amended by Directive 2008/35/EC of 11 March 2008.
142 Arts. 8 and 12 of Directive 2006/66/EC.
143 Art. 16, Directive 2006/66/EC.
144 Art. 17, Directive 2006/66/EC.
145 <http://ec.europa.eu/environment/waste/studies/>.

7   Opportunities and Pitfalls for Sustainable Materials Management in EU Waste Law

Geert van Calster

Sustainable materials management ('SMM') is

> an approach to promote sustainable materials use, integrating actions targeted at reducing negative environmental impacts and preserving natural capital throughout the lifecycle of materials, taking into account economic efficiency and social equity.[1]

The Environment Council of the EU adopted SMM at its meeting of December 2010,[2] linking it to sustainable production and consumption. SMM has many aspects, which altogether represent almost the entire plethora of legal challenges associated with a successful EU environmental policy. In this contribution, I highlight what in my view are some of the most relevant legal considerations of SMM considerations in EU waste law. The list and analysis below is not meant to be conclusive.[3]

7.1   The First Elephant in the Room: Definition of Waste

In EU waste law, 'waste' means

> any substance or object which the holder discards or intends or is required to discard (Art. 3(1) of Directive 2008/98).

Notwithstanding extensive case-law in the Court of Justice[4] and even more extensively in the courts of the Member States, practice stubbornly keeps on challenging the application

---

[1]   OECD, Working Group on Waste Prevention and Recycling, Outcome of the first workshop on SMM, Seoul, 28-30 November 2005.
[2]   <www.consilium.europa.eu/uedocs/cms_data/docs/pressdata/en/envir/118642.pdf>, last consulted on 20 February 2013.
[3]   *See* more detail in G. Van Calster, *Handbook of EU Waste Law*, forthcoming with OUP in 2014.
[4]   *See inter alia,* G. Van Calster, 'If It Ain't Broke, Don't Fix It? Commission Efforts to Manage the Definitions of Waste, Recycling and Recovery', in *Compendium 2006: annual anthology of diverse papers on key contemporary issues in European policies on wastes, products and resources/Association of Cities and Regions*, ACR, Brussel, 2006, pp. 115-119.

of the definition in old and new examples of industrial practice. The newest edition of the waste framework Directive, Directive 2008/98,[5] aims to assist practice *inter alia* with the prospect of practice-oriented criteria for two categories: industrial by-products, which per *Palin Granit*[6] are not waste, and end-of-waste criteria[7]: *i.e.* the technical parameters which have to be met for waste to cease being 'waste' and becoming secondary raw materials. These parameters have already been defined for iron, steel, and aluminium scrap.[8] The Joint Research Centre has moreover submitted reports with technical proposals for the end-of-waste criteria on copper scrap metal, recovered paper, glass cullet and is conducting further studies on biodegradable waste/compost and plastic.

Development of these end-of-waste criteria and criteria for by-products, is subject to a lot of discussion, with an inherent danger that they lock-in existing, incumbent technology. Over and above the particular challenges for these categories, problems remain with the application of the waste definition more generally. One particular issue at the ECJ recently is the application of the waste definition in the context of so-called 'reverse logistics', with 'off-spec products' being a subcategory of same. In joined Cases C-241/12 and C-242/12, the Court of Justice was asked to clarify the application of the Waste Framework Directive's concept of 'waste' in the context of reverse logistics /off-spec (or 'off

---

5 OJ 2008 L 312/3.
6 Case C-9/00, *Palin Granit Oy v. Vehmassalon kansanterveystyön kuntayhtymän hallitus*, 18 April 2002 [2002] ECR I-3533: materials resulting from a manufacturing or extraction process, the primary aim of which is not the production of that item, may be regarded not as a residue (a secondary material and hence 'waste'), but as a by-product which the undertaking does not wish to discard, but intends to exploit or market on terms which are advantageous to it, in a subsequent process, without any further processing prior to reuse.
   The Court found that this interpretation would not be incompatible with the aims of Directive 75/442. There is no reason to hold that the provisions of Directive 75/442 apply to goods, materials or raw materials which have an economic value as products regardless of any form of processing and which, as such, are subject to the legislation applicable to those products. However, the Court has regard to the obligation to interpret the concept of waste widely in order to limit its inherent risks and pollution. It held that the reasoning applicable to by-products should be confined to situations in which the reuse of the goods, materials or raw materials *is not a mere possibility but a certainty*, without any further processing prior to reuse, and as an integral part of the production process. In subsequent cases, it stuck to these conditions strictly.
7 This is a clarification of the concept of so-called 'full recovery'. The Directive deals with this under the heading 'end of waste'. The ECJ in *Arco Chemie* also briefly considered the concept of 'full recovery'. In particular (at 94), it noted that even where waste has undergone a complete recovery operation, which has the consequence that the substance in question has acquired the same properties and characteristics as a raw material, that substance may none the less be regarded as waste if, in accordance with the definition in Art. 1(a), its holder discards it or intends or is required to discard it. Classification as a waste is *a fortiori* not excluded where the objects at issue are merely pre-sorted or pre-treated, without the effect of transforming those objects into a product analogous to a raw material, with the same characteristics as that raw material and capable of being used in the same conditions of environmental protection (at 96).
   UK practice in particular, lays some emphasis on the notion of 'full recovery', especially after the High Court judgment in Mayer Parry, which held *inter alia* that materials which are made ready for re-use by a recovery operation, cease to be waste when the recovery operation is complete. The Directive foresees the drafting of guidelines, within the Directive's comitology procedure, so as to specify the moment when a waste has been fully recovered and hence ceases to be waste.
8 Council Regulation 333/2011, OJ 2011 L 94/2.

specification') products. These are products which after shipment, turn out not to meet the agreed specifications (because they are defective, or even if in working order, do not meet the agreed parameters). In the logistics chain, such products are often sent back upstream (whence 'reverse logistics') and sold to other customers, whether or not after modification or repair. The Court was asked specifically the extent of relevance of the contractual context. Under the terms of the contract (and indeed under general contract and warranty law), off-spec products are routinely sent back to the wholesaler or brought back to the point of sale. Any finding of such goods meeting the waste concept, may turn an important part of daily logistics operations into waste transport operations. The court held on 12 December 2013. Important is the finding by the Court (at 46) that in order to determine whether the client who received the off-spec product, discards it, particular attention needs to be paid to the fact that the client returned the off-specification fuel with a view to obtaining repayment in accordance with the sales agreement.

7.2 The Second Elephant in the Room: Delineation with REACH

The REACH Regulation[9] – the Regulation on the registration, evaluation and authorisation of chemicals – explicitly exempts waste from its scope of application,

> To ensure workability and to maintain the incentives for waste recycling and recovery, wastes should not be regarded as substances, preparations or articles within the meaning of this Regulation.

At the time of adoption of the Regulation, this led to the rather interesting development of clients seeking arguments to have their products considered waste (until then not a preferred option). Compliance under the Waste regulations was /is perceived as less onerous than REACH. The Waste framework Directive, in the revised 2008 version, as noted includes a specific regime in Article 6 for end-of-waste criteria. It is worth citing it here in full:

1. Certain specified waste shall cease to be waste within the meaning of point (1) of Article 3 when it has undergone a recovery, including recycling, operation and complies with specific criteria to be developed in accordance with the following conditions:
   (a) the substance or object is commonly used for specific purposes;
   (b) a market or demand exists for such a substance or object;
   (c) the substance or object fulfils the technical requirements for the specific purposes and meets the existing legislation and standards applicable to products; and

---

9 Regulation 1907/2006, OJ 2006 L 396/1.

(d) the use of the substance or object will not lead to overall adverse environmental or human health impacts.

The criteria shall include limit values for pollutants where necessary and shall take into account any possible adverse environmental effects of the substance or object.

2. The measures designed to amend non-essential elements of this Directive by supplementing it relating to the adoption of the criteria set out in paragraph 1 and specifying the type of waste to which such criteria shall apply shall be adopted in accordance with the regulatory procedure with scrutiny referred to in Article 39(2). End-of-waste specific criteria should be considered, among others, at least for aggregates, paper, glass, metal, tyres and textiles.

3. Waste which ceases to be waste in accordance with paragraphs 1 and 2, shall also cease to be waste for the purpose of the recovery and recycling targets set out in Directives 94/62/EC, 2000/53/EC, 2002/96/EC and 2006/66/EC and other relevant Community legislation when the recycling or recovery requirements of that legislation are satisfied.

4. Where criteria have not been set at Community level under the procedure set out in paragraphs 1 and 2, Member States may decide case by case whether certain waste has ceased to be waste taking into account the applicable case law. They shall notify the Commission of such decisions in accordance with Directive 98/34/EC of the European Parliament and of the Council of 22 June 1998 laying down a procedure for the provision of information in the field of technical standards and regulations and of rules on Information Society services [24] where so required by that Directive.

Intriguingly, Article 6(4) [Member States deciding end-of-waste status on a case-by-case basis in the absence of Union harmonisation], does not refer to the four criteria which Article 6(1) puts forward as binding in the event of Union harmonisation on same. In contrast with the Commission, AG Kokott has suggested in *Lapin elinkeino*, Case C-358/11, that this difference has to be taken at face value. The only benchmark for the Member States is the case-law of the ECJ on the end-of-waste status and on the very definition of waste. Once a Member State decides on that basis that even dangerous waste no longer is waste (or indeed never was waste), it can allow the use of such substance under application of relevant product legislation (here: the rules on CCA-treated wood under REACH). Importantly, therefore, the AG suggested that dangerous waste can be returned to use as products, in the case at issue under discipline of REACH, in accordance with national law. Member States need not wait for Union criteria to be developed. REACH therefore comes to the rescue of the Member States wishing to encourage the return of even hazardous wastes to product status. The ECJ agreed on 7 March 2013.[10] In the alternative, product use explicitly allowed under REACH for virgin material, would not so be allowed for recovered material. That would not be very sustainable.

Over and above the demarcation of REACH and waste law, there is a pressing concern with the application of the requirements under REACH, once a waste has been fully recovered. From that moment on, it does fall under REACH and needs to meet with all relevant requirements. This is a tall order however for products incorporating recovered wastes. It may not always be possible to determine the exact composition of the various substances present, given their history as waste,[11] thus making REACH compliance all but impossible. Relevant guidance from the European Chemicals Agency[12] goes some way to clarifying applicability, however it does not provide enough specific guidance to assist industry in achieving the level of regulatory certainty it requires to truly commit to sustainable materials management. Industry often understandably shies away from new applications if insufficient safeguards can be given that new solutions will not breach regulation.

7.3 A Herd of Elephants: The Application of the Waste Shipments Regulation and the Relationship with the Treaty Articles on the Free Movement of Goods. Similar Discussions at the Level of the WTO

Waste is a 'good' and as such protected by the relevant European Treaty Articles on the free movement of goods. The Treaty of course allows Member States to restrict free movement for reasons of environmental protection, subject to principles of necessity and proportionality. Member States have attempted to harmonise their approach in the Waste Shipments Regulation, Regulation 1013/2006,[13] specifically for the free movement of wastes. The very application of some of the provisions of the Regulation is not straightforward in and of itself.[14] However some of the provisions of the Regulation are also controversial in view of the protection to free movement, granted by the Treaty. Industry has long complained that there is at the very least an impression of partiality in the application of the Regulation,

---

10 Judgment in Case C-358/11, *Lapin elinkeino*.
11 Especially in the interim period, with REACH being a relatively new Regulation and hence the substances used in new applications.
12 ECHA, 'Guidance on Waste and Recovered Substances', 2010, available via <http://echa.europa.eu/documents/10162/13632/waste_rec_en.pdf>.
13 OJ 2006 L 90/1.
14 *See, e.g.,* 's-Gravenhage, 20 April 2012: a container filled with discarded material was not to be regarded as waste as the bulk of the shipment could be re-used without any repair. For export to Cameroon, therefore, no permit was required.

given the role of public authorities in allowing or barring export and import, and their own long-term investments in waste management facilities.

This intra-EU debate on waste movements is beginning to be paralleled at the WTO. A truism holds that there is more gold in one ton of mobile phones than there is in one ton of gold ore. For an environmental as well as trade lawyer, the watershed moment[15] which touches Article 35 TFEU (prohibition of exports: until recently unheard of, and revived precisely for environmental and public health reasons), now also touches the WTO. Restrictions on exports are a hot topic in the WTO, and the European Commission are pondering avenues to keep waste in the EU. If the recent China – Raw Materials report is anything to go by, however, justifying such export restrictions at the WTO level will not be straightforward.[16]

7.4 Ownership of Waste

Jurisdictions worldwide are fast moving away from a 'waste' society to one of 'resources'. However, amidst all of this renewed interest in many materials which until recently we could not wait to get rid off, there is no consensus on the legal definition of 'ownership' of waste. European law does not help: neither European nor regional waste legislation contain any provisions on the ownership of waste. Rather they apply the concepts of 'waste producer' and 'waste holder'. While these concepts are decisive in imposing particular legal liabilities, they are not directly decisive for the ownership of the waste. By way of example one can refer to the judgement of the European Court of Justice in the *Van de Walle et al.*-case, wherein Texaco was considered as a holder of the waste, despite the fact that it never had any possession over the waste.[17]

The provisions of standard civil law therefore determine ownership. To my knowledge (I would love to hear from readers if they have any case-law from across the EU), case-law on this is scarce to non-existent. The criminal court of first instance at Antwerp came close recently-ish, in a case involving the collection of waste paper from private households.[18] Prosecution was based however on carrying out a licensed activity without a permit – not on theft. The case will now be continued in civil proceedings, for

---

15 See G. Van Calster, 'Export Restrictions – A Watershed for Article 30', *European Law Review*, 2000, pp. 335-352.
16 See G. Van Calster, 'China, Minerals Export, Raw and Rare Earth Materials: A Perfect Storm for WTO Dispute Settlement', *Review of European Community & International Environmental Law*, 2013, 117-122.
17 Case C-1/03, *Criminal proceedings against Paul van de Walle et al.* [2004] ECR I-7613.
18 *Openbaar Ministerie supported by Stad Antwerpen v. G.F., H.M., and A.E.*, held 22 December 2011 – case on file with the author.

the City of Antwerp dragged its feet in calculating damage. A suggested defence might be that it was not theirs to keep?

7.5 USE RESTRICTIONS AND WASTE MANAGEMENT

Successful waste management of course requires more than just end-of-the road solutions. Above I have already made reference to the international trade obligations of the EU. Within the EU and indeed within specific Member States, there is moreover an interesting amount of restrictions on the use of equipment, which has otherwise been authorised to be marketed in the EU. For instance, some Member States (or regions within Member States) do not allow the use of waste shredders in household sinks. Others do not allow waste to be burnt in garden waste incinerators, in particular in metropolitan areas. Still others have banned the use of 'do it yourself' pellet manufacturing (these turn plastic wastes into pellets that are subsequently used in fireplaces or stoves).

When reviewing restrictions of use for environmental purposes, it immediately becomes fairly apparent that very little recourse is made to them, either by national or by European authorities. The *Mickelsson* Case below is one of very few examples (restrictions on the lighting of bonfires in private gardens in some Member States, another).

In the case of European law, this is in no small measure due to subsidiarity considerations. The instrument of choice for European environmental law are those Directives which are either process-based or relate to product standards. Those that are process-based, are all the so-called 'procedural' or 'horizontal' laws which aim to regulate (in the main) manufacturing processes and are likely to have an impact on the environment. The preference for product standards as a legal instrument is a legacy of the early stages of EC environmental law, when the European Commission had to justify its interference in national environmental matters by reference to the Internal Market implications of divergent national environmental laws (this is prior to the introduction of an environmental title proper in the Treaty). Evidently, many of the product standards have an immediate impact on the question as to whether further, specific restrictions to use have any residual value. Consider *e.g.* the case of noise pollution. Where EC law already provides for a noise emission standard for mopeds, it sharply reduces the need for the introduction of local laws to deal with the nuisance caused by the revving engines.

Further restrictions to use for environmental purposes which are not an implied consequence of EU-defined product standards, are considered to be apt only in the face of local circumstances, and therefore fall foul of the subsidiarity principle (which suggests or indeed in the case of EU law, proscribes, that regulatory action be taken as close as possible to the level where it is going to have the maximum impact. In the case of the EU this has led to a general presumption against the EC being the appropriate level for action).

Indeed there are other areas of regulatory concern where restrictions of use have either taken flight some time ago or are being increasingly mooted, and which may well inspire more such examples in the environmental sector. As the examples below illustrate, public and occupational health and safety for the time being would seem to be the driving factor behind these initiatives:

- Telecoms, health and use restrictions: see *e.g.* the tendency in a number of schools to scale back or completely remove the use of wireless internet technology; government guidelines on the safe use of mobile phones; restrictions on the *installations* of mobile phone masts;
- Public safety, human health and use restrictions: these relate in particular to road safety, and refer to *e.g.* the obligatory wearing of cycling helmets, and the prohibition of MP3 players in traffic;
- Food and health: *e.g.* limiting sales options in fast food restaurants (mooted only so far as far as the author is aware), restrictions on the use of alcohol and tobacco products;
- Infotainment and health, *e.g.* the widely publicised idea of the German federal government to prohibit paintball, or sales restrictions on computer games (in particular because of their violent or sexually explicit contents);
- Healthcare, and general welfare: *e.g.* restrictions on points of sales for medicines, restrictions on the use of nanotechnology in food processing.

As a result of there not being enough examples of use restrictions for environmental purposes at the national level, inevitably of course there is not much ECJ case-law on them either. In *Commission v. Austria* (Tiroler lorry restrictions),[19] Austria was rapped for not having even considered less trade-restrictive alternatives to far-reaching use restrictions, other than a ban on specific types of transport during specific periods. This judgment underlines the need for sound science that is properly prepared science as a requirement for use restrictions with trade impact to be acceptable. Whereas in the *Tiroler* case though the trade impact of the measure was clear, this is different in those cases were restrictions of use are applied indiscriminately and without even a hint of protectionism. It is in this context that calls have been made to simply regard such modalities or restrictions of use as not being covered by the prohibitions of Articles 34 and 35 TFEU, much like in the case of 'modalities of sale' in the *Keck* route. In *Commission v. Italy* (motorcycle trailers),[20] the Court refused to rule on that question, opting instead for a market access test. If restrictions of use (in the case at issue: a prohibition) has a considerable influence on the behaviour of consumers, it affects the access of that product to the market of that Member States

---

19 Case C-320/03, *Commission v. Austria* [2005] ECR I-9871.
20 Case C-110/05 [2009] ECR I-519.

and falls foul of Article 34 TFEU. However the Court granted Italy the right to introduce the ban on public interest /mandatory requirements grounds, in the process however giving Italy a very easy ride on the least-trade restrictiveness test (it would seem that the Commission could have pressed Italy more on the issue of proportionality).

Mickelsson[21] is the case which might shed some light on the exact amount of room for Member States to seek restrictions of use (as opposed to *Italy v. Commission* – moped trailers, which concerned a product prohibition). Swedish jet-ski regulations prohibit the use of personal watercraft other than on a general navigable waterway or waters in respect of which the local authority has issued rules permitting their use (on the basis of environmental considerations). Kokott AG on 14 December 2006 already gave as opinion that restrictions of use, as long as they are not product-related, apply to all relevant traders operating within the Member State. They affect in the same manner in law and in fact the marketing of domestic and import products and do not qualify as quantitative restrictions to trade. The Court disagreed, an unusually long 4 years later, and held that the measures at issue did fall under Articles 34 and 35 TFEU on principle, however it could be justified in certain circumstances.[22] The Mickelsson judgment underlines that Member States better get their homework right when considering use restrictions. In the aforementioned waste shredder (in sinks) example, for instance, it is not entirely certain that the absence of kitchen waste in the wastewater stream process is beneficial. Quite the opposite: the presence of relevant bacteria may actually assist with the purification process.

---

21 Case C-142/05, *Aklagaren v. Percy Mickelsson and Joakim Roos* [2009] ECR I-4273.
22 *See* for more detail P. Oliver, 'Of Trailers and Jet Skis: Is the Case-Law on Article 34 TFEU Hurtling in a New Direction?', *Fordham International Law Journal*, 2011, p. 1423.

ANNEXES

Directive 2008/98/EC of the European Parliament and of the Council

of 19 November 2008 on waste and repealing certain Directives (Text with EEA relevance)

THE EUROPEAN PARLIAMENT AND THE COUNCIL OF THE EUROPEAN UNION,

Having regard to the Treaty establishing the European Community, and in particular Article 175(1) thereof,

Having regard to the proposal from the Commission,

Having regard to the opinion of the European Economic and Social Committee[1],

Having regard to the opinion of the Committee of the Regions[2],

Acting in accordance with the procedure laid down in Article 251 of the Treaty[3],

WHEREAS:

1. Directive 2006/12/EC of the European Parliament and of the Council of 5 April 2006 on waste[4] establishes the legislative framework for the handling of waste in the Community. It defines key concepts such as waste, recovery and disposal and puts in place the essential requirements for the management of waste, notably an obligation for an establishment or undertaking carrying out waste management operations to have a permit or to be registered and an obligation for the Member States to draw up waste management plans. It also establishes major principles such as an obligation to handle waste in a way that does not have a negative impact on the environment or human health, an encouragement to apply the waste hierarchy and, in accordance with the polluter-pays principle, a requirement that the costs of disposing of waste must be borne by the holder of waste, by previous holders or by the producers of the product from which the waste came.

2. Decision No 1600/2002/EC of the European Parliament and of the Council of 22 July 2002 laying down the Sixth Community Environment Action Programme[5] calls for

---

1 OJ C 309, 16.12.2006, p. 55.
2 OJ C 229, 22.9.2006, p. 1.
3 Opinion of the European Parliament of 13 February 2007 (OJ C 287 E, 29.11.2007, p. 135), Council Common Position of 20 December 2007 (OJ C 71 E, 18.3.2008, p. 16) and Position of the European Parliament of 17 June 2008 (not yet published in the Official Journal). Council Decision of 20 October 2008.
4 OJ L 114, 27.4.2006, p. 9.
5 OJ L 242, 10.9.2002, p. 1.

the development or revision of the legislation on waste, including a clarification of the distinction between waste and non-waste, and for the development of measures regarding waste prevention and management, including the setting of targets.

3. The Commission communication of 27 May 2003 towards a Thematic Strategy on the prevention and recycling of waste noted the need to assess the existing definitions of recovery and disposal, the need for a generally applicable definition of recycling and a debate on the definition of waste.

4. In its resolution of 20 April 2004 on the abovementioned communication[6], the European Parliament called on the Commission to consider extending Council Directive 96/61/EC of 24 September 1996 concerning integrated pollution prevention and control[7] to the waste sector as a whole. It also asked the Commission to differentiate clearly between recovery and disposal and to clarify the distinction between waste and non-waste.

5. In its conclusions of 1 July 2004, the Council called on the Commission to bring forward a proposal for the revision of certain aspects of Directive 75/442/EEC, repealed and replaced by Directive 2006/12/EC, in order to clarify the distinction between waste and non-waste and that between recovery and disposal.

6. The first objective of any waste policy should be to minimise the negative effects of the generation and management of waste on human health and the environment. Waste policy should also aim at reducing the use of resources, and favour the practical application of the waste hierarchy.

7. In its Resolution of 24 February 1997 on a Community strategy for waste management[8], the Council confirmed that waste prevention should be the first priority of waste management, and that re-use and material recycling should be preferred to energy recovery from waste, where and insofar as they are the best ecological options.

8. It is therefore necessary to revise Directive 2006/12/EC in order to clarify key concepts such as the definitions of waste, recovery and disposal, to strengthen the measures that must be taken in regard to waste prevention, to introduce an approach that takes into account the whole life-cycle of products and materials and not only the waste phase, and to focus on reducing the environmental impacts of waste generation and waste management, thereby strengthening the economic value of waste. Furthermore, the recovery of waste and the use of recovered materials should be encouraged in order to conserve natural resources. In the interests of clarity and readability, Directive 2006/12/EC should be repealed and replaced by a new directive.

---

6   OJ C 104 E, 30.4.2004, p. 401.
7   OJ L 257, 10.10.1996, p. 26. Directive replaced by Directive 2008/1/EC of the European Parliament and of the Council (OJ L 24, 29.1.2008, p. 8).
8   OJ C 76, 11.3.1997, p. 1.

9. Since most significant waste management operations are now covered by Community legislation in the field of environment, it is important that this Directive be adapted to that approach. An emphasis on the environmental objectives laid down in Article 174 of the Treaty would bring the environmental impacts of waste generation and waste management more sharply into focus throughout the life-cycle of resources. Consequently, the legal basis for this Directive should be Article 175.

10. Effective and consistent rules on waste treatment should be applied, subject to certain exceptions, to movable property which the holder discards or intends or is required to discard.

11. The waste status of uncontaminated excavated soils and other naturally occurring material which are used on sites other than the one from which they were excavated should be considered in accordance with the definition of waste and the provisions on by-products or on the end of waste status under this Directive.

12. Regulation (EC) No 1774/2002 of the European Parliament and of the Council of 3 October 2002 laying down health rules concerning animal by-products not intended for human consumption[9] provides, inter alia, for proportionate controls as regards the collection, transport, processing, use and disposal of all animal by-products including waste of animal origin, preventing it from presenting a risk to animal and public health. It is therefore necessary to clarify the link with that Regulation, avoiding duplication of rules by excluding from the scope of this Directive animal by-products where they are intended for uses that are not considered waste operations.

13. In the light of the experience gained in applying Regulation (EC) No 1774/2002, it is appropriate to clarify the scope of waste legislation and of its provisions on hazardous waste as regards animal by-products regulated by Regulation (EC) No 1774/2002. Where animal by-products pose potential health risks, the appropriate legal instrument to address these risks is Regulation (EC) No 1774/2002 and unnecessary overlaps with waste legislation should be avoided.

14. The classification of waste as hazardous waste should be based, inter alia, on the Community legislation on chemicals, in particular concerning the classification of preparations as hazardous, including concentration limit values used for that purpose. Hazardous waste should be regulated under strict specifications in order to prevent or limit, as far as possible, the potential negative effects on the environment and on human health due to inappropriate management. Furthermore, it is necessary to maintain the system by which waste and hazardous waste have been classified in accordance with the list of the types of waste as last established by Commission

---

9 OJ L 273, 10.10.2002, p. 1.

Decision 2000/532/EC[10], in order to encourage a harmonised classification of waste and ensure the harmonised determination of hazardous waste within the Community.

15. It is necessary to distinguish between the preliminary storage of waste pending its collection, the collection of waste and the storage of waste pending treatment. Establishments or undertakings that produce waste in the course of their activities should not be regarded as engaged in waste management and subject to authorisation for the storage of their waste pending its collection.

16. Preliminary storage of waste within the definition of collection is understood as a storage activity pending its collection in facilities where waste is unloaded in order to permit its preparation for further transport for recovery or disposal elsewhere. The distinction between preliminary storage of waste pending collection and the storage of waste pending treatment should be made, in view of the objective of this Directive, according to the type of waste, the size and time period of storage and the objective of the collection. This distinction should be made by the Member States. The storage of waste prior to recovery for a period of three years or longer and the storage of waste prior to disposal for a period of one year or longer is subject to Council Directive 1999/31/EC of 26 April 1999 on the landfill of waste[11].

17. Waste collection schemes which are not conducted on a professional basis should not be subject to registration as they present a lower risk and contribute to the separate collection of waste. Examples of such schemes are waste medicines collected by pharmacies, take-back schemes in shops for consumer goods and community schemes in schools.

18. Definitions of prevention, re-use, preparing for re-use, treatment and recycling should be included in this Directive, in order to clarify the scope of these concepts.

19. The definitions of recovery and disposal need to be modified in order to ensure a clear distinction between the two concepts, based on a genuine difference in environmental impact through the substitution of natural resources in the economy and recognising the potential benefits to the environment and human health of using waste as a resource. In addition, guidelines may be developed in order to clarify cases where this distinction is difficult to apply in practice or where the classification of the activity as recovery does not match the real environmental impact of the operation.

20. This Directive should also clarify when the incineration of municipal solid waste is energy-efficient and may be considered a recovery operation.

---

10 Decision 2000/532/EC of 3 May 2000 replacing Decision 94/3/EC establishing a list of wastes pursuant to Article 1(a) of Council Directive 75/442/EEC on waste and Council Decision 94/904/EC establishing a list of hazardous waste pursuant to Article 1(4) of Council Directive 91/689/EEC on hazardous waste (OJ L 226, 6.9.2000, p. 3).
11 OJ L 182, 16.7.1999, p. 1.

21. Disposal operations consisting of release to seas and oceans including sea bed insertion are also regulated by international conventions, in particular the Convention on the Prevention of Marine Pollution by Dumping of Wastes and Other Matter, done at London on 13 November 1972, and the 1996 Protocol thereto as amended in 2006.
22. There should be no confusion between the various aspects of the waste definition, and appropriate procedures should be applied, where necessary, to by-products that are not waste, on the one hand, or to waste that ceases to be waste, on the other hand. In order to specify certain aspects of the definition of waste, this Directive should clarify:
    - when substances or objects resulting from a production process not primarily aimed at producing such substances or objects are by-products and not waste. The decision that a substance is not waste can be taken only on the basis of a coordinated approach, to be regularly updated, and where this is consistent with the protection of the environment and human health. If the use of a by-product is allowed under an environmental licence or general environmental rules, this can be used by Member States as a tool to decide that no overall adverse environmental or human health impacts are expected to occur; an object or substance should be regarded as being a by-product only when certain conditions are met. Since by-products fall into the category of products, exports of by-products should meet the requirements of the relevant Community legislation; and
    - when certain waste ceases to be waste, laying down end-of-waste criteria that provide a high level of environmental protection and an environmental and economic benefit; possible categories of waste for which "end-of-waste" specifications and criteria should be developed are, among others, construction and demolition waste, some ashes and slags, scrap metals, aggregates, tyres, textiles, compost, waste paper and glass. For the purposes of reaching end-of-waste status, a recovery operation may be as simple as the checking of waste to verify that it fulfils the end-of-waste criteria.
23. In order to verify or calculate if the recycling and recovery targets set in European Parliament and Council Directive 94/62/EC of 20 December 1994 on packaging and packaging waste[12], Directive 2000/53/EC of the European Parliament and of the Council of 18 September 2000 on end-of life vehicles[13], Directive 2002/96/EC of the European Parliament and of the Council of 27 January 2003 on waste electrical and electronic equipment (WEEE)[14] and Directive 2006/66/EC of the European Parliament and of the Council of 6 September 2006 on batteries and accumulators and waste batteries and accumulators[15] as well as other relevant Community legislation are met, the amounts

---

12 OJ L 365, 31.12.1994, p. 10.
13 OJ L 269, 21.10.2000, p. 34.
14 OJ L 37, 13.2.2003, p. 24.
15 OJ L 266, 26.9.2006, p. 1.

of waste which have ceased to be waste should be accounted for as recycled and recovered waste when the recycling or recovery requirements of that legislation are satisfied.
24. On the basis of the definition of waste, in order to promote certainty and consistency, the Commission may adopt guidelines to specify in certain cases when substances or objects become waste. Such guidelines may be developed inter alia for electrical and electronic equipment and vehicles.
25. It is appropriate that costs be allocated in such a way as to reflect the real costs to the environment of the generation and management of waste.
26. The polluter-pays principle is a guiding principle at European and international levels. The waste producer and the waste holder should manage the waste in a way that guarantees a high level of protection of the environment and human health.
27. The introduction of extended producer responsibility in this Directive is one of the means to support the design and production of goods which take into full account and facilitate the efficient use of resources during their whole life-cycle including their repair, re-use, disassembly and recycling without compromising the free circulation of goods on the internal market.
28. This Directive should help move the EU closer to a "recycling society", seeking to avoid waste generation and to use waste as a resource. In particular, the Sixth Community Environment Action Programme calls for measures aimed at ensuring the source separation, collection and recycling of priority waste streams. In line with that objective and as a means to facilitating or improving its recovery potential, waste should be separately collected if technically, environmentally and economically practicable, before undergoing recovery operations that deliver the best overall environmental outcome. Member States should encourage the separation of hazardous compounds from waste streams if necessary to achieve environmentally sound management.
29. Member States should support the use of recyclates, such as recovered paper, in line with the waste hierarchy and with the aim of a recycling society, and should not support the landfilling or incineration of such recyclates whenever possible.
30. In order to implement the precautionary principle and the principle of preventive action enshrined in Article 174(2) of the Treaty, it is necessary to set general environmental objectives for the management of waste within the Community. By virtue of those principles, it is for the Community and the Member States to establish a framework to prevent, reduce and, in so far as is possible, eliminate from the outset the sources of pollution or nuisance by adopting measures whereby recognised risks are eliminated.
31. The waste hierarchy generally lays down a priority order of what constitutes the best overall environmental option in waste legislation and policy, while departing from such hierarchy may be necessary for specific waste streams when justified for reasons of, inter alia, technical feasibility, economic viability and environmental protection.

32. It is necessary, in order to enable the Community as a whole to become self-sufficient in waste disposal and in the recovery of mixed municipal waste collected from private households and to enable the Member States to move towards that aim individually, to make provision for a network of cooperation as regards disposal installations and installations for the recovery of mixed municipal waste collected from private households, taking into account geographical circumstances and the need for specialised installations for certain types of waste.

33. For the purposes of applying Regulation (EC) No 1013/2006 of the European Parliament and of the Council of 14 June 2006 on shipments of waste[16], mixed municipal waste as referred to in Article 3(5) of that Regulation remains mixed municipal waste even when it has been subject to a waste treatment operation that has not substantially altered its properties.

34. It is important that hazardous waste be labelled in accordance with international and Community standards. However, where such waste is collected separately from households, this should not result in householders being obliged to complete the requisite documentation.

35. It is important, in accordance with the waste hierarchy, and for the purpose of reduction of greenhouse gas emissions originating from waste disposal on landfills, to facilitate the separate collection and proper treatment of bio-waste in order to produce environmentally safe compost and other bio-waste based materials. The Commission, after an assessment on the management of bio-waste, will submit proposals for legislative measures, if appropriate.

36. Technical minimum standards concerning waste treatment activities not covered by Directive 96/61/EC may be adopted where there is evidence that a benefit would be gained in terms of protecting human health and the environment and where a coordinated approach to the implementation of this Directive would ensure the protection of human health and the environment.

37. It is necessary to specify further the scope and content of the waste management planning obligation, and to integrate into the process of developing or revising waste management plans the need to take into account the environmental impacts of the generation and management of waste. Account should also be taken, where appropriate, of the waste planning requirements laid down in Article 14 of Directive 94/62/EC and of the strategy for the reduction of biodegradable waste going to landfills, referred to in Article 5 of Directive 1999/31/EC.

38. Member States may apply environmental authorisations or general environmental rules to certain waste producers without compromising the proper functioning of the internal market.

---

16 OJ L 190, 12.7.2006, p. 1.

Annexes

39. According to Regulation (EC) No 1013/2006, Member States may take the measures necessary to prevent shipments of waste which are not in accordance with their waste management plans. By way of derogation from that Regulation, Member States should be allowed to limit incoming shipments to incinerators classified as recovery, where it has been established that national waste would have to be disposed of or that waste would have to be treated in a way that is not consistent with their waste management plans. It is recognised that certain Member States may not be able to provide a network comprising the full range of final recovery facilities within their territory.

40. In order to improve the way in which waste prevention actions are taken forward in the Member States and to facilitate the circulation of best practice in this area, it is necessary to strengthen the provisions relating to waste prevention and to introduce a requirement for the Member States to develop waste prevention programmes concentrating on the key environmental impacts and taking into account the whole life-cycle of products and materials. Such measures should pursue the objective of breaking the link between economic growth and the environmental impacts associated with the generation of waste. Stakeholders, as well as the general public, should have the opportunity to participate in the drawing up of the programmes, and should have access to them once drawn up, in line with Directive 2003/35/EC of the European Parliament and of the Council of 26 May 2003 providing for public participation in respect of the drawing up of certain plans and programmes relating to the environment[17]. Waste prevention and decoupling objectives should be developed covering, as appropriate, the reduction of the adverse impacts of waste and of the amounts of waste generated.

41. In order to move towards a European recycling society with a high level of resource efficiency, targets for preparing for re-use and recycling of waste should be set. Member States maintain different approaches to the collection of household wastes and wastes of a similar nature and composition. It is therefore appropriate that such targets take account of the different collection systems in different Member States. Waste streams from other origins similar to household waste include waste referred to in entry 20 of the list established by Commission Decision 2000/532/EC.

42. Economic instruments can play a crucial role in the achievement of waste prevention and management objectives. Waste often has value as a resource, and the further application of economic instruments may maximise environmental benefits. The use of such instruments at the appropriate level should therefore be encouraged while stressing that individual Member States can decide on their use.

43. Certain provisions on the handling of waste, laid down in Council Directive 91/689/EEC of 12 December 1991 on hazardous waste[18], should be amended in order to

---

17 OJ L 156, 25.6.2003, p. 17.
18 OJ L 377, 31.12.1991, p. 20.

remove obsolete provisions and to improve the clarity of the text. In the interests of simplifying Community legislation, they should be integrated into this Directive. In order to clarify the operation of the mixing ban laid down in Directive 91/689/EEC, and to protect the environment and human health, the exemptions to the mixing ban should additionally comply with best available techniques as defined in Directive 96/61/EC. Directive 91/689/EEC should therefore be repealed.

44. In the interests of the simplification of Community legislation and the reflection of environmental benefits, the relevant provisions of Council Directive 75/439/EEC of 16 June 1975 on the disposal of waste oils[19] should be integrated into this Directive. Directive 75/439/EEC should therefore be repealed. The management of waste oils should be conducted in accordance with the priority order of the waste hierarchy, and preference should be given to options that deliver the best overall environmental outcome. The separate collection of waste oils remains crucial to their proper management and the prevention of damage to the environment from their improper disposal.

45. Member States should provide for effective, proportionate and dissuasive penalties to be imposed on natural and legal persons responsible for waste management, such as waste producers, holders, brokers, dealers, transporters and collectors, establishments or undertakings which carry out waste treatment operations and waste management schemes, in cases where they infringe the provisions of this Directive. Member States may also take action to recover the costs of non-compliance and remedial measures, without prejudice to Directive 2004/35/EC of the European Parliament and of the Council of 21 April 2004 on environmental liability with regard to the prevention and remedying of environmental damage[20].

46. The measures necessary for the implementation of this Directive should be adopted in accordance with Council Decision 1999/468/EC of 28 June 1999 laying down the procedures for the exercise of implementing powers conferred on the Commission[21].

47. In particular, the Commission should be empowered to establish criteria regarding a number of issues such as the conditions under which an object is to be considered a by-product, the end-of-waste status and the determination of waste which is considered as hazardous, as well as to establish detailed rules on the application and calculation methods for verifying compliance with the recycling targets set out in this Directive. Furthermore, the Commission should be empowered to adapt the annexes to technical and scientific progress and to specify the application of the formula for incineration facilities referred to in Annex II, R1. Since those measures are of general

---

19 OJ L 194, 25.7.1975, p. 23.
20 OJ L 143, 30.4.2004, p. 56.
21 OJ L 184, 17.7.1999, p. 23.

scope and are designed to amend non-essential elements of this Directive, by supplementing it with new non-essential elements, they must be adopted in accordance with the regulatory procedure with scrutiny provided for in Article 5a of Decision 1999/468/EC.

48. In accordance with paragraph 34 of the interinstitutional agreement on better lawmaking[22], Member States are encouraged to draw up, for themselves and in the interest of the Community, their own tables, illustrating, as far as possible, the correlation between this Directive and the transposition measures and to make them public.

49. Since the objective of this Directive, namely the protection of the environment and human health, cannot be sufficiently achieved by the Member States and can therefore, by reasons of the scale or effects of the Directive, be better achieved at Community level, the Community may adopt measures, in accordance with the principle of subsidiarity as set out in Article 5 of the Treaty. In accordance with the principle of proportionality, as set out in that Article, this Directive does not go beyond what is necessary in order to achieve that objective,

HAVE ADOPTED THIS DIRECTIVE:

CHAPTER I

SUBJECT MATTER, SCOPE AND DEFINITIONS

Article 1

Subject matter and scope

This Directive lays down measures to protect the environment and human health by preventing or reducing the adverse impacts of the generation and management of waste and by reducing overall impacts of resource use and improving the efficiency of such use.

Article 2

Exclusions from the scope

1. The following shall be excluded from the scope of this Directive:
   (a) gaseous effluents emitted into the atmosphere;
   (b) land (in situ) including unexcavated contaminated soil and buildings permanently connected with land;
   (c) uncontaminated soil and other naturally occurring material excavated in the course of construction activities where it is certain that the material will be used

---

22 OJ C 321, 31.12.2003, p. 1.

for the purposes of construction in its natural state on the site from which it was excavated;
   (d) radioactive waste;
   (e) decommissioned explosives;
   (f) faecal matter, if not covered by paragraph 2(b), straw and other natural non-hazardous agricultural or forestry material used in farming, forestry or for the production of energy from such biomass through processes or methods which do not harm the environment or endanger human health.
2. The following shall be excluded from the scope of this Directive to the extent that they are covered by other Community legislation:
   (a) waste waters;
   (b) animal by-products including processed products covered by Regulation (EC) No 1774/2002, except those which are destined for incineration, landfilling or use in a biogas or composting plant;
   (c) carcasses of animals that have died other than by being slaughtered, including animals killed to eradicate epizootic diseases, and that are disposed of in accordance with Regulation (EC) No 1774/2002;
   (d) waste resulting from prospecting, extraction, treatment and storage of mineral resources and the working of quarries covered by Directive 2006/21/EC of the European Parliament and of the Council of 15 March 2006 on the management of waste from extractive industries[23].
3. Without prejudice to obligations under other relevant Community legislation, sediments relocated inside surface waters for the purpose of managing waters and waterways or of preventing floods or mitigating the effects of floods and droughts or land reclamation shall be excluded from the scope of this Directive if it is proved that the sediments are non-hazardous.
4. Specific rules for particular instances, or supplementing those of this Directive, on the management of particular categories of waste, may be laid down by means of individual Directives.

Article 3

Definitions

For the purposes of this Directive, the following definitions shall apply:
1. "waste" means any substance or object which the holder discards or intends or is required to discard;
2. "hazardous waste" means waste which displays one or more of the hazardous properties listed in Annex III;

---

23 OJ L 102, 11.4.2006, p. 15.

3. "waste oils" means any mineral or synthetic lubrication or industrial oils which have become unfit for the use for which they were originally intended, such as used combustion engine oils and gearbox oils, lubricating oils, oils for turbines and hydraulic oils;
4. "bio-waste" means biodegradable garden and park waste, food and kitchen waste from households, restaurants, caterers and retail premises and comparable waste from food processing plants;
5. "waste producer" means anyone whose activities produce waste (original waste producer) or anyone who carries out pre-processing, mixing or other operations resulting in a change in the nature or composition of this waste;
6. "waste holder" means the waste producer or the natural or legal person who is in possession of the waste;
7. "dealer" means any undertaking which acts in the role of principal to purchase and subsequently sell waste, including such dealers who do not take physical possession of the waste;
8. "broker" means any undertaking arranging the recovery or disposal of waste on behalf of others, including such brokers who do not take physical possession of the waste;
9. "waste management" means the collection, transport, recovery and disposal of waste, including the supervision of such operations and the after-care of disposal sites, and including actions taken as a dealer or broker;
10. "collection" means the gathering of waste, including the preliminary sorting and preliminary storage of waste for the purposes of transport to a waste treatment facility;
11. "separate collection" means the collection where a waste stream is kept separately by type and nature so as to facilitate a specific treatment;
12. "prevention" means measures taken before a substance, material or product has become waste, that reduce:
    (a) the quantity of waste, including through the re-use of products or the extension of the life span of products;
    (b) the adverse impacts of the generated waste on the environment and human health; or
    (c) the content of harmful substances in materials and products;
13. "re-use" means any operation by which products or components that are not waste are used again for the same purpose for which they were conceived;
14. "treatment" means recovery or disposal operations, including preparation prior to recovery or disposal;
15. "recovery" means any operation the principal result of which is waste serving a useful purpose by replacing other materials which would otherwise have been used to fulfil a particular function, or waste being prepared to fulfil that function, in the plant or in the wider economy. Annex II sets out a non-exhaustive list of recovery operations;

16. "preparing for re-use" means checking, cleaning or repairing recovery operations, by which products or components of products that have become waste are prepared so that they can be re-used without any other pre-processing;
17. "recycling" means any recovery operation by which waste materials are reprocessed into products, materials or substances whether for the original or other purposes. It includes the reprocessing of organic material but does not include energy recovery and the reprocessing into materials that are to be used as fuels or for backfilling operations;
18. "regeneration of waste oils" means any recycling operation whereby base oils can be produced by refining waste oils, in particular by removing the contaminants, the oxidation products and the additives contained in such oils;
19. "disposal" means any operation which is not recovery even where the operation has as a secondary consequence the reclamation of substances or energy. Annex I sets out a non-exhaustive list of disposal operations;
20. "best available techniques" means best available techniques as defined in Article 2(11) of Directive 96/61/EC.

Article 4

Waste hierarchy

1. The following waste hierarchy shall apply as a priority order in waste prevention and management legislation and policy:
   (a) prevention;
   (b) preparing for re-use;
   (c) recycling;
   (d) other recovery, e.g. energy recovery; and
   (e) disposal.
2. When applying the waste hierarchy referred to in paragraph 1, Member States shall take measures to encourage the options that deliver the best overall environmental outcome. This may require specific waste streams departing from the hierarchy where this is justified by life-cycle thinking on the overall impacts of the generation and management of such waste.

   Member States shall ensure that the development of waste legislation and policy is a fully transparent process, observing existing national rules about the consultation and involvement of citizens and stakeholders.

   Member States shall take into account the general environmental protection principles of precaution and sustainability, technical feasibility and economic viability, protection of resources as well as the overall environmental, human health, economic and social impacts, in accordance with Articles 1 and 13.

Article 5

By-products

1. A substance or object, resulting from a production process, the primary aim of which is not the production of that item, may be regarded as not being waste referred to in point (1) of Article 3 but as being a by-product only if the following conditions are met:
   (a) further use of the substance or object is certain;
   (b) the substance or object can be used directly without any further processing other than normal industrial practice;
   (c) the substance or object is produced as an integral part of a production process; and
   (d) further use is lawful, i.e. the substance or object fulfils all relevant product, environmental and health protection requirements for the specific use and will not lead to overall adverse environmental or human health impacts.
2. On the basis of the conditions laid down in paragraph 1, measures may be adopted to determine the criteria to be met for specific substances or objects to be regarded as a by-product and not as waste referred to in point (1) of Article 3. Those measures, designed to amend non-essential elements of this Directive by supplementing it, shall be adopted in accordance with the regulatory procedure with scrutiny referred to in Article 39(2).

Article 6

End-of-waste status

1. Certain specified waste shall cease to be waste within the meaning of point (1) of Article 3 when it has undergone a recovery, including recycling, operation and complies with specific criteria to be developed in accordance with the following conditions:
   (a) the substance or object is commonly used for specific purposes;
   (b) a market or demand exists for such a substance or object;
   (c) the substance or object fulfils the technical requirements for the specific purposes and meets the existing legislation and standards applicable to products; and
   (d) the use of the substance or object will not lead to overall adverse environmental or human health impacts.
   The criteria shall include limit values for pollutants where necessary and shall take into account any possible adverse environmental effects of the substance or object.
2. The measures designed to amend non-essential elements of this Directive by supplementing it relating to the adoption of the criteria set out in paragraph 1 and specifying the type of waste to which such criteria shall apply shall be adopted in accordance with the regulatory procedure with scrutiny referred to in Article 39(2). End-of-waste

specific criteria should be considered, among others, at least for aggregates, paper, glass, metal, tyres and textiles.

3. Waste which ceases to be waste in accordance with paragraphs 1 and 2, shall also cease to be waste for the purpose of the recovery and recycling targets set out in Directives 94/62/EC, 2000/53/EC, 2002/96/EC and 2006/66/EC and other relevant Community legislation when the recycling or recovery requirements of that legislation are satisfied.

4. Where criteria have not been set at Community level under the procedure set out in paragraphs 1 and 2, Member States may decide case by case whether certain waste has ceased to be waste taking into account the applicable case law. They shall notify the Commission of such decisions in accordance with Directive 98/34/EC of the European Parliament and of the Council of 22 June 1998 laying down a procedure for the provision of information in the field of technical standards and regulations and of rules on Information Society services[24] where so required by that Directive.

Article 7

List of waste

1. The measures designed to amend non-essential elements of this Directive relating to the updating of the list of waste established by Decision 2000/532/EC shall be adopted in accordance with the regulatory procedure with scrutiny referred to in Article 39(2). The list of waste shall include hazardous waste and shall take into account the origin and composition of the waste and, where necessary, the limit values of concentration of hazardous substances. The list of waste shall be binding as regards determination of the waste which is to be considered as hazardous waste. The inclusion of a substance or object in the list shall not mean that it is waste in all circumstances. A substance or object shall be considered to be waste only where the definition in point (1) of Article 3 is met.

2. A Member State may consider waste as hazardous waste where, even though it does not appear as such on the list of waste, it displays one or more of the properties listed in Annex III. The Member State shall notify the Commission of any such cases without delay. It shall record them in the report provided for in Article 37(1) and shall provide the Commission with all relevant information. In the light of notifications received, the list shall be reviewed in order to decide on its adaptation.

3. Where a Member State has evidence to show that specific waste that appears on the list as hazardous waste does not display any of the properties listed in Annex III, it may consider that waste as non-hazardous waste. The Member State shall notify the

---

24 OJ L 204, 21.7.1998, p. 37.

Commission of any such cases without delay and shall provide the Commission with the necessary evidence. In the light of notifications received, the list shall be reviewed in order to decide on its adaptation.

4. The reclassification of hazardous waste as non-hazardous waste may not be achieved by diluting or mixing the waste with the aim of lowering the initial concentrations of hazardous substances to a level below the thresholds for defining waste as hazardous.

5. The measures designed to amend non-essential elements of this Directive relating to the revision of the list in order to decide on its adaptation pursuant to paragraphs 2 and 3 shall be adopted in accordance with the regulatory procedure with scrutiny referred to in Article 39(2).

6. Member States may consider waste as non-hazardous waste in accordance with the list of waste referred to in paragraph 1.

7. The Commission shall ensure that the list of waste and any review of this list adhere, as appropriate, to principles of clarity, comprehensibility and accessibility for users, particularly small and medium-sized enterprises (SMEs).

Chapter II

General Requirements

Article 8

Extended producer responsibility

1. In order to strengthen the re-use and the prevention, recycling and other recovery of waste, Member States may take legislative or non-legislative measures to ensure that any natural or legal person who professionally develops, manufactures, processes, treats, sells or imports products (producer of the product) has extended producer responsibility.

   Such measures may include an acceptance of returned products and of the waste that remains after those products have been used, as well as the subsequent management of the waste and financial responsibility for such activities. These measures may include the obligation to provide publicly available information as to the extent to which the product is re-usable and recyclable.

2. Member States may take appropriate measures to encourage the design of products in order to reduce their environmental impacts and the generation of waste in the course of the production and subsequent use of products, and in order to ensure that the recovery and disposal of products that have become waste take place in accordance with Articles 4 and 13.

Such measures may encourage, inter alia, the development, production and marketing of products that are suitable for multiple use, that are technically durable and that are, after having become waste, suitable for proper and safe recovery and environmentally compatible disposal.
3. When applying extended producer responsibility, Member States shall take into account the technical feasibility and economic viability and the overall environmental, human health and social impacts, respecting the need to ensure the proper functioning of the internal market.
4. The extended producer responsibility shall be applied without prejudice to the responsibility for waste management as provided for in Article 15(1) and without prejudice to existing waste stream specific and product specific legislation.

Article 9

Prevention of waste

Following the consultation of stakeholders, the Commission shall submit to the European Parliament and the Council the following reports accompanied, if appropriate, by proposals for measures required in support of the prevention activities and the implementation of the waste prevention programmes referred to in Article 29 covering:

(a) by the end of 2011, an interim report on the evolution of waste generation and the scope of waste prevention, including the formulation of a product eco-design policy addressing both the generation of waste and the presence of hazardous substances in waste, with a view to promoting technologies focusing on durable, re-usable and recyclable products;

(b) by the end of 2011, the formulation of an action plan for further support measures at European level seeking, in particular, to change current consumption patterns;

(c) by the end of 2014, the setting of waste prevention and decoupling objectives for 2020, based on best available practices including, if necessary, a revision of the indicators referred to in Article 29(4).

Article 10

Recovery

1. Member States shall take the necessary measures to ensure that waste undergoes recovery operations, in accordance with Articles 4 and 13.
2. Where necessary to comply with paragraph 1 and to facilitate or improve recovery, waste shall be collected separately if technically, environmentally and economically practicable and shall not be mixed with other waste or other material with different properties.

Article 11

Re-use and recycling

1. Member States shall take measures, as appropriate, to promote the re-use of products and preparing for re-use activities, notably by encouraging the establishment and support of re-use and repair networks, the use of economic instruments, procurement criteria, quantitative objectives or other measures.

    Member States shall take measures to promote high quality recycling and, to this end, shall set up separate collections of waste where technically, environmentally and economically practicable and appropriate to meet the necessary quality standards for the relevant recycling sectors.

    Subject to Article 10(2), by 2015 separate collection shall be set up for at least the following: paper, metal, plastic and glass.

2. In order to comply with the objectives of this Directive, and move towards a European recycling society with a high level of resource efficiency, Member States shall take the necessary measures designed to achieve the following targets:

    (a) by 2020, the preparing for re-use and the recycling of waste materials such as at least paper, metal, plastic and glass from households and possibly from other origins as far as these waste streams are similar to waste from households, shall be increased to a minimum of overall 50% by weight;

    (b) by 2020, the preparing for re-use, recycling and other material recovery, including backfilling operations using waste to substitute other materials, of non-hazardous construction and demolition waste excluding naturally occurring material defined in category 17 05 04 in the list of waste shall be increased to a minimum of 70% by weight.

3. The Commission shall establish detailed rules on the application and calculation methods for verifying compliance with the targets set out in paragraph 2 of this Article, considering Regulation (EC) No 2150/2002 of the European Parliament and of the Council of 25 November 2002 on waste statistics[25]. These can include transition periods for Member States which, in 2008, recycled less than 5% of either categories of waste referred to in paragraph 2. Those measures, designed to amend non-essential elements of this Directive by supplementing it, shall be adopted in accordance with the regulatory procedure with scrutiny referred to in Article 39(2) of this Directive.

4. By 31 December 2014 at the latest, the Commission shall examine the measures and the targets referred to in paragraph 2 with a view to, if necessary, reinforcing

---

25 OJ L 332, 9.12.2002, p. 1.

the targets and considering the setting of targets for other waste streams. The report of the Commission, accompanied by a proposal if appropriate, shall be sent to the European Parliament and the Council. In its report, the Commission shall take into account the relevant environmental, economic and social impacts of setting the targets.
5. Every three years, in accordance with Article 37, Member States shall report to the Commission on their record with regard to meeting the targets. If targets are not met, this report shall include the reasons for failure and the actions the Member State intends to take to meet those targets.

Article 12

Disposal

Member States shall ensure that, where recovery in accordance with Article 10(1) is not undertaken, waste undergoes safe disposal operations which meet the provisions of Article 13 on the protection of human health and the environment.

Article 13

Protection of human health and the environment

Member States shall take the necessary measures to ensure that waste management is carried out without endangering human health, without harming the environment and, in particular:
(a) without risk to water, air, soil, plants or animals;
(b) without causing a nuisance through noise or odours; and
(c) without adversely affecting the countryside or places of special interest.

Article 14

Costs

1. In accordance with the polluter-pays principle, the costs of waste management shall be borne by the original waste producer or by the current or previous waste holders.
2. Member States may decide that the costs of waste management are to be borne partly or wholly by the producer of the product from which the waste came and that the distributors of such product may share these costs.

Chapter III

Waste Management

Article 15

Responsibility for waste management

1. Member States shall take the necessary measures to ensure that any original waste producer or other holder carries out the treatment of waste himself or has the treatment handled by a dealer or an establishment or undertaking which carries out waste treatment operations or arranged by a private or public waste collector in accordance with Articles 4 and 13.

2. When the waste is transferred from the original producer or holder to one of the natural or legal persons referred to in paragraph 1 for preliminary treatment, the responsibility for carrying out a complete recovery or disposal operation shall not be discharged as a general rule.
Without prejudice to Regulation (EC) No 1013/2006, Member States may specify the conditions of responsibility and decide in which cases the original producer is to retain responsibility for the whole treatment chain or in which cases theresponsibility of the producer and the holder can be shared or delegated among the actors of the treatment chain.

3. Member States may decide, in accordance with Article 8, that the responsibility for arranging waste management is to be borne partly or wholly by the producer of the product from which the waste came and that distributors of such product may share this responsibility.

4. Member States shall take the necessary measures to ensure that, within their territory, the establishments or undertakings which collect or transport waste on a professional basis deliver the waste collected and transported to appropriate treatment installations respecting the provisions of Article 13.

Article 16

Principles of self-sufficiency and proximity

1. Member States shall take appropriate measures, in cooperation with other Member States where this is necessary or advisable, to establish an integrated and adequate network of waste disposal installations and of installations for the recovery of mixed municipal waste collected from private households, including where such collection also covers such waste from other producers, taking into account best available techniques. By way of derogation from Regulation (EC) No 1013/2006, Member States may, in order to protect their network, limit incoming shipments of waste destined to incinerators that are classified as recovery, where it has been established that such

shipments would result in national waste having to be disposed of or waste having to be treated in a way that is not consistent with their waste management plans. Member States shall notify the Commission of any such decision. Member States may also limit outgoing shipments of waste on environmental grounds as set out in Regulation (EC) No 1013/2006.
2. The network shall be designed to enable the Community as a whole to become self-sufficient in waste disposal as well as in the recovery of waste referred to in paragraph 1, and to enable Member States to move towards that aim individually, taking into account geographical circumstances or the need for specialised installations for certain types of waste.
3. The network shall enable waste to be disposed of or waste referred to in paragraph 1 to be recovered in one of the nearest appropriate installations, by means of the most appropriate methods and technologies, in order to ensure a high level of protection for the environment and public health.
4. The principles of proximity and self-sufficiency shall not mean that each Member State has to possess the full range of final recovery facilities within that Member State.

Article 17

Control of hazardous waste

Member States shall take the necessary action to ensure that the production, collection and transportation of hazardous waste, as well as its storage and treatment, are carried out in conditions providing protection for the environment and human health in order to meet the provisions of Article 13, including action to ensure traceability from production to final destination and control of hazardous waste in order to meet the requirements of Articles 35 and 36.

Article 18

Ban on the mixing of hazardous waste

1. Member States shall take the necessary measures to ensure that hazardous waste is not mixed, either with other categories of hazardous waste or with other waste, substances or materials. Mixing shall include the dilution of hazardous substances.
2. By way of derogation from paragraph 1, Member States may allow mixing provided that:
   (a) the mixing operation is carried out by an establishment or undertaking which has obtained a permit in accordance with Article 23;
   (b) the provisions of Article 13 are complied with and the adverse impact of the waste management on human health and the environment is not increased; and
   (c) the mixing operation conforms to best available techniques.

3. Subject to technical and economic feasibility criteria, where hazardous waste has been mixed in a manner contrary to paragraph 1, separation shall be carried out where possible and necessary in order to comply with Article 13.

Article 19

Labelling of hazardous waste

1. Member States shall take the necessary measures to ensure that, in the course of collection, transport and temporary storage, hazardous waste is packaged and labelled in accordance with the international and Community standards in force.
2. Whenever hazardous waste is transferred within a Member State, it shall be accompanied by an identification document, which may be in electronic format, containing the appropriate data specified in Annex IB to Regulation (EC) No 1013/2006.

Article 20

Hazardous waste produced by households

Articles 17, 18, 19 and 35 shall not apply to mixed waste produced by households. Articles 19 and 35 shall not apply to separate fractions of hazardous waste produced by households until they are accepted for collection, disposal or recovery by an establishment or an undertaking which has obtained a permit or has been registered in accordance with Articles 23 or 26.

Article 21

Waste oils

1. Without prejudice to the obligations related to the management of hazardous waste laid down in Articles 18 and 19, Member States shall take the necessary measures to ensure that:
   (a) waste oils are collected separately, where this is technically feasible;
   (b) waste oils are treated in accordance with Articles 4 and 13;
   (c) where this is technically feasible and economically viable, waste oils of different characteristics are not mixed and waste oils are not mixed with other kinds of waste or substances, if such mixing impedes their treatment.
2. For the purposes of separate collection of waste oils and their proper treatment, Member States may, according to their national conditions, apply additional measures such as technical requirements, producer responsibility, economic instruments or voluntary agreements.
3. If waste oils, according to national legislation, are subject to requirements of regeneration, Member States may prescribe that such waste oils shall be regenerated if

technically feasible and, where Articles 11 or 12 of Regulation (EC) No 1013/2006 apply, restrict the transboundary shipment of waste oils from their territory to incineration or co-incineration facilities in order to give priority to the regeneration of waste oils.

Article 22

Bio-waste

Member States shall take measures, as appropriate, and in accordance with Articles 4 and 13, to encourage:
(a) the separate collection of bio-waste with a view to the composting and digestion of bio-waste;
(b) the treatment of bio-waste in a way that fulfils a high level of environmental protection;
(c) the use of environmentally safe materials produced from bio-waste.

The Commission shall carry out an assessment on the management of bio-waste with a view to submitting a proposal if appropriate. The assessment shall examine the opportunity of setting minimum requirements for bio-waste management and quality criteria for compost and digestate from bio-waste, in order to guarantee a high level of protection for human health and the environment.

CHAPTER IV

PERMITS AND REGISTRATIONS

Article 23

Issue of permits

1. Member States shall require any establishment or undertaking intending to carry out waste treatment to obtain a permit from the competent authority.
   Such permits shall specify at least the following:
   (a) the types and quantities of waste that may be treated;
   (b) for each type of operation permitted, the technical and any other requirements relevant to the site concerned;
   (c) the safety and precautionary measures to be taken;
   (d) the method to be used for each type of operation;
   (e) such monitoring and control operations as may be necessary;
   (f) such closure and after-care provisions as may be necessary.
2. Permits may be granted for a specified period and may be renewable.

3. Where the competent authority considers that the intended method of treatment is unacceptable from the point of view of environmental protection, in particular when the method is not in accordance with Article 13, it shall refuse to issue the permit.
4. It shall be a condition of any permit covering incineration or co-incineration with energy recovery that the recovery of energy take place with a high level of energy efficiency.
5. Provided that the requirements of this Article are complied with, any permit produced pursuant to other national or Community legislation may be combined with the permit required under paragraph 1 to form a single permit, where such a format obviates the unnecessary duplication of information and the repetition of work by the operator or the competent authority.

Article 24

Exemptions from permit requirements

Member States may exempt from the requirement laid down in Article 23(1) establishments or undertakings for the following operations:
(a) disposal of their own non-hazardous waste at the place of production; or
(b) recovery of waste.

Article 25

Conditions for exemptions

1. Where a Member State wishes to allow exemptions, as provided for in Article 24, it shall lay down, in respect of each type of activity, general rules specifying the types and quantities of waste that may be covered by an exemption, and the method of treatment to be used.

   Those rules shall be designed to ensure that waste is treated in accordance with Article 13. In the case of disposal operations referred to in point (a) of Article 24 those rules should consider best available techniques.
2. In addition to the general rules provided for in paragraph 1, Member States shall lay down specific conditions for exemptions relating to hazardous waste, including types of activity, as well as any other necessary requirement for carrying out different forms of recovery and, where relevant, the limit values for the content of hazardous substances in the waste as well as the emission limit values.
3. Member States shall inform the Commission of the general rules laid down pursuant to paragraphs 1 and 2.

Article 26

Registration

Where the following are not subject to permit requirements, Member States shall ensure that the competent authority keeps a register of:
(a) establishments or undertakings which collect or transport waste on a professional basis;
(b) dealers or brokers; and
(c) establishments or undertakings which are subject to exemptions from the permit requirements pursuant to Article 24.

Where possible, existing records held by the competent authority shall be used to obtain the relevant information for this registration process in order to reduce the administrative burden.

Article 27

Minimum standards

1. Technical minimum standards for treatment activities which require a permit pursuant to Article 23 may be adopted where there is evidence that a benefit in terms of the protection of human health and the environment would be gained from such minimum standards. Those measures, designed to amend non-essential elements of this Directive by supplementing it, shall be adopted in accordance with the regulatory procedure with scrutiny referred to in Article 39(2).
2. Such minimum standards shall cover only those waste treatment activities that are not covered by Directive 96/61/EC or are not appropriate for coverage by that Directive.
3. Such minimum standards shall:
   (a) be directed to the main environmental impacts of the waste treatment activity;
   (b) ensure that the waste is treated in accordance with Article 13;
   (c) take into account best available techniques; and
   (d) as appropriate, include elements regarding the quality of treatment and the process requirements.
4. Minimum standards for activities that require registration pursuant to points (a) and (b) of Article 26 shall be adopted where there is evidence that a benefit in terms of the protection of human health and the environment or in avoiding disruption to the internal market would be gained from such minimum standards, including elements regarding the technical qualification of collectors, transporters, dealers or brokers.

   Those measures, designed to amend non-essential elements of this Directive by supplementing it, shall be adopted in accordance with the regulatory procedure with scrutiny referred to in Article 39(2).

Chapter V

Plans and Programmes

Article 28

Waste management plans

1. Member States shall ensure that their competent authorities establish, in accordance with Articles 1, 4, 13 and 16, one or more waste management plans.
   Those plans shall, alone or in combination, cover the entire geographical territory of the Member State concerned.
2. The waste management plans shall set out an analysis of the current waste management situation in the geographical entity concerned, as well as the measures to be taken to improve environmentally sound preparing for re-use, recycling, recovery and disposal of waste and an evaluation of how the plan will support the implementation of the objectives and provisions of this Directive.
3. The waste management plans shall contain, as appropriate and taking into account the geographical level and coverage of the planning area, at least the following:
   (a) the type, quantity and source of waste generated within the territory, the waste likely to be shipped from or to the national territory, and an evaluation of the development of waste streams in the future;
   (b) existing waste collection schemes and major disposal and recovery installations, including any special arrangements for waste oils, hazardous waste or waste streams addressed by specific Community legislation;
   (c) an assessment of the need for new collection schemes, the closure of existing waste installations, additional waste installation infrastructure in accordance with Article 16, and, if necessary, the investments related thereto;
   (d) sufficient information on the location criteria for site identification and on the capacity of future disposal or major recovery installations, if necessary;
   (e) general waste management policies, including planned waste management technologies and methods, or policies for waste posing specific management problems.
4. The waste management plan may contain, taking into account the geographical level and coverage of the planning area, the following:
   (a) organisational aspects related to waste management including a description of the allocation of responsibilities between public and private actors carrying out the waste management;

(b) an evaluation of the usefulness and suitability of the use of economic and other instruments in tackling various waste problems, taking into account the need to maintain the smooth functioning of the internal market;

(c) the use of awareness campaigns and information provision directed at the general public or at a specific set of consumers;

(d) historical contaminated waste disposal sites and measures for their rehabilitation.

5. Waste management plans shall conform to the waste planning requirements laid down in Article 14 of Directive 94/62/EC and the strategy for the implementation of the reduction of biodegradable waste going to landfills, referred to in Article 5 of Directive 1999/31/EC.

Article 29

Waste prevention programmes

1. Member States shall establish, in accordance with Articles 1 and 4, waste prevention programmes not later than 12 December 2013.

   Such programmes shall be integrated either into the waste management plans provided for in Article 28 or into other environmental policy programmes, as appropriate, or shall function as separate programmes. If any such programme is integrated into the waste management plan or into other programmes, the waste prevention measures shall be clearly identified.

2. The programmes provided for in paragraph 1 shall set out the waste prevention objectives. Member States shall describe the existing prevention measures and evaluate the usefulness of the examples of measures indicated in Annex IV or other appropriate measures. The aim of such objectives and measures shall be to break the link between economic growth and the environmental impacts associated with the generation of waste.

3. Member States shall determine appropriate specific qualitative or quantitative benchmarks for waste prevention measures adopted in order to monitor and assess the progress of the measures and may determine specific qualitative or quantitative targets and indicators, other than those referred to in paragraph 4, for the same purpose.

4. Indicators for waste prevention measures may be adopted in accordance with the regulatory procedure referred to in Article 39(3).

5. The Commission shall create a system for sharing information on best practice regarding waste prevention and shall develop guidelines in order to assist the Member States in the preparation of the Programmes.

Article 30

Evaluation and review of plans and programmes

1. Member States shall ensure that the waste management plans and waste prevention programmes are evaluated at least every sixth year and revised as appropriate and, where relevant, in accordance with Articles 9 and 11.
2. The European Environment Agency is invited to include in its annual report a review of progress in the completion and implementation of waste prevention programmes.

Article 31

Public participation

Member States shall ensure that relevant stakeholders and authorities and the general public have the opportunity to participate in the elaboration of the waste management plans and waste prevention programmes, and have access to them once elaborated, in accordance with Directive 2003/35/EC or, if relevant, Directive 2001/42/EC of the European Parliament and of the Council of 27 June 2001 on the assessment of the effects of certain plans and programmes on the environment[26]. They shall place the plans and programmes on a publicly available website.

Article 32

Cooperation

Member States shall cooperate as appropriate with the other Member States concerned and the Commission to draw up the waste management plans and the waste prevention programmes in accordance with Articles 28 and 29.

Article 33

Information to be submitted to the Commission

1. Member States shall inform the Commission of the waste management plans and waste prevention programmes referred to in Articles 28 and 29, once adopted, and of any substantial revisions to the plans and programmes.
2. The format for notifying the information on the adoption and substantial revisions of those plans and programmes shall be adopted in accordance with the regulatory procedure referred to in Article 39(3).

---

26 OJ L 197, 21.7.2001, p. 30.

Chapter VI

Inspections and Records

Article 34

Inspections

1. Establishments or undertakings which carry out waste treatment operations, establishments or undertakings which collect or transport waste on a professional basis, brokers and dealers, and establishments or undertakings which produce hazardous waste shall be subject to appropriate periodic inspections by the competent authorities.
2. Inspections concerning collection and transport operations shall cover the origin, nature, quantity and destination of the waste collected and transported.
3. Member States may take account of registrations obtained under the Community Eco-Management and Audit Scheme (EMAS), in particular regarding the frequency and intensity of inspections.

Article 35

Record keeping

1. The establishments or undertakings referred to in Article 23(1), the producers of hazardous waste and the establishments and undertakings which collect or transport hazardous waste on a professional basis, or act as dealers and brokers of hazardous waste, shall keep a chronological record of the quantity, nature and origin of the waste, and, where relevant, the destination, frequency of collection, mode of transport and treatment method foreseen in respect of the waste, and shall make that information available, on request, to the competent authorities.
2. For hazardous waste, the records shall be preserved for at least three years except in the case of establishments and undertakings transporting hazardous waste which must keep such records for at least 12 months.
   Documentary evidence that the management operations have been carried out shall be supplied at the request of the competent authorities or of a previous holder.
3. Member States may require the producers of non-hazardous waste to comply with paragraphs 1 and 2.

Article 36

Enforcement and penalties

1. Member States shall take the necessary measures to prohibit the abandonment, dumping or uncontrolled management of waste.
2. Members States shall lay down provisions on the penalties applicable to infringements of the provisions of this Directive and shall take all measures necessary to ensure that they are implemented. The penalties shall be effective, proportionate and dissuasive.

CHAPTER VII

FINAL PROVISIONS

Article 37

Reporting and reviewing

1. Every three years, Member States shall inform the Commission of the implementation of this Directive by submitting a sectoral report in an electronic form. This report shall also contain information on the management of waste oil and on the progress achieved in the implementation of the waste prevention programmes and, as appropriate, information on measures as foreseen by Article 8 on extended producer responsibility.
   The report shall be drawn up on the basis of a questionnaire or outline established by the Commission in accordance with the procedure referred to in Article 6 of Council Directive 91/692/EEC of 23 December 1991 standardising and rationalising reports on the implementation of certain Directives relating to the environment[27]. The report shall be submitted to the Commission within nine months of the end of the three year period covered by it.
2. The Commission shall send the questionnaire or outline to the Member States six months before the start of the period covered by the sectoral report.
3. The Commission shall publish a report on the implementation of this Directive within nine months of receiving the sectoral reports from the Member States in accordance with paragraph 1.
4. In the first report that intervenes by 12 December 2014, the Commission shall review the implementation of this Directive, including the energy efficiency provisions, and will present a proposal for revision if appropriate. The report shall also assess the existing Member State waste prevention programmes, objectives and indicators and shall review the opportunity of Community level programmes, including producer responsibility schemes for specific waste streams, targets, indicators and measures related to recycling, as well as material and energy recovery operations that may contribute to fulfilling the objectives set out in Articles 1 and 4 more effectively.

---

27 OJ L 377, 31.12.1991, p. 48.

Article 38

Interpretation and adaptation to technical progress

1. The Commission may develop guidelines for the interpretation of the definitions of recovery and disposal.

   If necessary, the application of the formula for incineration facilities referred to in Annex II, R1, shall be specified. Local climatic conditions may be taken into account, such as the severity of the cold and the need for heating insofar as they influence the amounts of energy that can technically be used or produced in the form of electricity, heating, cooling or processing steam. Local conditions of the outermost regions as recognised in the fourth subparagraph of Article 299(2) of the Treaty and of the territories mentioned in Article 25 of the 1985 Act of Accession may also be taken into account. This measure, designed to amend non-essential elements of this Directive, shall be adopted in accordance with the regulatory procedure with scrutiny referred to in Article 39(2).

2. The Annexes may be amended in the light of scientific and technical progress. Those measures, designed to amend non-essential elements of this Directive, shall be adopted in accordance with the regulatory procedure with scrutiny referred to in Article 39(2).

Article 39

Committee procedure

1. The Commission shall be assisted by a committee.
2. Where reference is made to this paragraph, Article 5a(1) to (4) and Article 7 of Decision 1999/468/EC shall apply, having regard to the provisions of Article 8 thereof.
3. Where reference is made to this paragraph, Articles 5 and 7 of Decision 1999/468/EC shall apply, having regard to the provisions of Article 8 thereof.

The period laid down in Article 5(6) of Decision 1999/468/EC shall be set at three months.

Article 40

Transposition

1. Member States shall bring into force the laws, regulations and administrative provisions necessary to comply with this Directive by 12 December 2010.

   When Member States adopt these measures, they shall contain a reference to this Directive or shall be accompanied by such reference on the occasion of their official publication. The methods of making such reference shall be laid down by Member States.

2. Member States shall communicate to the Commission the text of the main provisions of national law which they adopt in the field covered by this Directive.

Article 41

Repeal and transitional provisions

Directives 75/439/EEC, 91/689/EEC and 2006/12/EC are hereby repealed with effect from 12 December 2010.

However, from 12 December 2008, the following shall apply:

(a) Article 10(4) of Directive 75/439/EEC shall be replaced by the following:

"4. The reference method of measurement to determine the PCB/PCT content of waste oils shall be fixed by the Commission. That measure, designed to amend non-essential elements of this Directive by supplementing it, shall be adopted in accordance with the regulatory procedure with scrutiny referred to in Article 18(4) of Directive 2006/12/EC of the European Parliament and of the Council of 5 April 2006 on waste*.";

(b) Directive 91/689/EEC is hereby amended as follows:

(i) Article 1(4) shall be replaced by the following:

"4. For the purpose of this Directive 'hazardous waste' means:

- waste classified as hazardous waste featuring on the list established by Commission Decision 2000/532/EC** on the basis of Annexes I and II to this Directive. This waste must have one or more of the properties listed in Annex III. The list shall take into account the origin and composition of the waste and, where necessary, limit values of concentration. This list shall be periodically reviewed and, if necessary revised. Those measures, designed to amend non-essential elements of this Directive by supplementing it, shall be adopted in accordance with the regulatory procedure with scrutiny referred to in Article 18(4) of Directive 2006/12/EC of the European Parliament and of the Council of 5 April 2006 on waste***,

- any other waste which is considered by a Member State to display any of the properties listed in Annex III. Such cases shall be notified to the Commission and reviewed with a view to adapting the list. Those measures, designed to amend non-essential elements of this Directive by supplementing it, shall be adopted in accordance with the regulatory procedure with scrutiny referred to in Article 18(4) of Directive 2006/12/EC.";

---

* OJ L 114, 27.4.2006, p. 9.
** OJ L 226, 6.9.2000, p. 3.
*** OJ L 114, 27.4.2006, p. 9.

(ii) Article 9 shall be replaced by the following:

"*Article 9*

The measures necessary for adapting the Annexes of this Directive to scientific and technical progress and for revising the list of wastes referred to in Article 1(4), designed to amend non-essential elements of this Directive, inter alia by supplementing it, shall be adopted in accordance with the regulatory procedure with scrutiny referred to in Article 18(4) of Directive 2006/12/EC.";

(c) Directive 2006/12/EC is hereby amended as follows:

(i) Article 1(2) shall be replaced by the following:

"2. For the purposes of paragraph 1, point (a), Commission Decision 2000/532/EC* featuring the list of waste belonging to the categories listed in Annex I to this Directive shall apply. This list shall be periodically reviewed and, if necessary, revised. Those measures, designed to amend non-essential elements of this Directive by supplementing it, shall be adopted in accordance with the regulatory procedure with scrutiny referred to in Article 18(4).";

(ii) Article 17 shall be replaced by the following:

"*Article 17*

The measures necessary for adapting the Annexes to scientific and technical progress, designed to amend non-essential elements of this Directive, shall be adopted in accordance with the regulatory procedure with scrutiny referred to in Article 18(4).";

(iii) Article 18(4) shall be replaced by the following:

"4. Where reference is made to this paragraph, Article 5a(1) to (4) and Article 7 of Decision 1999/468/EC shall apply, having regard to the provisions of Article 8 thereof."

References to the repealed Directives shall be construed as references to this Directive and shall be read in accordance with the correlation table set out in Annex V.

Article 42

Entry into force

This Directive shall enter into force on the twentieth day following that of its publication in the Official Journal of the European Union.

---

* OJ L 226, 6.9.2000, p. 3.

Article 43

Addressees

This Directive is addressed to the Member States.

Done at Strasbourg, 19 November 2008.

For the European Parliament	*For the Council*
The President	*The President*
H.-G. PÖTTERING	J.-P. JOUYET

Annex I

Disposal Operations

D 1   Deposit into or on to land (e.g. landfill, etc.)

D 2   Land treatment (e.g. biodegradation of liquid or sludgy discards in soils, etc.)

D 3   Deep injection (e.g. injection of pumpable discards into wells, salt domes or naturally occurring repositories, etc.)

D 4   Surface impoundment (e.g. placement of liquid or sludgy discards into pits, ponds or lagoons, etc.)

D 5   Specially engineered landfill (e.g. placement into lined discrete cells which are capped and isolated from one another and the environment, etc.)

D 6   Release into a water body except seas/oceans

D 7   Release to seas/oceans including sea-bed insertion

D 8   Biological treatment not specified elsewhere in this Annex which results in final compounds or mixtures which are discarded by means of any of the operations numbered D 1 to D 12

D 9   Physico-chemical treatment not specified elsewhere in this Annex which results in final compounds or mixtures which are discarded by means of any of the operations numbered D 1 to D 12 (e.g. evaporation, drying, calcination, etc.)

D 10 Incineration on land

D 11 Incineration at sea*

D 12 Permanent storage (e.g. emplacement of containers in a mine, etc.)

D 13 Blending or mixing prior to submission to any of the operations numbered D 1 to D 12**

D 14 Repackaging prior to submission to any of the operations numbered D 1 to D 13

D 15 Storage pending any of the operations numbered D 1 to D 14 (excluding temporary storage, pending collection, on the site where the waste is produced)***

---

* This operation is prohibited by EU legislation and international conventions.

** If there is no other D code appropriate, this can include preliminary operations prior to disposal including pre-processing such as, inter alia, sorting, crushing, compacting, pelletising, drying, shredding, conditioning or separating prior to submission to any of the operations numbered D1 to D12.

*** Temporary storage means preliminary storage according to point (10) of Article 3.

Annex II

Recovery Operations

R 1   Use principally as a fuel or other means to generate energy*

R 2   Solvent reclamation/regeneration

R 3   Recycling/reclamation of organic substances which are not used as solvents (including composting and other biological transformation processes)**

R 4   Recycling/reclamation of metals and metal compounds

R 5   Recycling/reclamation of other inorganic materials***

R 6   Regeneration of acids or bases

R 7   Recovery of components used for pollution abatement

R 8   Recovery of components from catalysts

R 9   Oil re-refining or other reuses of oil

R 10 Land treatment resulting in benefit to agriculture or ecological improvement

R 11 Use of waste obtained from any of the operations numbered R 1 to R 10

R 12 Exchange of waste for submission to any of the operations numbered R 1 to R 11****

R 13 Storage of waste pending any of the operations numbered R 1 to R 12 (excluding temporary storage, pending collection, on the site where the waste is produced)*****

---

* This includes incineration facilities dedicated to the processing of municipal solid waste only where their energy efficiency is equal to or above:
- 0,60 for installations in operation and permitted in accordance with applicable Community legislation before 1 January 2009,
- 0,65 for installations permitted after 31 December 2008, using the following formula: Energy efficiency = $(Ep - (Ef + Ei))/(0,97 \times (Ew + Ef))$ In which:
- Ep means annual energy produced as heat or electricity. It is calculated with energy in the form of electricity being multiplied by 2,6 and heat produced for commercial use multiplied by 1,1 (GJ/year)
- Ef means annual energy input to the system from fuels contributing to the production of steam (GJ/year)
- Ew means annual energy contained in the treated waste calculated using the net calorific value of the waste (GJ/year)
- Ei means annual energy imported excluding Ew and Ef (GJ/year)
- 0,97 is a factor accounting for energy losses due to bottom ash and radiation. This formula shall be applied in accordance with the reference document on Best Available Techniques for waste incineration.

** This includes gasification and pyrolisis using the components as chemicals.

*** This includes soil cleaning resulting in recovery of the soil and recycling of inorganic construction materials.

**** If there is no other R code appropriate, this can include preliminary operations prior to recovery including pre-processing such as, inter alia, dismantling, sorting, crushing, compacting, pelletising, drying, shredding, conditioning, repackaging, separating, blending or mixing prior to submission to any of the operations numbered R1 to R11.

***** Temporary storage means preliminary storage according to point (10) of Article 3.

Annex III

Properties of Waste which Render It Hazardous

H 1   "Explosive": substances and preparations which may explode under the effect of flame or which are more sensitive to shocks or friction than dinitrobenzene.

H 2   "Oxidizing": substances and preparations which exhibit highly exothermic reactions when in contact with other substances, particularly flammable substances.

H 3-A   "Highly flammable"
- liquid substances and preparations having a flash point below 21 °C (including extremely flammable liquids), or
- substances and preparations which may become hot and finally catch fire in contact with air at ambient temperature without any application of energy, or
- solid substances and preparations which may readily catch fire after brief contact with a source of ignition and which continue to burn or to be consumed after removal of the source of ignition, or
- gaseous substances and preparations which are flammable in air at normal pressure, or
- substances and preparations which, in contact with water or damp air, evolve highly flammable gases in dangerous quantities.

H 3-B   "Flammable": liquid substances and preparations having a flash point equal to or greater than 21 °C and less than or equal to 55 °C.

H 4   "Irritant": non-corrosive substances and preparations which, through immediate, prolonged or repeated contact with the skin or mucous membrane, can cause inflammation.

H 5   "Harmful": substances and preparations which, if they are inhaled or ingested or if they penetrate the skin, may involve limited health risks.

H 6   "Toxic": substances and preparations (including very toxic substances and preparations) which, if they are inhaled or ingested or if they penetrate the skin, may involve serious, acute or chronic health risks and even death.

H 7   "Carcinogenic": substances and preparations which, if they are inhaled or ingested or if they penetrate the skin, may induce cancer or increase its incidence.

H 8   "Corrosive": substances and preparations which may destroy living tissue on contact.

H 9   "Infectious": substances and preparations containing viable micro-organisms or their toxins which are known or reliably believed to cause disease in man or other living organisms.

	H 10	"Toxic for reproduction": substances and preparations which, if they are inhaled or ingested or if they penetrate the skin, may induce non-hereditary congenital malformations or increase their incidence.
	H 11	"Mutagenic": substances and preparations which, if they are inhaled or ingested or if they penetrate the skin, may induce hereditary genetic defects or increase their incidence.
	H 12	Waste which releases toxic or very toxic gases in contact with water, air or an acid.
	H 13*	"Sensitizing": substances and preparations which, if they are inhaled or if they penetrate the skin, are capable of eliciting a reaction of hypersensitization such that on further exposure to the substance or preparation, characteristic adverse effects are produced.
	H 14	"Ecotoxic": waste which presents or may present immediate or delayed risks for one or more sectors of the environment.
	H 15	Waste capable by any means, after disposal, of yielding another substance, e.g. a leachate, which possesses any of the characteristics listed above.

Notes
1. Attribution of the hazardous properties "toxic" (and "very toxic"), "harmful", "corrosive", "irritant", "carcinogenic", "toxic to reproduction", "mutagenic" and "eco-toxic" is made on the basis of the criteria laid down by Annex VI, to Council Directive 67/548/EEC of 27 June 1967 on the approximation of laws, regulations and administrative provisions relating to the classification, packaging and labelling of dangerous substances[1].
2. Where relevant the limit values listed in Annex II and III to Directive 1999/45/EC of the European Parliament and of the Council of 31 May 1999 concerning the approximation of the laws, regulations and administrative provisions of the Member States relating to the classification, packaging and labelling of dangerous preparations[2] shall apply.

Test methods
The methods to be used are described in Annex V to Directive 67/548/EEC and in other relevant CEN-notes.

---

*   As far as testing methods are available.
1   OJ 196, 16.8.1967, p. 1.
2   OJ L 200, 30.7.1999, p. 1.

Annex IV

Examples of Waste Prevention Measures Preferred to in Article 29

Measures that can affect the framework conditions related to the generation of waste

1. The use of planning measures, or other economic instruments promoting the efficient use of resources.

2. The promotion of research and development into the area of achieving cleaner and less wasteful products and technologies and the dissemination and use of the results of such research and development.

3. The development of effective and meaningful indicators of the environmental pressures associated with the generation of waste aimed at contributing to the prevention of waste generation at all levels, from product comparisons at Community level through action by local authorities to national measures.

Measures that can affect the design and production and distribution phase

4. The promotion of eco-design (the systematic integration of environmental aspects into product design with the aim to improve the environmental performance of the product throughout its whole life cycle).

5. The provision of information on waste prevention techniques with a view to facilitating the implementation of best available techniques by industry.

6. Organise training of competent authorities as regards the insertion of waste prevention requirements in permits under this Directive and Directive 96/61/EC.

7. The inclusion of measures to prevent waste production at installations not falling under Directive 96/61/EC. Where appropriate, such measures could include waste prevention assessments or plans.

8. The use of awareness campaigns or the provision of financial, decision making or other support to businesses. Such measures are likely to be particularly effective where they are aimed at, and adapted to, small and medium sized enterprises and work through established business networks.

9. The use of voluntary agreements, consumer/producer panels or sectoral negotiations in order that the relevant businesses or industrial sectors set their own waste prevention plans or objectives or correct wasteful products or packaging.

10. The promotion of creditable environmental management systems, including EMAS and ISO 14001.

Measures that can affect the consumption and use phase

11. Economic instruments such as incentives for clean purchases or the institution of an obligatory payment by consumers for a given article or element of packaging that would otherwise be provided free of charge.

12. The use of awareness campaigns and information provision directed at the general public or a specific set of consumers.

13. The promotion of creditable eco-labels.

14. Agreements with industry, such as the use of product panels such as those being carried out within the framework of Integrated Product Policies or with retailers on the availability of waste prevention information and products with a lower environmental impact.

15. In the context of public and corporate procurement, the integration of environmental and waste prevention criteria into calls for tenders and contracts, in line with the Handbook on environmental public procurement published by the Commission on 29 October 2004.

16. The promotion of the reuse and/or repair of appropriate discarded products or of their components, notably through the use of educational, economic, logistic or other measures such as support to or establishment of accredited repair and reuse-centres and networks especially in densely populated regions.

Annex V

Correlation Table

Directive 2006/12/EC	This Directive
Article 1(1)(a)	Article 3(1)
Article 1(1)(b)	Article 3(5)
Article 1(1)(c)	Article 3(6)
Article 1(1)(d)	Article 3(9)
Article 1(1)(e)	Article 3(19)
Article 1(1)(f)	Article 3(15)
Article 1(1)(g)	Article 3(10)
Article 1(2)	Article 7
Article 2(1)	Article 2(1)
Article 2(1)(a)	Article 2(1)(a)
Article 2(1)(b)	Article 2(2)
Article 2(1)(b)(i)	Article 2(1)(d)
Article 2(1)(b)(ii)	Article 2(2)(d)
Article 2(1)(b)(iii)	Article 2(1)(f) and (2)(c)
Article 2(1)(b)(iv)	Article 2(2)(a)
Article 2(1)(b)(v)	Article 2(1)(e)
Article 2(2)	Article 2(4)
Article 3(1)	Article 4
Article 4(1)	Article 13
Article 4(2)	Article 36(1)
Article 5	Article 16
Article 6	—
Article 7	Article 28
Article 8	Article 15
Article 9	Article 23
Article 10	Article 23
Article 11	Articles 24 and 25
Article 12	Article 26
Article 13	Article 34
Article 14	Article 35
Article 15	Article 14

Directive 2006/12/EC	This Directive
Article 16	Article 37
Article 17	Article 38
Article 18(1)	Article 39(1)
—	Article 39(2)
Article 18(2)	—
Article 18(3)	Article 39(3)
Article 19	Article 40
Article 20	—
Article 21	Article 42
Article 22	Article 43
Annex I	—
Annex IIA	Annex I
Annex IIB	Annex II

Directive 75/439/EEC	This Directive
Article 1(1)	Article 3(18)
Article 2	Articles 13 and 21
Article 3(1) and (2)	—
Article 3(3)	Article 13
Article 4	Article 13
Article 5(1)	—
Article 5(2)	—
Article 5(3)	—
Article 5(4)	Articles 26 and 34
Article 6	Article 23
Article 7(a)	Article 13
Article 7(b)	—
Article 8(1)	—
Article 8(2)(a)	—
Article 8(2)(b)	—
Article 8(3)	—
Article 9	—
Article 10(1)	Article 18
Article 10(2)	Article 13

Directive 75/439/EEC	This Directive
Article 10(3) and (4)	—
Article 10(5)	Articles 19, 21, 25, 34 and 35
Article 11	—
Article 12	Article 35
Article 13(1)	Article 34
Article 13(2)	—
Article 14	—
Article 15	—
Article 16	—
Article 17	—
Article 18	Article 37
Article 19	—
Article 20	—
Article 21	—
Article 22	—
Annex I	—

Directive 91/689/EEC	This Directive
Article 1(1)	—
Article 1(2)	—
Article 1(3)	—
Article 1(4)	Articles 3(2) and 7
Article 1(5)	Article 20
Article 2(1)	Article 23
Article 2(2)-(4)	Article 18
Article 3	Articles 24, 25 and 26
Article 4(1)	Article 34(1)
Article 4(2)(3)	Article 35
Article 5(1)	Article 19(1)
Article 5(2)	Article 34(2)
Article 5(3)	Article 19(2)
Article 6	Article 28
Article 7	—
Article 8	—

Directive 91/689/EEC	This Directive
Article 9	—
Article 10	—
Article 11	—
Article 12	—
Annexes I and II	—
Annex III	Annex III

Affaire Di Sarno et Autres c. Italie

Requete n° 30765/08

En l'affaire di Sarno et autres c. Italie,

La Cour européenne des droits de l'homme (deuxième section), siégeant en une chambre composée de :

Françoise Tulkens, *présidente*,
Danutė Jočienė,
Dragoljub Popović,
Isabelle Berro-Lefèvre,
András Sajó,
Işıl Karakaş,
Guido Raimondi, *juges*,

et de Stanley Naismith, *greffier de section*,

Après en avoir délibéré en chambre du conseil le 29 novembre 2011,

Rend l'arrêt que voici, adopté à cette date :

PROCÉDURE

1. A l'origine de l'affaire se trouve une requête (n° 30765/08) dirigée contre la République italienne et dont dix-huit ressortissants de cet Etat, (« les requérants »), ont saisi la Cour le 9 janvier 2008 en vertu de l'article 34 de la Convention de sauvegarde des droits de l'homme et des libertés fondamentales (« la Convention »).

2. Devant la Cour, les requérants, dont les noms figurent dans la liste annexée au présent arrêt, ont été représentés par l'un d'eux, Mᵉ Errico di Lorenzo, avocat à Somma Vesuviana (Naples).

3. Le gouvernement italien (« le Gouvernement ») a été représenté par son agent, Mᵐᵉ E. Spatafora, et son ancien coagent, M. N. Lettieri.

4. Dans leur requête, les requérants alléguaient que la mauvaise gestion, par les autorités italiennes, du service de collecte, de traitement et d'élimination des déchets en Campanie, ainsi que le manque de diligence des autorités judiciaires à poursuivre les responsables de cette situation, avaient porté atteinte à leurs droits garantis par les articles 2, 6, 8 et 13 de la Convention.

5. Le 2 juin 2009, la Cour a décidé de communiquer la requête au Gouvernement et de la traiter en priorité (article 41 du règlement de la Cour). Comme le permettait l'ancien article 29 § 3 de la Convention, elle a en outre décidé que seraient examinés en même temps la recevabilité et le fond de l'affaire.

ANNEXES

EN FAIT

I. LES CIRCONSTANCES DE L'ESPÈCE

6. Treize des requérants résident dans la commune de Somma Vesuviana, en Campanie. Cinq y travaillent.
7. Du 11 février 1994 au 31 décembre 2009, la région Campanie fut soumise à l'état d'urgence (*stato di emergenza*) sur décision du président du Conseil des ministres en raison de graves problèmes d'élimination des déchets solides urbains.
8. Du 11 février 1994 au 23 mai 2008, la gestion de l'état d'urgence fut confiée à des « commissaires délégués » désignés par le président du Conseil des ministres et secondés par des sous-commissaires. Neuf hauts responsables – dont quatre présidents de la région de Campanie et le chef du service de la protection civile de la présidence des Conseil des ministres – furent nommés aux fonctions de commissaire.
9. Du 23 mai 2008 au 31 décembre 2009, la gestion de l'état d'urgence fut confiée à un sous-secrétariat d'Etat à la présidence du Conseil des ministres attribué au chef du service de la protection civile.

A. **La gestion des déchets en Campanie et dans la commune de Somma Vesuviana jusqu'en 2004**

10. La loi régionale n° 10 du 10 février 1993 (« la loi n° 10/93 ») fixa les lignes directrices pour l'adoption d'un plan d'élimination des déchets en Campanie, lequel devait prévoir la valorisation des déchets solides urbains et des matériaux recyclables ainsi que la réduction de moitié du nombre et de la capacité des décharges – grâce à des techniques de compactage et de tri sélectif des déchets – sur la période 1993-1995.
11. Le 9 juin 1997, le président de la région agissant en qualité de commissaire délégué arrêta un plan régional d'élimination des déchets. Ce plan prévoyait notamment la construction de cinq incinérateurs – dont quatre sur les bans communaux de Marcianise, Battipaglia, Giugliano et Nola-Marigliano (ces deux derniers étant destinés à desservir les communes de résidence des requérants), et le cinquième sur un site à définir ultérieurement – ainsi que de cinq décharges principales et de six décharges secondaires.
12. Le 12 juin 1998, le président de la région agissant en qualité de commissaire délégué lança un appel d'offres pour la concession décennale du service de traitement et d'élimination des déchets produits dans la province de Naples. En application du cahier des charges, le concessionnaire retenu devait assurer la réception régulière des déchets collectés, leur tri, leur transformation en « combustible dérivé de déchets » (*combustibile derivato da rifiuti*, ci-après : « CDR ») et l'incinération du CDR. Pour ce faire, il devait construire et gérer trois centres destinés au tri des déchets et

à la production de CDR (« centres de production de CDR ») à Caivano, Tufino et Giugliano et réaliser, avant le 31 décembre 2000, une usine de production d'énergie électrique par combustion de CDR (« usine de thermo-valorisation du CDR »).

13. A l'issue de la procédure d'adjudication, clôturée le 20 mars 2000, la concession de ce service fut confiée à un consortium d'entreprises composé des sociétés Fisia Impianti S.p.A. (ayant qualité de chef de file), Impregilo S.p.A., Babcock Kommunal GmbH, Deutsche Babcock Anlagen GmbH et Evo Oberhausen AG (ayant qualité de mandataires).

14. Aux termes d'un contrat de concession de services conclu le 7 juin 2000, les cinq entreprises adjudicataires s'engageaient à construire deux centres de production de CDR à Caivano et à Tufino dans un délai de 300 jours à compter des 10 et 14 avril 2000 respectivement, et un autre à Giugliano dans un délai de 270 jours à compter du 30 mars 2000. L'usine de thermo-valorisation du CDR, à ériger dans la localité d'Acerra, devait être bâtie dans un délai de 24 mois à compter d'une date à préciser ultérieurement.

15. Entre-temps, le 22 avril 1999, le commissaire délégué avait lancé un appel d'offres pour la concession du service d'élimination des déchets produits en Campanie. La procédure d'adjudication fut remportée par le consortium FIBE S.p.A., qui avait été constitué par les entreprises concessionnaires. A une date non précisée, celles-ci créèrent la société FIBE Campania S.p.A.

16. En exécution d'un contrat de concession de services conclu le 5 septembre 2001, FIBE S.p.A. devait construire et gérer sept centres de production de CDR et deux usines de thermo-valorisation de ce produit. Elle devait assurer la réception, le tri et le traitement des déchets produits dans la région en vue d'en transformer 32% en CDR et 33% en compost, et de produire 14% de déchets non réutilisables et 3% de déchets ferreux.

17. En janvier 2001, la fermeture de la décharge de Tufino provoqua la suspension temporaire de l'élimination des déchets dans la province de Naples. Pour faire face à leur accumulation, les maires des autres communes de la province autorisèrent à titre provisoire leur stockage dans leurs décharges respectives aux fins de l'article 13 du décret législatif n° 22 du 5 février 1997 (voir paragraphe 65 ci-dessous).

18. De fin 2001 à mai 2003, sept centres de production de CDR furent construits à Caivano, Pianodardine, Santa Maria Capua Vetere, Giugliano, Casalduni, Tufino et Battipaglia.

19. Le 22 mai 2001, le service de ramassage, de collecte et de transport des déchets urbains de la commune de Somma Vesuviana fut confié à un consortium d'entreprises composé des sociétés C.I.C.-Clin Industrie Città S.p.A. et Ecologia Bruscino S.r.l. Le 26 octobre 2004, la gestion de ce service fut attribuée à M.I.T.A S.p.A., une société à capital public.

B. L'enquête pénale relative à la situation du service d'élimination des déchets après la conclusion des contrats de concession du 7 juin 2000 et du 5 septembre 2001

20. En 2003, le parquet près le tribunal de Naples ouvrit une enquête pénale (RGNR n° 15940/03) sur la situation de la gestion du service d'élimination des déchets en Campanie après la conclusion des contrats de concession du 7 juin 2000 et du 5 septembre 2001.

21. Le 31 juillet 2007, le parquet demanda le renvoi en jugement des administrateurs et de certains employés des sociétés Fisia Italimpianti S.p.A., FIBE S.p.A., FIBE Campania S.p.A., Impregilo S.p.A., Gestione Napoli S.p.A. (« les sociétés »), du commissaire délégué en exercice de 2000 à 2004 et de plusieurs fonctionnaires du bureau de celui-ci pour avoir commis, de 2001 à 2005, les délits de fraude, d'inexécution de contrats publics, d'escroquerie, d'interruption d'un service public ou d'utilité publique, d'abus de fonctions, de faux idéologique dans l'exercice de fonctions publiques et d'opérations de gestion de déchets non autorisées.

22. Les membres des sociétés en question étaient notamment accusés d'avoir violé, avec la complicité du commissaire délégué et des fonctionnaires de son bureau, l'obligation de réceptionner et de traiter les déchets produits dans la région imposée par les contrats de concession. Pour leur part, les sociétés étaient accusées d'avoir ralenti, et parfois interrompu, la réception régulière des déchets collectés dans les centres de production de CDR, provoquant ainsi l'accumulation des déchets dans les rues et les sites de stockage provisoire mis en place par les maires ou le commissaire délégué.

23. En outre, le parquet reprochait aux sociétés mises en causes d'avoir 1) produit du CDR et du compost de manière non conforme aux conditions contractuelles, 2) omis d'effectuer les opérations de récupération énergétique du CDR requises dans l'attente de la construction de l'usine de thermo-valorisation, 3) sous-traité l'activité de transport des déchets valorisés issus des centres de production de CDR, au mépris des dispositions du contrat de concession, 4) stocké des matériaux polluants issus de la production de CDR dans des décharges illicites sans aucune protection de l'environnement.

24. Pour leur part, les fonctionnaires visés par la demande de renvoi étaient accusés d'avoir faussement attesté du respect, par les sociétés mises en cause, des dispositions légales et des conditions contractuelles régissant l'élimination des déchets ainsi que d'avoir autorisé l'ouverture de décharges non conformes à la législation en vigueur, le stockage provisoire du CDR jusqu'à l'ouverture des usines de thermo-valorisation, la mise en décharge des matériaux polluants issus des centres de production de CDR et des dérogations aux critères contenus dans le cahier des charges pour la production du CDR.

25. Le 29 février 2008, le juge de l'audience préliminaire ordonna le renvoi en jugement des accusés et fixa l'audience devant le tribunal de Naples au 14 mai 2008.

C. La gestion des déchets en Campanie et dans la commune de Somma Vesuviana de 2005 à 2007

26. Le décret-loi n° 245 du 30 novembre 2005, converti en la loi n° 21 du 27 janvier 2006, prévoyait la résiliation des contrats de concession du service d'élimination des déchets en Campanie conclus par le commissaire délégué en 2000 et 2001 ainsi que l'organisation en urgence d'une nouvelle adjudication publique. Afin d'assurer la continuité du service, les sociétés concessionnaires étaient tenues de poursuivre leurs activités jusqu'à la clôture de la procédure d'adjudication, mais pas au-delà du 31 décembre 2007.

27. Un premier appel d'offres, lancé le 27 mars 2006 par le commissaire délégué en exercice, échoua faute d'un nombre suffisant d'offres valides.

28. Le 2 août 2006, le commissaire délégué lança un deuxième appel d'offres portant sur vingt ans.

29. Le décret-loi n° 263 du 9 octobre 2006, converti en la loi n° 290 du 6 décembre 2006, nomma le chef du service de la protection civile aux fonctions de commissaire délégué à la gestion de la crise des déchets en Campanie. Le deuxième appel d'offres ayant été annulé, le commissaire délégué fut chargé de confier le service d'élimination des déchets à de nouvelles entreprises adjudicataires.

30. Le 28 mars 2007, la région adopta la loi n° 4, qui prévoyait la création d'une section régionale du cadastre des déchets, d'un observatoire régional des déchets, d'un plan régional de gestion du cycle intégré des déchets, d'un plan régional de gestion des déchets spéciaux, y compris les déchets dangereux, ainsi que d'un plan régional pour l'assainissement des sites pollués.

31. Le 6 juillet 2007, le préfet de Naples fut nommé commissaire délégué à la gestion de la crise.

32. Le décret-loi n° 61 du 11 mai 2007, converti en la loi n° 87 du 5 juillet 2007 (« le décret-loi n° 61/07 »), autorisa la création, dans les communes de Serre (Salerne), Savignano Irpino (Avellino), Terzigno (Naples), Sant'Arcangelo Trimonte (Bénévent), de décharges dérogeant aux dispositions en vigueur en matière environnementale, d'hygiène et de santé, et interdit la création de nouveaux sites d'élimination des déchets notamment dans les communes de Giugliano in Campania, Villaricca, Qualiano et Quarto (Naples) au moins jusqu'à l'assainissement du territoire. Ce texte confia au commissaire délégué la charge d'identifier d'urgence de nouvelles entreprises auxquelles attribuer le service de traitement et d'élimination des déchets.

33. Le 21 novembre 2007, un troisième appel d'offres fut lancé. Faute d'offres, il fut déclaré infructueux.

34. Le 28 décembre 2007, le commissaire délégué arrêta un plan régional pour les déchets urbains de la Campanie aux fins de l'article 9 du décret-loi n° 61/07. Ce plan proposait une stratégie de sortie de crise, notamment grâce au développement de la collecte

sélective des déchets, à la transparence de leur cycle de vie, à la rationalisation et la mise en conformité des structures existantes – en particulier d'au moins un des centres de production de CDR –, à la création de structures destinées à produire du compost et à l'emploi de nouvelles technologies et de méthodes de traitement biologique des déchets.

35. Le 19 avril 2008, le service de collecte et de transport des déchets organiques dans la commune de Somma Vesuviana fut confié à Pomigliano Ambiente S.p.A, une société à capital public.

D. La gestion des déchets en Campanie et dans la commune de Somma Vesuviana de 2008 à 2010

36. Une nouvelle crise se produisit à la fin de l'année 2007. Des tonnes de déchets furent abandonnées pendant des semaines dans les rues de Naples et de plusieurs villes de sa province, y compris celles où les requérants résident (voir la liste annexée au présent arrêt).

37. Le 11 janvier 2008, le président du Conseil des ministres nomma par ordonnance (n° 3639/08) un haut fonctionnaire de police aux fonctions de commissaire délégué (article 1). Celui-ci fut chargé d'ouvrir les décharges prévues par le décret-loi n° 61/07 et de repérer de nouveaux sites de stockage et d'élimination des déchets, avec l'assistance de la force publique, armée comprise (article 2). Les communes de la région furent invitées à préparer des plans pour la collecte sélective des déchets (article 3).

38. Le décret-loi n° 90 du 23 mai 2008 (« le décret-loi n° 90/08 ») – converti en la loi n° 123 du 14 juillet 2008 (intitulée « Mesures extraordinaires en réponse à la crise de l'élimination des déchets en Campanie et dispositions ultérieures de protection civile ») – nomma le chef du service de la protection civile aux fonctions de sous-secrétaire d'Etat à la présidence du Conseil des ministres et le chargea de la gestion de la crise jusqu'au 31 décembre 2009, en remplacement du commissaire délégué. Le sous-secrétaire fut autorisé à ouvrir dix nouvelles décharges dans la région, dont deux à Terzigno et à Chiaiano, par dérogation aux dispositions en vigueur en matière environnementale, d'hygiène et de santé.

39. Le décret-loi n° 90/08 autorisa aussi le traitement de certaines catégories de déchets dans l'usine de thermo-valorisation du CDR d'Acerra contre l'avis rendu le 9 février 2005 par la commission d'évaluation de l'impact sur l'environnement, ainsi que la réalisation d'usines de thermo-valorisation du CDR à Santa Maria La Fossa (Caserte) et dans les communes de Naples et Salerne.

40. Ledit décret-loi attribuait aux provinces de la Campanie la propriété des centres de tri et de traitement des déchets, mais en confiait la gestion provisoire à l'armée (article 6 bis).

41. Les alinéas 4 et 7 de l'article 2 de ce texte qualifiaient les sites, les zones, les usines et les sièges des services de gestion des déchets de zones d'intérêt stratégique national placées sous la surveillance de la police et de l'armée. Il fut demandé aux forces armées de participer à la mise en service des chantiers et des sites ainsi qu'à la collecte et au transport des déchets.

42. L'article 2, alinéa 9, qualifiait le fait d'empêcher, d'entraver ou de rendre plus difficile la gestion des déchets d'interruption du service public passible de sanction.
43. Enfin, le décret-loi chargea le sous-secrétaire d'Etat de contrôler le respect par les communes des objectifs de collecte sélective des déchets urbains fixés dans le plan régional pour les déchets urbains de la Campanie établi le 28 décembre 2007.
44. Pour sa part, le décret-loi n° 172 du 6 novembre 2008 (« le décret-loi n° 172/08 »), converti en la loi n° 210 du 30 décembre 2008 (intitulée « Mesures extraordinaires en réponse à la crise de l'élimination des déchets en Campanie et dispositions urgentes en matière de protection de l'environnement ») prévoyait que, dans les territoires visés par l'état d'urgence en rapport avec l'élimination des déchets, les maires, les présidents de province, les membres des conseils municipaux ou provinciaux et ceux des commissions communales ou provinciales pouvaient être destitués par décret du ministre de l'Intérieur en cas de manquement grave, entre autres, aux obligations de planification et d'organisation du service de collecte, de transport, de valorisation, d'élimination et de collecte sélective des déchets (article 3). En outre, dans ces mêmes territoires, il prévoyait des sanctions pénales spéciales réprimant en particulier 1) l'abandon ou l'incendie de déchets, 2) la collecte, le transport, la valorisation, l'élimination et le commerce de déchets sans autorisation, 3) la création et la gestion de décharges illégales ainsi que le mélange de déchets dangereux et non dangereux (article 6).
45. Selon les informations fournies par le Gouvernement et non contestées par les requérants, deux décharges avaient déjà été ouvertes à Savignano Irpino et Sant'Arcangelo Trimonte fin octobre 2009, d'autres étaient sur le point d'ouvrir à Chiaiano, Terzigno, San Tammaro, et les travaux préliminaires en vue de l'ouverture d'une décharge à Andretta (Avellino) étaient en cours. Les travaux d'achèvement de l'usine de thermo-valorisation d'Acerra étaient en voie de réalisation, un appel d'offres pour la construction d'une usine de thermo-valorisation du CDR à Salerne avait été lancé et un site pour l'implantation d'une usine de thermo-valorisation dans la province de Naples avait été choisi. Du 14 janvier au 1er mars 2008, 269 000 tonnes de déchets avaient été enlevées des rues des villes de la région et 79 000 tonnes de CDR avaient été stockées. 530 communes avaient entamé le tri sélectif des déchets en application de l'ordonnance n° 3639/08.
46. Le 3 juin 2008, en application de l'ordonnance n° 3804/09 prise par le président du Conseil des ministres et après approbation d'un programme de tri sélectif, le service de collecte de la commune de Somma Vesuviana aurait été confié à la société L'Igiene Urbana S.r.l. sur appel d'offres.
47. Le 15 mars 2009, le président du Conseil des ministres enjoignit par ordonnance (n° 3746) aux provinces de la région de constituer des sociétés à capital public majoritaire pour la gestion des sites de stockage des déchets, des décharges et des structures de traitement, d'élimination, de valorisation et de recyclage des déchets.

E. L'enquête pénale relative à la gestion du service d'élimination des déchets postérieure à décembre 2005

48. En 2006, à une date non précisée, le parquet près le tribunal de Naples ouvrit une enquête pénale (RGNR n° 40246/06) sur les opérations d'élimination des déchets réalisées à titre provisoire par les sociétés FIBE S.p.A. et FIBE Campania S.p.A. pendant la phase transitoire consécutive à la résiliation des contrats de concession.

49. Le 22 mai 2008, à la demande du parquet, le juge des investigations préliminaires du tribunal de Naples ordonna l'assignation à résidence de l'administrateur délégué de FIBE S.p.A. et FIBE Campania S.p.A., de plusieurs cadres et employés de ces sociétés, des responsables des centres de tri de déchets gérés par Fisia Italimpianti S.p.A., du gérant de la décharge de Villaricca, des représentants de la société de transports FS Cargo S.p.A. et de plusieurs fonctionnaires du bureau du commissaire délégué.

50. Les prévenus étaient accusés, entre autres, d'association de malfaiteurs en vue du trafic illégal de déchets et de la réalisation de faux en écritures publiques, d'escroquerie, de faux idéologique dans l'exercice de fonctions publiques et d'activités organisées pour le trafic illicite de déchets.

51. En 2008, à une date non précisée, le parquet près le tribunal de Naples ouvrit une enquête pénale (RGNR n° 32722/08, dite « Rompiballe ») sur des opérations d'élimination de déchets réalisées après décembre 2005. Selon les informations fournies par le Gouvernement et non contestées par les requérants, l'enquête, encore pendante au 26 octobre 2009, portait sur de nombreux délits contre l'environnement et l'administration publique et était dirigée contre plusieurs employés de FIBE S.p.A. et autres entreprises du consortium, ainsi que contre des fonctionnaires du bureau du commissaire délégué.

F. Les arrêts de la Cour de justice de l'Union européenne

52. Le 22 mars 2005, la Commission des Communautés européennes (« la Commission ») introduisit devant la Cour de justice un recours en manquement contre l'Italie au titre de l'article 226 du traité instituant la Communauté européenne (« TCE ») (affaire C-135/05). Dénonçant l'existence d'un grand nombre de décharges illégales et non contrôlées en Italie, la Commission alléguait que les autorités italiennes avaient manqué à leurs obligations au titre des articles 4, 8 et 9 de la directive 75/442/CEE relative aux déchets, de l'article 2 § 1 de la directive 91/689/CEE relative aux déchets dangereux et de l'article 14, lettres a) à c), de la directive 1999/31/CE concernant la mise en décharge des déchets.

53. Dans l'arrêt qu'elle rendit le 26 avril 2007, la Cour de justice constata « la non-conformité générale des décharges au regard desdites dispositions », observant notamment que le gouvernement italien « ne contest[ait] pas l'existence (...) sur son territoire, d'au moins 700 décharges illégales contenant des déchets dangereux, qui n'[étaient] (...) soumis à aucun contrôle ».

54. Elle conclut, entre autres, que la République italienne avait manqué aux obligations découlant des dispositions invoquées par la Commission, au motif qu'elle n'avait pas

pris toutes les mesures nécessaires pour assurer que les déchets soient valorisés ou éliminés sans mettre en danger la santé de l'homme et sans que soient utilisés des procédés ou des méthodes susceptibles de porter préjudice à l'environnement, et pour interdire l'abandon, le rejet et l'élimination incontrôlée des déchets.

55. Le 3 juillet 2008, la Commission introduisit un nouveau recours en manquement devant la Cour de justice sur le fondement de l'article 226 TCE (affaire C-297/08).

56. Par un arrêt du 4 mars 2010, la Cour de justice, tout en prenant acte des mesures adoptées par l'Etat italien en 2008 pour surmonter la « crise des déchets », constata l'existence d'un « déficit structurel en termes d'installations nécessaires à l'élimination des déchets urbains produits en Campanie », comme le démontraient « les quantités importantes de déchets s'étant accumulées sur les voies publiques de cette région ».

Elle estima que l'Italie avait « failli à son obligation d'établir un réseau adéquat et intégré d'installations d'élimination (...) de ses déchets, et [avait], par conséquent, manqué aux obligations lui incombant en vertu de l'article 5 de la directive 2006/12 ». Selon la Cour, ledit manquement ne pouvait être justifié par des circonstances telles que l'opposition de la population à l'installation de décharges, l'existence d'activités criminelles dans la région et les inexécutions contractuelles de la part des entreprises chargées de la réalisation de certaines structures d'élimination des déchets. Elle précisa que cette dernière circonstance ne relevait pas de la force majeure car cette notion désignait « des circonstances étrangères à celui qui l'invoque, anormales et imprévisibles, dont les conséquences n'auraient pu être évitées malgré toutes les diligences déployées », et qu'une administration diligente devait prendre les mesures nécessaires soit pour se prémunir contre les inexécutions contractuelles, soit pour s'assurer de la réalisation effective et en temps voulu des structures nécessaires malgré les inexécutions en question. De surcroît, la Cour de Justice releva que « la République italienne ne contest[ait] pas que (...) les déchets jonchant la voie publique s'élevaient à 55 000 tonnes, s'ajoutant aux 110 000 à 120 000 tonnes de déchets en attente de traitement dans les sites municipaux de stockage ». En ce qui concerne le risque environnemental, la Cour de justice rappela notamment que l'accumulation des déchets constituait, compte tenu de la capacité limitée de chaque région ou localité à les recevoir, un danger pour l'environnement. Elle conclut que l'accumulation sur la voie publique et dans les aires de stockage temporaires de quantités si importantes de déchets avait créé un « risque pour l'eau, l'air, le sol » ainsi que « pour la faune et la flore » (article 4, paragraphe 1, sous a), de la directive 2006/12), avait provoqué des « incommodités par les odeurs » (paragraphe 1, sous b) de cet article) et était susceptible de porter « atteinte aux paysages et aux sites présentant un intérêt particulier » (article 4, paragraphe 1, sous c), de la directive 2006/12). Quant au risque pour la santé humaine, la Cour de justice releva que « la situation préoccupante d'accumulation de déchets sur les voies publiques a[vait] exposé la santé des populations à un danger certain, et ce en méconnaissance de l'article 4, paragraphe 1, de la directive 2006/12 ».

Annexes

G. Les commissions parlementaires d'enquête sur le cycle des déchets et sur les activités illégales connexes

57. De 1997 à 2008, trois commissions parlementaires d'enquête sur le cycle des déchets et sur les activités illégales connexes furent constituées en application des lois n° 97 du 10 avril 1997, n° 399 du 31 octobre 2001 et n° 271 du 20 octobre 2006.

58. Dans son rapport sur la Campanie établi le 13 juin 2007, la troisième commission releva notamment que « la situation du cycle des déchets présent[ait] les signes d'une dangereuse régression ayant conduit à la désagrégation de la capacité opérationnelle du service et entraîné des risques sérieux pour la santé de la population ».

59. Dans son deuxième rapport, établi le 19 décembre 2007, elle émit notamment les observations suivantes : « une bonne partie du territoire demeure souillée par des amas de déchets laissés à l'abandon, les collectivités locales sont de moins en moins disposées à ouvrir de nouveaux sites destinés à la décharge ou à l'installation de structures de service et la confiance dans la capacité des institutions centrales à engager des programmes d'assainissement et de développement des territoires les plus atteints par la dégradation de l'environnement est devenue pratiquement nulle. (...) à cela s'ajoute fatalement l'enracinement quasi-immuable de la criminalité organisée dans le circuit des déchets qui s'oppose au caractère largement inefficace du dispositif administratif de contrôle ». Elle fit état de son « jugement strictement négatif sur le bureau du commissaire délégué, dont l'inefficacité structurelle s'est révélée tellement manifeste au cours de ces dernières années que sa capacité à remplir ses fonctions en est irréversiblement atteinte ». Elle indiqua avoir « le sentiment que la crise a laissé place au drame ».

H. Les études scientifiques

60. Selon une étude publiée en septembre 2004 par la revue *The Lancet Oncology*, le taux de mortalité par cancer dans le ressort de l'unité sanitaire locale n° 4 (« l'ASL n° 4 ») de Naples a constamment augmenté au cours des années 1970-1974 et 1995-2000.

61. Par ailleurs, il ressortirait du registre des tumeurs tenu par l'ASL n° 4 que, en février 2002, le taux de mortalité par cancer colorectal, cancer du foie, leucémie et lymphome était plus élevé dans l'arrondissement n° 73 – comprenant les villes de Nola, Marigliano et Acerra (limitrophe à la commune de Somma Vesuviana) – que dans le reste du territoire de son ressort. Le taux de cancers du foie, de leucémie et de lymphome était très élevé par rapport à celui observé dans le reste de l'Italie. Ces données démontreraient que la pollution provoquée par le traitement non approprié des déchets et l'existence de décharges illégales présente un lien de causalité avec le taux élevé de mortalité par cancer dans la région.

62. A une date non précisée mais ultérieure à la publication de l'étude, le service de la protection civile demanda à l'Organisation mondiale de la santé (OMS) d'effectuer une

étude de l'impact sanitaire des déchets dans les provinces de Naples et de Caserte. Les résultats de la première phase des recherches (*Studio Pilota*), réalisées en coopération avec l'Institut supérieur de la santé italien (ISS), le Conseil supérieur de la recherche italien (CNR), l'Agence régionale pour la protection environnementale (ARPA) de Campanie et l'Observatoire épidémiologique régional (OER), furent présentés publiquement à Naples en 2005. Ils révélaient que le risque de mortalité associé aux tumeurs de l'estomac, du foie, des canaux biliaires, de la trachée, des bronches, des poumons, de la plèvre et de la vessie, ainsi que le risque de malformations cardiovasculaires, uro-génitales et des membres étaient plus élevés dans une zone à cheval sur les provinces de Naples et de Caserte que dans le reste de la Campanie. Les résultats de la deuxième phase de cette étude (*Studio di correlazione tra rischio ambientale da rifiuti, mortalità e malformazioni congenite*) furent publiés en 2007 sur le site internet du service de la protection civile. Il en ressortait que la zone présentant les taux de mortalité par cancer et de malformations les plus élevés était celle qui était la plus atteinte par l'élimination illégale de déchets dangereux et la combustion incontrôlée de déchets solides urbains. Cette corrélation donnerait à penser que l'exposition au traitement des déchets a une incidence sur le risque de mortalité observé en Campanie, bien que la prévalence de certaines infections et virus ainsi que la diffusion du tabagisme dans la région puissent aussi avoir une influence sur le taux de mortalité.

63. Début 2008, à la demande du commissaire délégué en exercice, le ministère de la Santé, l'ISS et les autorités sanitaires de Campanie réalisèrent une étude intitulée « *Santé et déchets en Campanie* », dont les résultats furent présentés lors d'un congrès tenu à Naples le 24 avril 2008. D'après cette étude, les données épidémiologiques collectées en Campanie ne permettaient pas d'établir un rapport de causalité entre l'exposition de la population aux déchets solides urbains et la prévalence de maladies. Il en ressortait en particulier que le taux élevé de la mortalité associée aux maladies cardiovasculaires et aux tumeurs du poumon et du foie observé en Campanie s'expliquait par le surpeuplement et la pauvreté de la région, par la diffusion du tabagisme, par de mauvaises habitudes alimentaires et par une endémie d'hépatites virales. Toutefois, l'étude n'excluait pas que des groupes limités de personnes se trouvant dans des situations particulières aient pu être exposés à des substances chimiques provenant de déchets toxiques éliminés de manière inappropriée ou illégale.

64. Une étude publiée en 2008 dans les annales de l'ISS releva un taux élevé de mortalité par cancer du poumon, du foie, de l'estomac, des reins et de la vessie, et de malformations congénitales générales, des membres, du système cardiovasculaire et de l'appareil uro-génital dans la partie septentrionale de la province Naples et la partie méridionale de la province de Caserte, zones de grande concentration de sites illégaux d'élimination de déchets toxiques.

II. LE DROIT ET LA PRATIQUE INTERNES ET INTERNATIONAUX PERTINENTS

A. Le cadre législatif italien relatif au traitement des déchets

65. Le décret-loi n° 22 du 5 février 1997 (« *le décret Ronchi* ») [(transposant les directives CEE/91/156, 91/689/CEE et 94/162/CE relatives respectivement aux déchets, aux déchets dangereux, aux emballages et aux déchets d'emballages)] qualifia la gestion de déchets d'activité d'utilité publique ayant pour but d'assurer une protection élevée de l'environnement et des contrôles effectifs. Aux termes de ce texte, en vigueur de 1997 à 2006, les déchets devaient être valorisés ou éliminés sans mettre en danger la santé de l'homme et sans que soient utilisés des procédés ou des méthodes susceptibles de porter préjudice à l'environnement. La gestion des déchets devait se conformer aux principes de responsabilisation et de coopération de tous les acteurs impliqués dans la production, la distribution, l'utilisation et la consommation des biens dont les déchets proviennent, dans le respect des principes des ordres juridiques national et communautaire.

66. Le *décret Ronchi* fut abrogé par le décret-législatif n° 152 du 3 avril 2006 intitulé « Normes en matière d'environnement » (« le décret-loi n°152/06 »). L'article 260 de ce texte créa le délit d'« activités organisées en vue du trafic illicite de déchets », défini comme des activités organisées et continues de cession, de réception, de transport, d'exportation, d'importation ou de gestion illicite d'importantes quantités de déchets effectuée dans le but d'obtenir un profit injuste. Le responsable de telles activités est passible d'une peine d'emprisonnement d'un à six ans et astreint à l'obligation de remettre en état l'environnement. La suspension conditionnelle de la peine peut être subordonnée à l'élimination du dommage ou du danger pour l'environnement.

67. L'article 300 du même décret-loi définit le dommage environnemental (*danno ambientale*) comme « toute détérioration, significative et mesurable, directe ou indirecte, d'une ressource naturelle ou de l'usage que l'on en fait ». Toute action ou omission contraire à une loi, à un règlement, à une décision administrative qui provoque un dommage à l'environnement en l'altérant, en le détériorant ou en le détruisant en tout ou partie oblige son auteur à la remise en état ou, à défaut, à verser une indemnisation à l'Etat. Le ministère de l'Environnement est compétent pour agir en vue d'obtenir l'indemnisation en question, notamment en se constituant partie civile à un procès pénal (article 311). Les personnes touchées ou pouvant l'être par le dommage environnemental peuvent s'en plaindre auprès du ministère de l'Environnement et demander l'intervention des autorités publiques.

B. **Le droit et la pratique internes pertinents en matière d'indemnisation des personnes du fait de la mauvaise gestion du service de traitement des déchets**

68. L'article 4 du décret-loi n° 90 du 24 mai 2008 attribue au juge administratif compétence pour trancher tout différend concernant l'ensemble des activités de gestion des déchets, y compris dans les cas où celles-ci sont du ressort de l'administration publique ou d'organismes assimilés. La compétence du juge administratif s'étend aux différends portant sur des droits protégés par la Constitution.

69. Statuant dans le cadre d'une procédure en dommages-intérêts introduite le 5 mai 2008 – avant l'entrée en vigueur de l'article 4 du décret-loi n° 90/08 – par un groupe de résidents contre la commune de Naples et la société chargée du service de collecte des déchets, le tribunal civil de Naples releva que seul le juge administratif pouvait se prononcer en la matière et adopter aussi toute mesure provisoire et urgente au sens de l'article 21 de la loi n° 1034 du 6 décembre 1971 (instituant les tribunaux administratifs régionaux).

70. Par deux arrêts déposés le 21 mai et le 23 novembre 2009, la Cour de cassation plénière jugea que le juge administratif était compétent pour statuer sur les actions indemnitaires exercées par les résidents d'une commune contre les autorités chargées du service de collecte, de traitement et d'élimination des déchets.

C. **Les sources de droit de l'Union européenne**

71. L'article 4 de la directive 75/442/CEE du Conseil de l'Union européenne, du 15 juillet 1975, relative aux déchets, telle que modifiée par la directive 91/156/CEE du Conseil du 18 mars 1991, se lit comme suit :

> « Les États membres prennent les mesures nécessaires pour assurer que les déchets seront valorisés ou éliminés sans mettre en danger la santé de l'homme et sans que soient utilisés des procédés ou méthodes susceptibles de porter préjudice à l'environnement, et notamment :
> - sans créer de risque pour l'eau, l'air ou le sol, ni pour la faune et la flore,
> - sans provoquer d'incommodités par le bruit ou les odeurs,
> - sans porter atteinte aux paysages et aux sites présentant un intérêt particulier.
>
> Les États membres prennent, en outre, les mesures nécessaires pour interdire l'abandon, le rejet et l'élimination incontrôlée des déchets. »

72. La disposition pertinente de l'article 2 de la directive 91/689/CEE du Conseil relative aux déchets dangereux, du 12 décembre 1991, est ainsi libellée :

> « 1. Les États membres prennent les mesures nécessaires pour exiger que, sur chaque site de déversement (décharge) de déchets dangereux, ces déchets soient inventoriés et identifiés.
> (...) »

73. La directive 1999/31/CE du Conseil concernant la mise en décharge des déchets, du 26 avril 1999, comporte les dispositions suivantes :

Article 14 – Décharges existantes

« Les États membres prennent des mesures afin que les décharges autorisées ou déjà en exploitation au moment de la transposition de la présente directive ne puissent continuer à fonctionner que si (...)

(a) Dans un délai d'un an à compter de la date fixée à l'article 18, paragraphe 1, [soit au plus tard le 16 juillet 2002], l'exploitant d'une décharge prépare et présente, pour approbation, à l'autorité compétente un plan d'aménagement du site comprenant les éléments énumérés à l'article 8 ainsi que toute mesure corrective qu'il estime nécessaire pour se conformer aux exigences de la présente directive (...).

(b) A la suite de la présentation du plan d'aménagement, l'autorité compétente prend une décision définitive quant à la poursuite de l'exploitation sur la base dudit plan d'aménagement et de la présente directive. Les États membres prennent les mesures nécessaires pour qu'il soit procédé, dans les meilleurs délais (...), à la désaffectation des sites qui n'ont pas obtenu (...) l'autorisation de poursuivre leurs opérations.

(c) Sur la base du plan d'aménagement du site approuvé, l'autorité compétente autorise les travaux nécessaires et fixe une période transitoire pour l'exécution du plan. (...) »

Article 18 – Transposition

« Les États membres mettent en vigueur les dispositions législatives, réglementaires et administratives nécessaires pour se conformer à la présente directive au plus tard dans les deux ans à compter de son entrée en vigueur [soit le 16 juillet 2001] et en informent immédiatement la Commission.
(...) »

74. La directive 2006/12/CE du Parlement européen et du Conseil du 5 avril 2006 relative aux déchets se lit ainsi dans ses dispositions pertinentes :

Article 4

« 1. Les États membres prennent les mesures nécessaires pour assurer que les déchets seront valorisés ou éliminés sans mettre en danger la santé de l'homme et sans que soient utilisés des procédés ou méthodes susceptibles de porter préjudice à l'environnement, et notamment :

(a) sans créer de risque pour l'eau, l'air ou le sol, ni pour la faune et la flore;
(b) sans provoquer d'incommodités par le bruit ou les odeurs;
(c) sans porter atteinte aux paysages et aux sites présentant un intérêt particulier.

2. Les États membres prennent les mesures nécessaires pour interdire l'abandon, le rejet et l'élimination incontrôlée des déchets. »

Article 5

« 1. Les États membres prennent les mesures appropriées, en coopération avec d'autres États membres lorsque cela s'avère nécessaire ou opportun, en vue de l'établissement d'un réseau intégré et adéquat d'installations d'élimination, en tenant compte des meilleures technologies disponibles qui n'entraînent pas de coûts excessifs. Ce réseau doit permettre à la Communauté dans son ensemble d'assurer elle-même l'élimination de ses déchets et aux États membres de tendre individuellement vers ce but, en tenant compte des conditions géographiques ou du besoin d'installations spécialisées pour certains types de déchets.

2. Le réseau visé au paragraphe 1 doit permettre l'élimination des déchets dans l'une des installations appropriées les plus proches, grâce à l'utilisation des méthodes et technologies les plus appropriées pour garantir un niveau élevé de protection de l'environnement et de la santé publique. »

75. En vertu du principe de précaution, inscrit à l'article 174 du Traité instituant la Communauté européenne, l'absence de certitude en l'état des connaissances scientifiques et techniques du moment ne saurait justifier que l'Etat retarde l'adoption de mesures effectives et proportionnées visant à prévenir un risque de dommages graves et irréversibles à l'environnement. La jurisprudence communautaire a fait application de ce principe principalement dans des affaires portant sur la santé, alors que le traité n'énonce le principe qu'en ce qui concerne la politique de la Communauté dans le domaine de l'environnement. Selon la jurisprudence de la Cour de justice des Communautés européennes (« CJCE »), lorsque « des incertitudes subsistent quant à l'existence ou à la portée des risques pour la santé des personnes, les institutions peuvent prendre des mesures sans avoir à attendre que la réalité et la gravité de ces risques soient pleinement démontrées » (CJCE, 5 mai 1998, *Royaume Uni/Commission*, Aff C-180/96, Rec. I-2265 et CJCE, 5 mai 1998, *National Farmer's Union*, C-157/96, Rec. I-2211).

D. Les sources de droit international

76. La Convention internationale du 25 juin 1998 (Aarhus, Danemark) sur l'accès à l'information, la participation du public au processus décisionnel et l'accès à la justice en matière d'environnement, ratifiée par l'Italie par la loi n°108 du 16 mars 2001, se lit ainsi dans sa partie pertinente :

Article 5 – Rassemblement et diffusion d'informations sur l'environnement

« 1. Chaque Partie fait en sorte :

  (a) Que les autorités publiques possèdent et tiennent à jour les informations sur l'environnement qui sont utiles à l'exercice de leurs fonctions;

  (b) Que des mécanismes obligatoires soient mis en place pour que les autorités publiques soient dûment informées des activités proposées ou en cours qui risquent d'avoir des incidences importantes sur l'environnement;

  (c) Qu'en cas de menace imminente pour la santé ou l'environnement, qu'elle soit imputable à des activités humaines ou qu'elle soit due à des causes naturelles, toutes les informations susceptibles de permettre au public de prendre des mesures pour prévenir ou limiter d'éventuels dommages qui sont en la possession d'une autorité publique soient diffusées immédiatement et sans retard aux personnes qui risquent d'être touchées.

2. Chaque Partie veille à ce que, dans le cadre de la législation nationale, les autorités publiques mettent les informations sur l'environnement à la disposition du public de façon transparente et à ce que ces informations soient réellement accessibles, notamment :

  (a) En fournissant au public des renseignements suffisants sur le type et la teneur des informations sur l'environnement détenues par les autorités publiques compétentes, sur les principales conditions auxquelles ces informations sont mises à sa disposition et lui sont accessibles et sur la procédure à suivre pour les obtenir; (...)

3. Chaque Partie veille à ce que les informations sur l'environnement deviennent progressivement disponibles dans des bases de données électroniques auxquelles le public peut avoir facilement accès par le biais des réseaux de télécommunications publics. (...)

4. Chaque Partie publie et diffuse à des intervalles réguliers ne dépassant pas trois ou quatre ans un rapport national sur l'état de l'environnement, y compris des informations sur la qualité de l'environnement et des informations sur les contraintes qui s'exercent sur l'environnement.

(...)

9. Chaque Partie prend des mesures pour mettre en place progressivement, compte tenu, le cas échéant, des processus internationaux, un système cohérent de portée nationale consistant à inventorier ou enregistrer les données relatives à la pollution dans une base de données informatisée structurée et accessible au public, ces données étant recueillies au moyen de formules de déclaration normalisées. Ce système pourra prendre en compte

les apports, les rejets et les transferts dans les différents milieux et sur les lieux de traitement et d'élimination sur le site et hors du site d'une série donnée de substances et de produits découlant d'une série donnée d'activités, y compris de l'eau, de l'énergie et des ressources utilisées aux fins de ces activités. »

77. L'article 23 des Articles de la Commission de droit international des Nations Unies sur la responsabilité de l'État pour fait internationalement illicite est ainsi libellé :

« 1. L'illicéité du fait d'un État non conforme à une obligation internationale de cet État est exclue si ce fait est dû à la force majeure, consistant en la survenance d'une force irrésistible ou d'un événement extérieur imprévu qui échappe au contrôle de l'État et fait qu'il est matériellement impossible, étant donné les circonstances, d'exécuter l'obligation.

2. Le paragraphe 1 ne s'applique pas :
a) Si la situation de force majeure est due, soit uniquement soit en conjonction avec d'autres facteurs, au comportement de l'État qui l'invoque; ou
b) Si l'État assumé le risque que survienne une telle situation. »

EN DROIT

I. SUR LES EXCEPTIONS PRÉLIMINAIRES DU GOUVERNEMENT

A. Sur la qualité de « victimes » des requérants

78. Le Gouvernement excipe d'abord du défaut de qualité de « victimes » des requérants, avançant qu'ils n'ont subi aucune atteinte à leurs droits au respect de la vie privée et familiale et du domicile, ni à leurs droits à la santé et à la vie. A la différence des requérants dans les affaires *López Ostra c. Espagne* (9 décembre 1994, série A n° 303-C) et *Guerra et autres c. Italie* (19 février 1998, *Recueil des arrêts et décisions* 1998-I), qui habitaient près d'usines polluantes, les requérants dans la présente affaire n'ont pas démontré qu'ils vivaient ou travaillaient à proximité de décharges ou de rues où l'abandon de déchets pourrait avoir causé un préjudice sérieux à leur santé ou à leur bien-être psychologique. La ville de Somma Vesuviana, dans laquelle les intéressés habitent ou travaillent, n'aurait même pas été touchée par la « crise des déchets ». Les requérants se plaindraient en réalité de la politique législative et administrative en matière de gestion de déchets, introduisant ainsi devant la Cour une *actio popularis* non admise dans le système de la Convention.

79. Les requérants affirment que Somma Vesuviana a été l'une des communes les plus gravement frappées par la « crise des déchets ». Cela ressortirait d'un article paru le 4 mai 2008 dans le quotidien *Corriere della Sera* faisant état d'un incendie de plusieurs

ANNEXES

tonnes de déchets déclenché par les habitants de cette commune, ainsi que la mention de la « crise des déchets » à l'ordre du jour de deux réunions du conseil municipal de la ville. En outre, Somma Vesuviana se trouverait près de la commune de Marigliano, qui, selon une étude scientifique de 2004 (voir paragraphe 60 ci-dessus), ferait partie d'une zone à haute concentration de tumeurs qui seraient liées à la présence de déchets.

80. La Cour rappelle que le mécanisme de contrôle de la Convention ne saurait admettre l'*actio populavis* (*Perez c. France* [GC], n° 47287/99, § 70, CEDH 2004-I; *Ada Rossi et autres c. Italie* (déc.), n° 55185/08, 55483/08, 55516/08, 55519/08, 56010/08, 56278/08, 58420/08 et 58424/08, CEDH 2008-…). Par ailleurs, ni l'article 8 ni aucune autre disposition de la Convention ne garantit spécifiquement une protection générale de l'environnement en tant que tel (*Kyrtatos c. Grèce*, n° 41666/98, § 52, CEDH 2003-VI (extraits)). Selon la jurisprudence de la Cour, l'élément crucial qui permet de déterminer si, dans les circonstances d'une affaire, des atteintes à l'environnement ont emporté violation de l'un des droits garantis par le paragraphe 1 de l'article 8 est l'existence d'un effet néfaste sur la sphère privée ou familiale d'une personne, et non simplement la dégradation générale de l'environnement (*Kyrtatos*, précité, § 52; *Fadeïeva c. Russie*, n° 55723/00, § 68, ECHR 2005-IV).

81. La Cour note que les requérants dénoncent une situation affectant l'ensemble de la population de la Campanie, à savoir l'atteinte à l'environnement provoquée par le mauvais fonctionnement du système de collecte, de traitement et d'élimination des déchets mis en place par les autorités publiques. Toutefois, elle relève qu'il ressort des documents fournis par les parties que Somma Vesuviana a été frappée par la « crise des déchets ». En particulier, une note de la présidence du Conseil des ministres du 16 novembre 2009 signale que, en raison du blocage d'un centre de production de CDR, les déchets de Somma Vesuviana n'ont pas pu y être transportés et que « les rues [...] ont été envahies par les déchets ». Les documents annexés aux observations du Gouvernement relatent que, de janvier 2008 à juillet 2009, 3 069 tonnes de déchets furent enlevées au cours de 94 opérations de ramassage auxquelles participa l'armée dans la commune de Somma Vesuviana et que, du 5 mai 2008 au 9 octobre 2009, les pompiers furent appelés pour éteindre trente-quatre incendies de déchets. Une note du service écologie et environnement de Somma Vesuviana indique que, « de novembre 2007 à février 2008, la crise était à son paroxysme » faute de moyens de transport suffisants pour déposer les déchets dans les décharges.

Dans ces conditions, la Cour estime que les dommages à l'environnement dénoncés par les requérants sont de nature à affecter directement leur propre bien-être (voir, *a contrario*, *Kyrtatos*, précité, § 53). Partant, il y a lieu de rejeter l'exception du Gouvernement.

B. Sur le non-épuisement allégué des voies de recours internes

82. Par ailleurs, le Gouvernement excipe du non-épuisement des voies de recours internes. Les requérants auraient pu exercer une action indemnitaire contre les organismes

gérant le service de collecte, de traitement et d'élimination des déchets pour leur demander réparation des préjudices découlant du mauvais fonctionnement dudit service, comme l'auraient fait d'autres habitants de la Campanie. Il ressortirait de la note du 16 novembre 2009 de la présidence du Conseil des ministres (voir paragraphe 81 ci-dessus) que, au 31 décembre 2008, 1 294 affaires portant sur les mêmes faits et griefs que ceux à l'origine de la présente requête avaient été introduites devant les juges de paix de Campanie contre plusieurs municipalités de la région, y compris celle de Somma Vesuviana, contre le commissaire délégué et contre la région. Certaines d'entre elles auraient abouti à la condamnation des communes et/ou du commissaire et au dédommagement des intéressés. Quatre habitants de Somma Vesuviana auraient assigné la commune, le commissaire et la société chargée de la collecte des déchets (MITA) devant le juge de paix de Sant'Anastasia. D'autres actions en dommages-intérêts auraient été introduites devant des juridictions administratives ou de droit commun hors de la région.

83. En outre, les requérants auraient pu demander au ministère de l'Environnement d'introduire, devant les juridictions civiles ou pénales, une action en réparation du préjudice environnemental au sens de l'article 18 de la loi n° 349/86 contre ces mêmes autorités et les administrateurs des sociétés concessionnaires du service. Enfin, il aurait été loisible aux intéressés de se constituer parties civiles dans les procédures pénales diligentées contre le personnel des entreprises adjudicataires du service de collecte des déchets en Campanie et contre les fonctionnaires du bureau du commissaire délégué (voir paragraphes 49 et 51 ci-dessus). Les requérants n'ayant exercé aucun des recours internes susmentionnés, ils auraient failli à l'obligation qui leur incombe en vertu de l'article 35 § 1 de la Convention.

84. Pour leur part, les requérants estiment qu'ils ne disposaient d'aucune voie de recours utile et effective au sens des articles 35 et 13 de la Convention. Ils affirment que, bien que la « crise des déchets » perdure en Campanie depuis 1994, aucune décision judiciaire reconnaissant la responsabilité civile ou pénale des autorités publiques ou des entreprises adjudicataires du service n'a été rendue. Ils concèdent qu'une procédure pénale a été diligentée en 2003 par le parquet près le tribunal de Naples contre les responsables présumés, mais signalent qu'elle est toujours pendante. Ils en concluent que les recours prévus par le droit italien ne leur offraient aucune chance d'obtenir une décision judiciaire, ni, d'ailleurs, de solliciter une solution à la « crise des déchets ».

85. La Cour rappelle que la règle de l'épuisement des voies de recours internes inscrite à l'article 35 § 1 de la Convention vise à ménager aux Etats contractants l'occasion de prévenir ou de redresser les violations alléguées contre eux avant que celles-ci ne lui soient soumises. Cette règle se fonde sur l'hypothèse, objet de l'article 13 de la Convention – et avec lequel elle présente d'étroites affinités – que l'ordre interne offre un recours effectif quant à la violation alléguée (*Selmouni c. France* [GC], n° 25803/94, § 74,

CEDH 1999-V). De la sorte, elle constitue un aspect important du principe voulant que le mécanisme de sauvegarde instauré par la Convention revête un caractère subsidiaire par rapport aux systèmes nationaux de garantie des droits de l'homme (*Aksoy c. Turquie*, 18 décembre 1996, § 51, *Recueil des arrêts et décisions* 1996-VI).

86. En outre, en vertu de la règle de l'épuisement des voies de recours internes énoncée à l'article 35 § 1 de la Convention, un requérant doit se prévaloir des recours normalement disponibles et suffisants pour lui permettre d'obtenir réparation des violations qu'il allègue, étant entendu qu'il incombe au Gouvernement excipant du non-épuisement de convaincre la Cour que le recours invoqué était effectif et disponible tant en théorie qu'en pratique à l'époque des faits, c'est-à-dire qu'il était accessible et susceptible d'offrir au requérant le redressement de ses griefs et qu'il présentait des perspectives raisonnables de succès (voir, parmi d'autres, *Akdivar et autres c. Turquie*, 16 septembre 1996, *Recueil des arrêts et décisions 1996-IV*, p. 1210, § 66, et *Giacobbe et autres c. Italie*, n° 16041/02, § 63, 15 décembre 2005). De plus, selon les « principes de droit international généralement reconnus », certaines circonstances particulières peuvent dispenser le requérant de l'obligation d'épuiser les recours internes qui s'offrent à lui (*Selmouni*, précité, § 75).

87. En ce qui concerne la possibilité pour les requérants d'exercer une action endommages-intérêts devant les juridictions civiles, la Cour note, d'une part, qu'une telle démarche aurait théoriquement pu aboutir au dédommagement des intéressés mais non à l'enlèvement des déchets des voies et lieux publics. D'autre part, même à supposer qu'une réparation du préjudice constituât un redressement adéquat des violations alléguées de la Convention, la Cour estime que le Gouvernement n'a pas démontré que les requérants auraient eu des chances de succès en exerçant cette voie de recours. Le Gouvernement s'est borné à fournir copie des assignations introduites devant le juge de paix par certains résidents de la Campanie contre les responsables de la gestion des déchets, et à indiquer que des affaires étaient pendantes devant les juridictions civiles et administratives. Aucune décision d'une juridiction civile accordant un dédommagement aux habitants des zones concernées par l'accumulation des déchets sur la voie publique n'a été fournie par le Gouvernement. Par ailleurs, la Cour de cassation a confirmé, en 2009, la compétence des juridictions administratives pour connaître des demandes d'indemnisation en rapport avec la « crise des déchets » (voir paragraphe 70 ci-dessus). Toutefois, le Gouvernement n'a pas non plus produit de décision juridictionnelle administrative octroyant une indemnité.

88. De même, le Gouvernement n'a cité aucune jurisprudence établissant que les résidents des zones touchées par la mauvaise gestion des déchets avaient qualité pour se constituer parties civiles dans le cadre de procédures pénales visant à sanctionner des délits contre l'administration publique et l'environnement.

89. Enfin, pour ce qui est de la possibilité de demander au ministère de l'Environnement d'exercer une action en réparation du préjudice environnemental au sens de l'article 18 de la loi n° 349/86, la Cour note d'emblée que la disposition évoquée par le Gouvernement a été abrogée par l'article 318 du décret-loi n° 152/06 et remplacée par l'article 311 dudit décret. Cette dernière disposition énonce, comme jadis l'article 18 de la loi n° 349/86, que seul le ministère de l'Environnement peut demander réparation du préjudice environnemental et que les particuliers ne peuvent que l'inviter à saisir les autorités judiciaires. Il s'ensuit que les recours prévus par ces dispositions n'auraient pas permis aux requérants de se prévaloir du préjudice découlant des dommages à l'environnement. En conséquence, ces recours ne sauraient passer pour des recours utiles au sens de l'article 35 § 1 de la Convention.

90. Au vu de ce qui précède, la Cour estime qu'il y a lieu de rejeter l'exception du Gouvernement tirée du non-épuisement des voies de recours internes.

C. Sur l'observation du délai de six mois

91. Le Gouvernement soutient que, en vertu de l'article 35 § 1 de la Convention, seuls des faits survenus dans les six mois précédant la date d'introduction de la requête – en l'occurrence le 9 janvier 2008 – peuvent être déférés à la Cour et que cette disposition interdit à celle-ci tout examen de la situation antérieure.

92. Les requérants n'ont pas pris position sur ce point.

93. La Cour relève que les requérants ne se plaignent pas d'un acte instantané mais d'une situation de crise dans la gestion du service de collecte, de transport, de traitement et d'élimination des déchets en Campanie. Elle rappelle que, lorsque la violation alléguée constitue, comme en l'espèce, une situation continue, le délai de six mois ne commence à courir qu'à partir du moment où cette situation continue a pris fin (voir parmi d'autres, (*Çınar c. Turquie*, n° 17864/91, décision de la Commission du 5 septembre 1994; (*Ülke c. Turquie* (déc.), n° 39437/98, 1ᵉʳ juin 2004). Dès lors, elle estime qu'il y a lieu de rejeter l'exception du Gouvernement.

II. SUR LA VIOLATION ALLÉGUÉE DE L'ARTICLE 8 DE LA CONVENTION

94. Invoquant les articles 2 et 8 de la Convention, les requérants avancent que, en s'abstenant d'adopter les mesures requises pour garantir le fonctionnement du service public de collecte des déchets et en appliquant une politique législative et administrative inadaptée, l'Etat a nui gravement à l'environnement de leur région et mis en danger leur vie et leur santé ainsi que celles de l'ensemble de la population locale. Les autorités publiques auraient, en outre, omis d'informer les intéressés des risques liés au fait d'habiter dans un territoire pollué.

95. Le Gouvernement s'oppose à cette thèse.

96. Maîtresse de la qualification juridique des faits de la cause (*Guerra et autres*, précité, § 44), la Cour estime, au vu de sa jurisprudence en la matière (*López Ostra*, précité, § 51, *Guerra et autres*, précité, § 57; *Moreno Gómez c. Espagne*, n° 4143/02, 16 novembre 2004; *Hatton et autres c. Royaume-Uni* [GC], n° 36022/97, § 96, CEDH 2003-VIII), que les griefs des requérants doivent être examinés sous l'angle du droit au respect de la vie privée et du domicile garanti par l'article 8 de la Convention, dont les dispositions pertinentes sont ainsi libellées :

« 1. Toute personne a droit au respect de sa vie privée (...), de son domicile (...).
2. Il ne peut y avoir ingérence d'une autorité publique dans l'exercice de ce droit que pour autant que cette ingérence est prévue par la loi et qu'elle constitue une mesure qui, dans une société démocratique, est nécessaire à la sécurité nationale, à la sûreté publique, au bien-être économique du pays, à la défense de l'ordre et à la prévention des infractions pénales, à la protection de la santé ou de la morale, ou à la protection des droits et libertés d'autrui. »

A. Sur la recevabilité

97. La Cour constate que ce grief n'est pas manifestement mal fondé au sens de l'article 35 § 3 de la Convention et qu'il ne se heurte à aucun autre motif d'irrecevabilité. Il convient donc de le déclarer recevable.

B. Sur le fond

1. Thèses des parties

(a) Thèse du Gouvernement

98. Le Gouvernement admet que « la gestion presque désastreuse du service de collecte, de traitement et d'élimination des déchets produits dans certaines zones de la province de Naples » a entraîné l'accumulation de déchets dans les rues de certaines villes ainsi que la création de décharges illégales. Toutefois, il avance que la phase aiguë de la crise n'a duré que cinq mois environ, à savoir de fin 2007 à mai 2008, et que, en tout état de cause, Somma Vesuviana n'a pas été touchée.

99. Il soutient en outre que les difficultés rencontrées en Campanie sont imputables à des causes relevant de la force majeure telles que la présence de la criminalité organisée dans la région, l'inexécution par les entreprises adjudicataires du service de collecte des déchets des obligations qui leur incombaient en vertu des contrats de concession, le manque d'entreprises disposées à assurer la continuité du service et l'opposition de la population à la création de décharges et de centres de production de CDR. Il précise en outre que les incendies de déchets dans les rues ont été déclenchés par les citoyens, raison pour laquelle l'Etat ne saurait en être tenu pour responsable.

100. Il souligne que, en tout état de cause, les autorités italiennes ont satisfait à leur devoir de vigilance et pris des mesures adéquates pour réagir à la « crise ». D'une

part, elles auraient diligenté des poursuites pénales à l'encontre des responsables de la mauvaise gestion de la situation. D'autre part, elles auraient adopté plusieurs mesures législatives, dont le décret-loi n° 90/08 par lequel aurait été mis en place un système efficace ayant abouti au ramassage des déchets, à l'élimination des décharges illégales et à la reprise du fonctionnement des usines de traitement et d'élimination des déchets (voir paragraphe 68 ci-dessus).

101. Par ailleurs, elles auraient réalisé plusieurs études sur les causes et les effets de la « crise des déchets » en Campanie et fourni à la population des informations qui lui auraient permis d'évaluer son degré d'exposition aux risques associés à la collecte, au traitement et à l'élimination des déchets. Les causes de la crise des déchets en Campanie auraient été analysées par trois commissions parlementaires, dont les conclusions figureraient dans des rapports publics. Le ministère de la Santé et le service de la protection civile auraient commandé diverses études d'impact de la crise sur l'environnement et la santé humaine (voir paragraphes 62-64 ci-dessus). Ces études auraient démontré que « la crise des déchets » n'avait pas eu d'impact significatif sur l'environnement – exceptée une augmentation sporadique des niveaux de pollution de l'eau non directement imputable à la présence de déchets – ni de conséquences négatives sur la santé humaine. Leurs résultats auraient été diffusés à l'occasion de séminaires et de conférences publics. Enfin, un centre de documentation sur la santé et la pollution environnementale provoquée par les déchets, géré par le Centre national pour la prévention et le contrôle des maladies (CCM) et la région de Campanie, serait en cours de création.

(b) Thèse des requérants

102. Les requérants soutiennent que les carences des autorités publiques dans la gestion de la crise ont causé des dommages à l'environnement et mis en danger leur santé.

103. L'Etat défendeur aurait aussi failli à l'obligation de fournir des informations permettant aux intéressés d'évaluer leur degré d'exposition aux risques associés à la collecte et à l'élimination des déchets faute d'avoir diffusé auprès du public les résultats de l'étude commandée par le service de la protection civile (paragraphe 62 ci-dessus). Par ailleurs, l'étude de l'ISS, présentée à la préfecture de Naples en janvier 2009 (paragraphe 63 ci-dessus), aurait mis en évidence un lien entre le taux de tumeurs et la présence de décharges dans la zone comprenant les communes d'Acerra, de Nola et de Marigliano (limitrophe de Somma Vesuviana).

2. Appréciation de la Cour

(a) Principes généraux

104. La Cour rappelle que des atteintes graves à l'environnement peuvent affecter le bien-être des personnes et les priver de la jouissance de leur domicile de manière à nuire à leur vie privée et familiale (*López Ostra*, précité, § 51; *Guerra et autres*, précité, § 60).

105. Par ailleurs, elle souligne que l'article 8 ne se borne pas à astreindre l'Etat à s'abstenir d'ingérences arbitraires : à cet engagement plutôt négatif peuvent s'ajouter des obligations positives inhérentes à un respect effectif de la vie privée. En tout état de cause, que l'on aborde la question sous l'angle de l'obligation positive de l'Etat d'adopter des mesures raisonnables et adéquates pour protéger les droits de l'individu en vertu du premier paragraphe de l'article 8 ou sous celui d'une ingérence d'une autorité publique, à justifier selon le second paragraphe, les principes applicables sont assez voisins (*López Ostra,* précité, § 51, et *Guerra,* précité, § 58).

106. Les Etats ont avant tout l'obligation positive, en particulier dans le cas d'une activité dangereuse, de mettre en place une réglementation adaptée aux spécificités de ladite activité, notamment au niveau du risque qui pourrait en résulter. Cette obligation doit régir l'autorisation, la mise en fonctionnement, l'exploitation, la sécurité et le contrôle de l'activité en question, ainsi qu'imposer à toute personne concernée par celle-ci l'adoption de mesures d'ordre pratique propres à assurer la protection effective des citoyens dont la vie risque d'être exposée aux dangers inhérents au domaine en cause (voir, *mutatis mutandis, Oneryildiz c. Turquie,* [GC], n° 48939/99, § 90, CEDH 2004-XII).

107. En ce qui concerne les obligations procédurales découlant de l'article 8, la Cour rappelle qu'elle attache une importance particulière à l'accès du public à des informations permettant d'évaluer le danger auquel il est exposé (*Guerra,* précité, § 60; *Taşkin et autres c. Turquie* n° 46117/99, § 119, CEDH 2004-X; *Giacomelli c. Italie,* n° 59909/00, § 83, CEDH 2006-XII; *Tătar c. Roumanie,* n° 67021/01, § 113, CEDH 2009-... (extraits)). Elle rappelle de surcroît que l'article 5 § 1 c) de la Convention d'Aarhus, ratifiée par l'Italie, prévoit que chaque Partie fait en sorte « qu'en cas de menace imminente pour la santé ou l'environnement, imputable à des activités humaines ou due à des causes naturelles, toutes les informations susceptibles de permettre au public de prendre des mesures pour prévenir ou limiter d'éventuels dommages qui sont en la possession d'une autorité publique soient diffusées immédiatement et sans retard aux personnes qui risquent d'être touchées » (paragraphe 76 ci-dessus).

(b) Application des principes précités au cas d'espèce

108. La Cour rappelle d'emblée qu'elle vient de constater (paragraphe 80 ci-dessus) que la commune de Somma Vesuviana, où les requérants habitent ou travaillent, a été frappée par la « crise des déchets ». Elle relève que la Campanie a connu l'état d'urgence du 11 février 1994 au 31 décembre 2009 et que les requérants ont été contraints de vivre dans un environnement pollué par les déchets abandonnés sur la voie publique au moins à compter de la fin de l'année 2007 jusqu'au mois de mai 2008. La Cour estime que cette situation a pu conduire à une détérioration de la qualité de vie des intéressés et, en particulier, nuire à leur droit au respect de la vie privée et du domicile. Dès lors,

l'article 8 trouve à s'appliquer en l'espèce. Par ailleurs, la Cour note que les requérants n'ont pas allégué être affectés par des pathologies liées à l'exposition aux déchets et que les études scientifiques fournies par les parties parviennent à des conclusions opposées quant à l'existence d'un lien de causalité entre l'exposition aux déchets et l'augmentation du risque de développement de pathologies telles que des cancers ou des malformations congénitales. Dans ces conditions, bien que la Cour de justice de l'Union européenne, appelée à se prononcer sur la question de l'élimination des déchets en Campanie, ait estimé que l'accumulation de quantités importantes de déchets sur la voie publique et des aires de stockage temporaires était susceptible d'exposer à un danger la santé de la population résidente (voir l'arrêt C-297/08, précité, paragraphes 55 et 56 ci-dessus), la Cour ne saurait conclure que la vie et la santé des requérants ont été menacées. Cela étant, l'article 8 peut être invoqué même en l'absence de la preuve d'un grave danger pour la santé des intéressés (voir *López Ostra*, précité, § 51).

109. La Cour considère que la présente affaire porte non sur une ingérence directe dans l'exercice du droit au respect de la vie privée et du domicile des requérants qui se serait matérialisée par un acte des autorités publiques, mais sur le manquement allégué de celles-ci à prendre des mesures adéquates pour assurer le fonctionnement régulier du service de collecte, de traitement et d'élimination des déchets dans la commune de Somma Vesuviana. Elle estime donc approprié de se placer sur le terrain des obligations positives découlant de l'article 8 de la Convention (voir *Guerra*, précité, § 58).

110. La collecte, le traitement et l'élimination des déchets constituent, à n'en pas douter, des activités dangereuses (voir, *mutatis mutandis*, *Oneryildiz*, précité, § 71). Dès lors, il pesait sur l'Etat l'obligation positive d'adopter des mesures raisonnables et adéquates capables de protéger les droits des intéressés au respect de leur vie privée et de leur domicile et, plus généralement, à la jouissance d'un environnement sain et protégé (voir *Tătar*, précité, § 107). La Cour rappelle, par ailleurs, la marge d'appréciation dont jouissent les Etats dans le choix des mesures concrètes à adopter pour s'acquitter des obligations positives découlant de l'article 8 de la Convention (voir *Fadeïeva*, précité, § 96).

En l'espèce, de 2000 à 2008, le service de traitement et d'élimination des déchets a été confié à des sociétés de droit privé, alors que le service de collecte des déchets dans la commune de Somma Vesuviana a été assuré par plusieurs sociétés à capital public. La circonstance que les autorités italiennes aient confié à des organismes tiers la gestion d'un service public ne saurait cependant les dispenser des obligations de vigilance leur incombant en vertu de l'article 8 de la Convention (voir *López Ostra*, précité, §§ 44-58).

111. La Cour relève que l'Etat italien a adopté, à partir de mai 2008, plusieurs mesures et pris des initiatives pour surmonter les difficultés rencontrées en Campanie et que l'état d'urgence, déclaré en Campanie le 11 février 1994, a été levé le 31 décembre

2009. Le gouvernement défendeur a, certes, admis l'existence d'un état de crise, mais il l'a qualifié de situation de force majeure. A ce propos, la Cour se borne à rappeler qu'aux termes de l'article 23 des Articles de la Commission de droit international des Nations Unies, sur la responsabilité de l'État pour fait internationalement illicite, la « force majeure » consiste en « (...) une force irrésistible ou (...) un événement extérieur imprévu qui échappe au contrôle de l'Etat et fait qu'il est matériellement impossible, étant donné les circonstances, d'exécuter [une] obligation [internationale] » (paragraphe 77 ci-dessus). Eu égard aussi aux conclusions de la Cour de justice de l'Union européenne dans l'affaire C-297/08 précitée, la Cour estime que les circonstances invoquées par l'Etat italien ne sauraient relever de la force majeure.

112. Selon la Cour, même si on considère, comme l'affirme le gouvernement, que la phase aiguë de la crise n'a duré que cinq mois – de fin 2007 à mai 2008 – et malgré la marge d'appréciation reconnue à l'Etat défendeur, force est de constater que l'incapacité prolongée des autorités italiennes à assurer le fonctionnement régulier du service de collecte, de traitement et d'élimination des déchets a porté atteinte au droit des requérants au respect de leur vie privée et de leur domicile, en violation de l'article 8 de la Convention sous son volet matériel.

113. En revanche, en ce qui concerne le volet procédural de l'article 8 et le grief tiré du manque allégué de diffusion d'informations propres à permettre aux requérants d'évaluer le risque auquel ils étaient exposés, la Cour souligne que les études commandées par le service de la protection civile ont été rendues publiques en 2005 et 2008. Dès lors, elle estime que les autorités italiennes se sont acquittées de l'obligation d'informer les personnes concernées, y compris les requérants, quant aux risques potentiels auxquels elles s'exposaient en continuant à résider en Campanie. Partant, il n'y a pas eu violation de l'article 8 de la Convention à cet égard.

III. SUR LES VIOLATIONS ALLÉGUÉES DES ARTICLES 6 ET 13 DE LA CONVENTION

114. Invoquant les articles 6 et 13 de la Convention, les requérants allèguent que les autorités italiennes n'ont pris aucune initiative visant à sauvegarder les droits des justiciables et reprochent à la justice d'avoir considérablement tardé à poursuivre pénalement les responsables de la « gestion » des déchets.

115. En ce qui concerne le grief portant sur l'ouverture de poursuites pénales, la Cour rappelle que ni les articles 6 et 13 ni aucune autre disposition de la Convention ne garantissent à un requérant le droit de faire poursuivre et condamner des tiers ou le droit à la « vengeance privée » (voir *Perez*, précité, § 70; *Oneryildiz*, précité, § 147). Dès lors, la Cour estime qu'il y lieu de déclarer cette partie du grief irrecevable pour incompatibilité *ratione materiae* avec les dispositions de la Convention, au sens des articles 35 §§ 3 b) et 4.

116. En revanche, pour autant que le grief des requérants porte sur l'absence, dans l'ordre juridique italien, de voies de recours effectives qui leur auraient permis d'obtenir réparation de leur préjudice, la Cour considère qu'il relève de l'article 13 de la Convention, qu'il est étroitement lié aux griefs examinés aux paragraphes 93-111 ci-dessus et qu'il doit donc être déclaré recevable.

117. La Cour rappelle que l'article 13 de la Convention garantit l'existence en droit interne d'un recours permettant à l'autorité nationale compétente de connaître du contenu d'un « grief défendable » fondé sur la Convention (*Z. et autres c. Royaume-Uni* [GC], n° 29392/95, § 108, CEDH 2001-V). L'objet de cet article est de fournir un moyen au travers duquel les justiciables puissent obtenir, au niveau national, le redressement des violations de leurs droits garantis par la Convention, avant d'avoir à mettre en œuvre le mécanisme international de plainte devant la Cour (*Kudła c. Pologne* [GC], n° 30210/96, § 152, CEDH 2000-XI).

118. Eu égard aux conclusions auxquelles elle est parvenue quant à l'existence de voies de recours utiles et effectives permettant de soulever, devant les autorités nationales, des griefs ayant trait aux conséquences préjudiciables pour les requérants de la mauvaise gestion du service de collecte, de traitement et d'élimination des déchets (paragraphes 84-89 ci-dessus), la Cour estime qu'il y lieu de conclure à la violation de l'article 13 de la Convention en l'espèce.

IV. SUR L'APPLICATION DE L'ARTICLE 41 DE LA CONVENTION

119. Aux termes de l'article 41 de la Convention,

« Si la Cour déclare qu'il y a eu violation de la Convention ou de ses Protocoles, et si le droit interne de la Haute Partie contractante ne permet d'effacer qu'imparfaitement les conséquences de cette violation, la Cour accorde à la partie lésée, s'il y a lieu, une satisfaction équitable. »

A. Dommage

120. Les requérants réclament chacun 15 000 euros (EUR) au titre du préjudice moral qu'ils auraient subi.

121. Le Gouvernement s'oppose à ces prétentions, soutenant que la demande ne concerne que Me Errico di Lorenzo, avocat agissant devant la Cour en son nom personnel.

122. La Cour relève que Me di Lorenzo a demandé réparation de son préjudice moral allégué non seulement pour lui-même mais aussi pour « chaque appelant », raison pour laquelle elle considère que la demande d'indemnisation s'étend à tous les requérants. Dans les circonstances de l'espèce, la Cour estime toutefois que le constat de violations de la Convention auquel elle est parvenue constitue une réparation suffisante pour dommage moral.

B. Frais et dépens

123. Notes d'honoraires à l'appui, les requérants demandent 23 263,72 EUR pour les frais et dépens engagés devant la Cour.
124. Le Gouvernement conteste cette prétention.
125. Selon la jurisprudence de la Cour, un requérant ne peut obtenir le remboursement de ses frais et dépens que dans la mesure où se trouvent établis leur réalité, leur nécessité et le caractère raisonnable de leur taux (*Iatridis c. Grèce* (satisfaction équitable) [GC], n° 31107/96, § 54, CEDH 2000-XI). En outre, les frais de justice ne sont recouvrables que dans la mesure où ils se rapportent à la violation constatée (*Beyeler c. Italie* (satisfaction équitable) [GC], n° 33202/96, § 27, 28 mai 2002; *Sahin c. Allemagne* [GC], n° 30943/96, § 105, CEDH 2003-VIII. En l'espèce, et compte tenu des documents en sa possession et de sa jurisprudence, la Cour estime raisonnable d'allouer à Me Errico di Lorenzo la somme de 2 500 EUR au titre des frais et dépens exposés pour les besoins de la procédure suivie devant elle.

C. Intérêts moratoires

126. La Cour juge approprié de calquer le taux des intérêts moratoires sur le taux d'intérêt de la facilité de prêt marginal de la Banque centrale européenne majoré de trois points de pourcentage.

PAR CES MOTIFS, LA COUR,

1. *Déclare*, à la majorité, la requête recevable quant aux griefs tirés des articles 8 et 13 de la Convention et, à l'unanimité, irrecevable pour le surplus;
2. *Dit*, par six voix contre une, qu'il y a eu violation de l'article 8 de la Convention en son volet matériel;
3. *Dit*, à l'unanimité, qu'il n'y a pas eu violation de l'article 8 de la Convention en son volet procédural;
4. *Dit*, par six voix contre une, qu'il y a eu violation de l'article 13 de la Convention;
5. *Dit*, par six voix contre une,
    (a). que l'Etat défendeur doit verser, dans les trois mois à compter du jour où l'arrêt sera devenu définitif conformément à l'article 44 § 2 de la Convention, 2 500 EUR (deux mille cinq cents euros) à Me Errico di Lorenzo pour frais et dépens;
    (b). qu'à compter de l'expiration dudit délai et jusqu'au versement, ce montant sera à majorer d'un intérêt simple à un taux égal à celui de la facilité de prêt marginal de la Banque centrale européenne applicable pendant cette période, augmenté de trois points de pourcentage;

6. *Rejette*, à l'unanimité, la demande de satisfaction équitable pour le surplus.

Fait en français, puis communiqué par écrit le 10 janvier 2012, en application de l'article 77 §§ 2 et 3 du règlement.

    Stanley Naismith   Françoise Tulkens
        Greffier   Présidente

Au présent arrêt se trouve joint, conformément aux articles 45 § 2 de la Convention et 74 § 2 du règlement, l'exposé de l'opinion séparée dissidente du juge Sajó.

F.T.
S.H.N.

ANNEXE
LISTE DES REQUÉRANTS

	Nom	Prénom	Année de naissance	Lieu de résidence
1.	Di Sarno	Francesco	1954	Sant'Anastasia (NA)
2.	Di Lorenzo	Errico	1974	Somma Vesuviana (NA)
3.	Raiola	Luigi	1974	Somma Vesuviana (NA)
4.	De Falco	Lucio	1939	Somma Vesuviana (NA)
5.	Esposito	Marianna	1978	Somma Vesuviana (NA)
6.	Buonuomo	Armando	1948	Somma Vesuviana (NA)
7.	Di Lorenzo	Domenico	1977	Somma Vesuviana (NA)
8.	Di Lorenzo	Giuseppina	1974	Somma Vesuviana (NA)
9.	Izzo	Ulderico	1940	Somma Vesuviana (NA)
10.	Vesce	Anna	1942	Somma Vesuviana (NA)
11.	Rippa	Mariano	1944	Somma Vesuviana (NA)
12.	Di Lorenzo	Mariano	1944	Somma Vesuviana (NA)
13.	Rippa	Giuseppe	1947	Somma Vesuviana (NA)
14.	Aliperta	Maria	1946	Somma Vesuviana (NA)
15.	Coppola	Angelo	1967	Palma Campania (NA)
16.	Raiola	Gaetano	1950	S. Giorgio a Cremano (NA)
17.	Galise	Armando	1976	Acerra (NA)
18.	Raiola	Giovanna	1980	Acerra (NA)

OPINION DISSIDENTE DU JUGE SAJÓ

(Traduction)

Bien que je partage les préoccupations exprimées par mes collègues sur le fond, je regrette de devoir me dissocier d'eux en l'espèce car j'estime que la requête est irrecevable.

La Cour, dans son arrêt, rejette l'exception du Gouvernement tirée du non-épuisement des voies de recours internes. Elle dit qu'il incombe au Gouvernement excipant du non-épuisement de convaincre la Cour que le recours invoqué était effectif et disponible tant en théorie qu'en pratique à l'époque des faits, c'est-à-dire qu'il était accessible et susceptible d'offrir au requérant le redressement de ses griefs et qu'il présentait des perspectives raisonnables de succès. Selon la Cour, « aucune décision d'une juridiction civile accordant un dédommagement aux habitants des zones concernées par l'accumulation des déchets sur la voie publique n'a été fournie par le Gouvernement. » (paragraphe 87 de l'arrêt). Il n'a jamais été conclu que le régime de la responsabilité civile en Italie était lacunaire en tant que tel ; dans les circonstances de l'espèce, il était tout simplement impossible de démontrer l'existence d'un recours, étant donné que les requérants n'ont pas attendu l'issue de leur recours civil (apparemment certains des requérants et d'autres personnes dans des situations analogues ont engagé une telle action devant les juridictions internes). Il est impossible de prouver l'existence d'un recours dans le cas d'espèce si on ne laisse pas à la justice le temps de connaître de l'affaire. Les événements en cause se sont déroulés au moins à compter de la fin de l'année 2007 et jusqu'au mois de mai 2008 (paragraphe 108 de l'arrêt). La requête a été introduite le 9 janvier 2008 et le Gouvernement a soumis ses observations le 23 octobre 2009. Je ne vois pas comment l'ordre judiciaire italien aurait pu produire entre mai 2008 et le 23 octobre 2009 (voire la date de nos délibérations) un jugement définitif, qui aurait démontré le caractère effectif ou non du recours.

En outre, je ne suis pas convaincu que les personnes qui prétendent travailler dans le village de Somma Vesuviana mais n'y résident pas puissent se prétendre victimes puisqu'elles n'ont pas démontré que la présence des déchets avait des répercussions sur la jouissance de leur vie privée et de leur domicile au point qu'il en résulterait une ingérence dans leur vie privée, sous l'angle du « bien-être » (paragraphe 81 de l'arrêt) ni indiqué comment cette situation a pu conduire à une détérioration de la qualité de vie des intéressés qui travaillent à Somma Vesuviana et, en particulier, nuire à leur droit au respect de la vie privée et du *domicile* (italique ajouté par moi).